The Payroll Book

The Payroll Book

A Guide for Small Businesses and Start-Ups

Charles J. Read, CPA

WILEY

Published by John Wiley & Sons, Inc., Hoboken, New Jersey.
Published simultaneously in Canada.

For general information on our other products and services or for technical support, please contact our Customer Care Department within the United States at (800) 762-2974, outside the United States at (317) 572-3993 or fax (317) 572-4002.

Wiley publishes in a variety of print and electronic formats and by print-on-demand. Some material included with standard print versions of this book may not be included in e-books or in print-on-demand. If this book refers to media such as a CD or DVD that is not included in the version you purchased, you may download this material at http://booksupport.wiley.com. For more information about Wiley products, visit www .wiley.com.

Library of Congress Cataloging-in-Publication Data.

Names: Read, Charles, author.
Title: The payroll book : a guide for small businesses and start ups / Charles Read.
Description: First Edition. | Hoboken : Wiley, 2020. | Includes index.
Identifiers: LCCN 2020021876 (print) | LCCN 2020021877 (ebook) | ISBN 9781119704430 (paperback) | ISBN 9781119704539 (adobe pdf) | ISBN 9781119704515 (epub)
Subjects: LCSH: Wages—Accounting. | Small business—Accounting. | Bookkeeping.
Classification: LCC HF5681.W3 R43 2020 (print) | LCC HF5681.W3 (ebook)| DDC 658.3/21—dc23
LC record available at https://lccn.loc.gov/2020021876
LC ebook record available at https://lccn.loc.gov/2020021877

Cover Design: Wiley
Cover Image: Courtesy of Charles J. Read

Printed in the United States of America

V10019672_070820

Contents

Preface

*T*he *Payroll Book* is the summation of 40-plus years of payroll experience, mostly with small businesses. From my first job as a controller to becoming a business owner to owning a national payroll service bureau, I have processed tens of thousands of payrolls for thousands of companies over the years. I have the professional qualifications to go with that experience, including being a certified public accountant (CPA) for over 40 years. I am also a United States Tax Court Practitioner, which allows me to represent clients in the US Tax Court without being an attorney. As a member of the Internal Revenue Service Advisory Council, I meet with the IRS to help provide recommendations for tax problems or concerns.

All of the information presented in this book is general in nature and you should consult with your trusted advisors on specific situations in your business.

Payroll is vital to the federal government's tax operations. Over 70% of the revenue collected by the IRS comes through payroll departments, either as withholding or payroll taxes.

In addition, the IRS issues over $6 billion a year in employment tax penalties on businesses large and small. Forty percent (40%) of small businesses are penalized every year, with the average penalty approaching $500. However, more than half the penalties get abated; I will show you how in Chapter 6.

Payroll is an integral part of your business. Do it wrong and it can cost you everything. There are lots of complexities in preparing payroll that I will walk you through. I'll also try to keep you out of trouble with the taxing authorities and keep your employees happy as well.

 ## HOW TO USE THIS BOOK

First of all, this book is designed for the small or new business. By small I mean those with 50 or fewer employees. I am not going to assume that you have a dedicated human resources department, a payroll department, or employees on staff who are specialists.

Everything here applies to larger businesses as well but a large business has additional problems and regulations that are not important to the small business owner. I include a section in the back (Chapter 17) that discusses the additional laws and regulations you will be subject to as you hit employee count milestones.

This book is broken into three parts.

Part 1 covers the details in setting up a payroll. Some of this material you will never need in your business and some will be absolutely critical. It is a truism in the payroll business that if a payroll client is set up correctly, it runs like clockwork forever. If the client is set up poorly, it is a disaster, and the client soon leaves.

Part 2 is about running the payroll and reporting. If you don't have time right now for the chapters on setting up a payroll, which at some point you really need to look at, Part 2 will help you to get a payroll done and out the door.

Part 3 offers a lot of additional essential components in the payroll arena. Some, such as record retention, you need to know in order to keep yourself out of hot water; next year or five years from now. Other items may or may not be important, depending on your business and how it and you operate.

In addition to this book there are some extra resources that you may find useful. There are also links to reference pages – some of them lead to our website, some to various governmental sites, and others to sites of third parties. They are subject to change and some handle lengthy technical areas, making it difficult to cover in a book. We keep the information in our links up to date and they are available to anyone who reads this book.

ICONS USED

String on Finger Icon: These will be important points that you need to remember as you move forward.

Light Bulb Icon: These are tips on doing payroll that will make your life easier. Many of these tips are the result of seeing mistakes and problems over the years and finding ways to avoid them the next time around.

Triangle with Exclamation Point Icon: This is a warning icon. There are lots of places in doing payroll and payroll taxes where things can go wrong and problems can get expensive if there is a problem. These are common mistake areas to be wary of.

Guy with Glasses Icon: This will designate a technical area, a detail that you will love to know about, but will probably not need all the time.

Hockey Mask Icon: This is a horror story to illustrate what can happen.

Resource Icon: These are resources that we have vetted and feel comfortable recommending to our clients and readers.

Experience Icon: This icon is for an important fact, lesson, or truth earned through years of experience.

The Payroll Book

PART ONE

Payroll Setup

CHAPTER ONE

Business Entity

The entity you choose for your business determines several things about the way you process payroll. There are four standard entities for businesses, and we will examine each one of them and their unique attributes in relation to payroll. If you have already chosen your entity type, then you can read only that section. The remaining sections may become useful if you change your entity type.

This is by no means a complete analysis of each type of entity. If you have not chosen the entity type for your business I suggest that you consult with a certified public accountant (CPA) who specializes in small business as well as an attorney who also specializes in small business to discuss not only the cost but also the legal, tax, accounting, and liability aspects of all types of entities in relationship to your particular needs and circumstances.

CORPORATION

Corporations are creatures of the state; that is, you must set up a corporation through a state government. A corporation is a business entity that is owned by a shareholder(s), people who own shares of stock. The shareholder(s) elect a board of directors to oversee the corporation's actions and hire executives to run the day-to-day operation. In many cases in small business corporations the shareholders, the board of directors, and the officers are the same people. The corporation is liable for the actions and finances of the business, but the shareholders are not.

There are two standard classifications of corporations: Subchapter C (C-Corp) corporations, which pay taxes as an entity, and Subchapter S corporations (S-Corp), which are pass-through entities. The S-Corp pays no federal income taxes. The gains and/or losses are "passed through" to the shareholders. Form 1120S, which is the federal corporation tax return for S-Corps, will have a form K1 for each shareholder. The K1 will be used to report the corporation's earnings/losses on the shareholders' personal tax returns. Many small business owners use S-Corps because they can reduce employment taxes, including Social Security and Medicare taxes, for the shareholders.

 For employment tax purposes, an S-Corp shareholder who works in the corporation (other than minor services) is an employee. He remains a shareholder as well. This allows for savings on Social Security and Medicare taxes because such taxes need not be paid on distributions of earnings and profits from the corporation to its shareholders. Thus, to the extent they pay themselves shareholder distributions instead of employee salaries, S-Corp shareholders/employees can save money on payroll taxes. The downside is that it may also reduce their Social Security benefits when (if) they are eligible to draw them.

It's up to the people who run an S-Corp, its officers and directors, to decide how much salary to pay the corporation's employees. When you are employed by an S corporation that you own (alone or with others), you may be the one making this decision. In fact, 70% of all S corporations are owned by just one person, so the owner has complete discretion to decide on his or her salary.

However, the Internal Revenue Service (IRS) insists that the employee/shareholder must be paid reasonable compensation, that employment tax is withheld and paid (see Chapter 5) for the work the employee/shareholder does. Only after reasonable compensation is paid can the corporation pay distributions to the employee/shareholder. Distributions are not subject to employment tax but will be reported as income on the employee's/shareholder's personal tax return.

A lot of S-Corp owners go too far and pay distributions pay to avoid any employment tax at all on what the employee/shareholder takes out of the corporation as compensation.

J. Russell George, Inspector General for Tax Administration, testified to the Senate Committee on Finance that "In tax year 2000, the owners of 36,000 single-shareholder S corporations received no salaries at all from their corporations, even though the operating profits of each of these corporations exceeded $100,000. This resulted in employment taxes not being paid on $13.2 billion in profits."

If the IRS feels that an employee/shareholder has taken too little in wages and too much in distributions, the IRS will "recharacterize" the distributions as wages and require payment of the employment taxes, plus penalties that can equal 100% of the taxes then due.

 A CPA who incorporated his accounting practice as an S-Corp took a salary of $24,000 and distributions of $220,000. The IRS said that his salary was not reasonable compensation and that $175,000 of the distributions should be treated as wages subject to employment taxes, and assessed almost $50,000 of taxes plus penalties. The court upheld the IRS's power to recharacterize the distributions as wages subject to employment tax. (*Watson v. United States* (DC IA 05/27/2010), 105 AFTR 2d)

 In my years of tax practice, my firm used a rule of thumb that distributions should never exceed wages for an employee/shareholder. We never had a problem with "reasonable compensation" for any audit.

PARTNERSHIP

The standard general partnership is an entity where two or more people combine money, assets, skills, and other resources. The partners then share the profits and/or losses in accordance with the agreement between the partners. If there is no agreement, then the assumption is that the partners share equally. General partners as opposed to limited partners are personally responsible for all the liabilities that the partnership incurs.

A partnership pays no income tax directly. The gains and/or losses are "passed through" to the partners. Form 1065, which is the federal partnership tax return, will have a form K1 for each partner. The K1 will be used to report the partnership earnings/losses on the shareholders personal tax returns.

General partners are never employees for payroll purposes. The partnership may have employees that the partnership will have on payroll and withhold as well as pay taxes on. The partners will pay self-employment tax on the profits reported by the partnership on their personal tax returns.

There are other forms of partnerships where there are limited partners who share based on the partnership agreement in the profits and/or losses but are not liable for the liabilities that the partnership may incur. They have "limited" liability.

SOLE PROPRIETORSHIP

The sole proprietorship is the simplest entity in which to operate a business. A sole proprietorship is not a separate legal entity. It just denotes an individual who owns and operates a business. A sole proprietor is personally responsible for all of the liabilities of the business they operate.

The sole proprietorship is a popular entity in that it is simple, cheap, and easy to setup. An entrepreneur can simply go into business, in many cases without any planning other than doing business.

Since a sole proprietorship is only its owner, taxation is simple. The sole proprietor reports all of their income and expenses on a Schedule C of their Form 1040. Self-employment taxes are calculated on any gain and are equivalent to employment taxes that they would pay, if on payroll.

 A sole proprietor is never on payroll in their own business. No employment taxes are withheld from distributions the sole proprietor takes. The sole proprietor pays self-employment tax, which is Social Security and Medicare taxes, on their individual Form 1040 every year.

LIMITED LIABILITY COMPANY (LLC)

An LLC is a hybrid entity. Like a corporation, it is a creature of the state – you must set up an LLC through a state government office. If you do nothing, and are the only member of the LLC, the LLC is treated as a disregarded entity for federal tax purposes. If there is one member (owner) it is treated as a sole proprietor for tax and payroll purposes; see the Sole Proprietorship section. If there is more than one member it is treated as a partnership for tax and payroll purposes; see the Partnership section.

An LLC, however, can elect to be treated as a S-Corp or a S-corporation for tax and payroll purposes, discussed earlier in this chapter. The election is made on IRS Form 8832 – Entity Classification Election.

The LLC has some advantages and disadvantages over the S-Corp structure. The advantages include:

- Creditor protection.
- Flexibility in organizational control.
- Fewer documents and fewer formalities.
- Built-in transfer restrictions.
- Disproportionate distributions.

The disadvantages include:

- Additional transaction costs to create.
- Built-in transfer restrictions.

Your legal and financial advisors can walk you through all of the complexities and help you select the best entity for your needs.

2

Employees and Nonemployees

D o you have employees? Are you sure? Who is an employee and who is not an employee? What are the special categories of employees? This is what we explore in this chapter.

YOU

Are you an employee? That depends. If you work in your business, you may be an employee, but it depends on the type of entity you selected. Go to chapter 1 and look at the type of entity you do business as. That will tell you if you are an employee and need to take a paycheck or not. If you are an employee, your payroll is basically calculated the same as any other employee's. There are a few items relating to benefits that may be different for income tax purposes, but they should not affect your payroll.

FAMILY MEMBERS

If you have family members working in your business, are they employees? The following extracts are from the IRS:

> One of the advantages of operating your own business is hiring family members. However, employment tax requirements for family employees may vary from those that apply to other employees. The following information may assist you with pointing out some differences to consider.

Child employed by parents

Payments for the services of a child under age 18 who works for his or her parent in a trade or business are not subject to Social Security and Medicare taxes if the trade or business is a sole proprietorship or a partnership in which each partner is a parent of the child. Refer to the "Covered services of a child" section below. Payments for the services of a child under age 21 who works for his or her parent in a trade or business are not subject to Federal Unemployment Tax Act (FUTA) tax. Payment for the services of a child are subject to income tax withholding, regardless of age.

Covered services of a child

The wages for the services of a child are subject to income tax withholding as well as Social Security, Medicare, and FUTA taxes if he or she works for:

- A corporation, even if it is controlled by the child's parent,
- A partnership, even if the child's parent is a partner, unless each partner is a parent of the child, or
- An estate, even if it is the estate of a deceased parent.

One spouse employed by another

A spouse is considered an employee if there is an employer/employee type of relationship, i.e., the first spouse substantially controls the business in terms of management decisions and the second spouse is under the direction and control of the first spouse. If such a relationship exists, then the second spouse is an employee subject to income tax and FICA (Social Security and Medicare) withholding. However, if the second spouse has an equal say in the affairs of the business, provides substantially equal services to the business, and contributes capital to the business, then a partnership type of relationship exists and the business's income should be reported on Form 1065, U.S. Return of Partnership Income (PDF).

Both spouses carrying on the trade or business

On May 25, 2007, the Small Business and Work Opportunity Tax Act of 2007 was signed into law and affected changes to the treatment of qualified joint ventures of married couples not treated as partnerships. The provision is effective for taxable years beginning after December 31, 2006.

The provision generally permits a qualified joint venture whose only members are a married couple filing a joint return not to be treated as a partnership for Federal tax purposes. A qualified joint venture is a joint venture involving the conduct of a trade or business, if (1) the only members of the joint venture are a married couple who file a joint tax return, (2) both spouses materially participate in the trade or business, (3) both spouses elect to have the provision apply, and the business is co-owned by both spouses and (4) isn't held in the name of a state law entity such as a partnership or limited liability company (LLC).

Under the provision, a qualified joint venture conducted by a married couple who file a joint return is not treated as a partnership for Federal tax purposes. All items of income, gain, loss, deduction, and credit are divided between the spouses in accordance with their respective interests in the venture. Each spouse takes into account his or her respective share of these items as a sole proprietor. Thus, it is anticipated that each spouse would account for his or her respective share on the appropriate form, such as Schedule C. For purposes of determining net earnings from self-employment, each spouse's share of income or loss from a qualified joint venture is taken into account, just as it is for Federal income tax purposes under the provision (i.e., in accordance with their respective interests in the venture).

This generally does not increase the total tax on the return, but it does give each spouse credit for Social Security earnings on which retirement benefits are based. However, this may not be true if either spouse exceeds the Social Security tax limitation. Refer to Publication 334, Tax Guide for Small Business, for further information about self-employment taxes. For more information on qualified joint ventures, refer to Election for Married Couples Unincorporated Businesses.

Parent employed by child

The wages for the services of a parent employed by his or her child in a trade or business are subject to income tax withholding and Social Security and Medicare taxes. Wages paid to a parent employed by his or her child are not subject to FUTA tax, regardless of the type of services provided. For additional employment tax information, refer to Publication 15, Circular E, Employer's Tax Guide, and Publication 51, Circular A, Agricultural Employer's Tax Guide.

If your parent works for you in your business, the wages you pay to him or her are subject to income tax withholding and Social Security and Medicare taxes. Social Security and Medicare taxes do not apply to wages paid to your parent for services not performed in your business, but they do apply to domestic services if all the following apply:

- You employ your parent;
- You have a child or stepchild living in the home;
- You are a widow or widower, divorced, or living with a spouse, who because of a mental or physical condition, can't care for the child or stepchild for at least 4 continuous weeks in a calendar quarter; and
- The child or stepchild is either under age 18 or requires the personal care of an adult for at least 4 continuous weeks in a calendar quarter due to a mental or physical condition."

EMPLOYEES VERSUS INDEPENDENT CONTRACTORS

 Let's start with one of the thornier questions about payroll and one that has great potential for harm: Is a person working for you an employee or an independent contractor? What is an independent contractor, you ask? There is no good answer. Let's look back a century.

Before the twentieth century this question was basically a tort law question concerning the liability of a master for their servant's actions. However, in the twentieth century, Congress adopted rules specifying the difference between an employee and an independent contractor. There has been a great deal of litigation concerning the issue and many updates of the statutes happening up to the current moment. There are also various additional regulations issued by the Treasury and Labor Departments.

In the past few decades, the number of independent contractors has mushroomed. The reason, in many cases, is to force workers to pay for an opportunity to work rather than paying them wages and overtime, for example, the worker who signs a contract to clean a building or a taxi driver who rents a cab for a 12-hour shift. There is very little difference in the work done between these independent contractors and full-time employees doing the same job. But the independent contractor label keeps workers from getting the protection of labor laws at the Federal and State levels as well as denying them the right to organize into a labor union.

The advantages to an employer in using independent contractors are large. There are reduced overhead costs, such as:

- Reduced payroll taxes
- No expenses of paying and accounting for payroll
- No benefits for independent contactors, which means:
    - No health insurance.
    - No vacation pay.
    - No jury duty pay or the like.
    - No time off with pay.

The independent contractor works when the employer wants him to. There is full flexibility about when they work, with no overtime pay for long hours and no pay for down times. In addition, an employer can find very experienced and well-trained contractors. If the employer were hiring workers, then they could be responsible for training their employees.

There are some disadvantages to hiring independent contractors over employees. These include employees' loyalty to the company, something an independent contractor may not have. Loyal and dedicated employees tend to be very productive. Loyal employees will also do other jobs as necessary for the company, even if the tasks are not necessarily in their job description. If the employee works for the company it is easier to schedule projects because the company controls the work schedule. Independent contractors may have to set their own schedules because of other contracts they are fulfilling at the same time.

There are also disadvantages to hiring employees. An employer now has a person who is depending on you to provide for them and their family. A company may be in an "employment-at-will" condition but employment generally connotes some permanency. If you do lay an employee off, the company then has to cover unemployment costs, which can be very expensive. Then there is extra overhead, facilities, taxes, benefits, and the like. The employee that stays with an employer is going to expect supervision, growth, training, and maybe a path to a better position in the future.

As there are downsides to employees, there are downsides to independent contractors besides the issues with scheduling mentioned previously. Independent contractors are not, as we discuss later, subject to your control. Their charges are subject to market variation and demand. You may pay them $25 an hour this month but with changes in the market and demands on their time, during the next month, you may find their rate has doubled. If you have misclassified workers as independent contractors and the IRS says they are really employees, then the back taxes, penalties, and interest owed can be devastating. Remember, the IRS and the Department of Labor would prefer that there be no independent contractors.

 Misclassifying workers can cost you big time! The state of California performed a routine employment audit on a client of ours, and discovered that the client was misclassifying workers. After the state audited several quarters crossing several years, the client was forced to pay back taxes plus penalties and interest for each quarter that the employee(s) were paid. The total amount due reached the mid-five-figure range. And this was just the state amounts. Regardless of whether a misclassification was done unintentionally or not, state agencies can be pretty ruthless when it comes to solving these matters, as we have seen time after time.

Now that we have discussed why you would want or not want an independent contractor let's talk about the definition of an independent contractor.

Common Law Test

The "common law test" of whether a worker is an employee for federal tax purposes has been made part of various federal law and regulations including the IRS Code relating to Social Security and Medicare taxes.

Through time, the judiciary has identified various factors which they felt were relevant in determining a worker's status to be that of an employee. In 1987, the IRS created a list of 20 factors they consider relevant after examining the case law.

The amount of weight given to each of the 20 factors depends on the job and the actual situation in which the worker operates. The list of 20 items is not exhaustive, and other relevant issues must be taken into account.

The following 20 items are listed in the IRS Revenue Ruling 87- 41 and are available with additional classification information in this document (https://www.irs.gov/pub/irs-utl/x-26-07.pdf).

1. *Instructions:* If the employer has the right to require that the worker comply with the employers' instructions, this indicates employee status.

2. *Training:* If the worker can be required to attend training as to how the work is done, this indicates employee status.

3. *Integration:* Integration of the worker's services into the normal business operations of the business indicates employee status.

4. *Service rendered personally:* The employer requires that the worker perform the services and the worker is not allowed to substitute another person (which indicates employee status).

5. *Hiring, supervising, and paying:* The employer hires, pays, and supervises assistants for the worker rather than the worker hiring, paying, and supervising his or her own assistants (which indicates employee status).

6. *Continuing relationship:* The employer and the worker maintain an ongoing and continuous relationship, which indicates employee status.

7. *Set hours of work:* The worker has established regular hours for work set by the employer (which indicates employee status).

8. *Full-time work required:* The worker must work full time for the employer rather than be free to work for whomever they want to and whenever they want to (which indicates employee status).

9. *Work on employer's premises:* The services performed by the worker occur in facilities controlled by the employer (which indicates employee status).

10. *Sequence test:* The worker performs tasks in the order that the employer specifies.

11. *Reporting:* The worker must submit reports either verbally or in writing on a regular basis.

12. *Payment:* The pay is based on a time unit (hour/day/week/etc.) as opposed to being paid by the job.

13. *Expenses:* If the employer pays the expenses for the worker, this leans toward employee status.

14. *Tools and materials:* If the worker's tools and materials are provided by the employer, this would indicate that the worker is an employee.

15. *Investment:* If the worker has made significant investment in the facilities where the work is performed, it indicates that the worker may be an independent contractor.

16. *Profit or loss:* A worker who is an employee does not normally make a profit or a loss in addition to his normal pay (which indicates employee status).

17. *One employer:* Normally a worker who performs the same service for multiple employers at the same time would be considered an independent contractor.

18. *Generally available:* If the worker makes his services available to the general public, this is indicative of an independent contractor status.
19. *Discharge:* The ability of an employer to fire a worker leans toward the worker being an employee.
20. *Termination:* If worker can quit at any time, this indicates that the worker is an employee.

IRS Rules

Since 1987 the IRS has been refining and trying to implement a system that is easier to use to make determinations than the 20 common law rules. More recently, the IRS has identified three types of conditions that could be used in determining the status of a worker as an independent contractor or an employee:

1. Behavioral control
2. Financial control
3. Relationship of the parties

The IRS makes the point that, in addition to the 20 common law tests, there other factors that may be relevant to the status of a worker, and that the weight allocated to each factor may vary based on the situation. Also, specific factors may change in relevance and weight over time, and all of the facts of every case need to be considered.

In general, the following is true. Individuals who offer the services they perform in the course of their professional work to the general public are normally independent contractors.

Courts realize that, in this day and age, highly skilled or highly educated workers don't require the minute-by-minute supervision of a bygone era, and so day-to-day control over a worker is not necessarily helpful in determining status. The courts are tending to focus on the worker's ability to realize the profit or loss from their services, particularly as shown by who pays expenses and who finances the business.

It all falls, in the end, to the single opinion of a judge. If the IRS says that your independent contractors are employees, you will have to spend time and money going to court to try and get that determination overturned by a judge's opinion.

There are some safe harbors if you think you will have a problem. Talk with a CPA who understands employment tax practice; they can explain what programs are in place. Programs change from time to time without warning and may have required a certain pattern of behavior to be effective. Beware of state laws about misclassification. In California, since January 1, 2012, if you misclassify a worker as an independent contractor instead of an employee, the potential fine is up to $15,000. Oklahoma, on the other hand, does not levy any fines for misclassification.

If you want to get the opinion of the IRS on how they are going to classify an employee, you can submit a Form SS-8 to receive a determination from the IRS. It may take six months or more to get your answer. In the meantime, if you have chosen wrong, the filing of the SS-8 is not going to relieve you of any liability. In fact, it raises a red flag to the IRS to come out and audit you. If a worker files a complaint about being treated as an independent contractor instead of as an employee, the IRS will ask you to fill out an SS-8. At that point, if all your paperwork is not in perfect order, you may lose not only the status determination, but also your safe harbor. If you're not sure exactly how to maintain your safe harbor for independent contract employees, contact a local trusted CPA who specializes in small business and employment taxes, and get on the straight and narrow.

 Another thing that happens on a fairly frequent basis is that you might terminate a worker that you classified and paid as an independent contractor. The worker files for unemployment, and lists your company as the former employer. The unemployment agency contacts you and wants to know why you were not reporting wages. You are now in a fight with your state unemployment agency, which is funded by the US Department of Labor. They are going to audit you for other workers who are really W-2 employees and whom you are treating as independent contractors.

If you are tempted by the financial gains of classifying workers as independent contractors instead of as employees, *beware*. Just one disgruntled ex-"independent contractor" can sink your business. They simply file for unemployment, even if they agreed to be treated as an independent contractor in writing. The rights of an employee are not something they can sign away. Again, if you have always paid them as independent contractors, filed their 1099s on a timely basis, used written contracts, acted consistently at all times, and never issued W-2s and 1099s to employees/independent contractors who hold the same job, you may be able to claim a safe harbor under Section 530. You still won't get off scot-free, but at least you will have a chance of surviving the ordeal.

 We had a client who hired independent contractors on a regular basis to use the client's equipment on assignment. One worker, when he or she was no longer getting jobs from the client, filed for unemployment. The state unemployment agency decided to immediately audit the client and then levied taxes, penalties, and interest charges on the client. We represented the client, first administratively, then to an administrative law judge, and finally to a Rule 13 hearing with the Unemployment Commission itself. At the Rule 13 hearing we were able to prevail. We showed that the client met the criteria to classify his workers as independent contractors and not employees. All the taxes, penalties, and interest costs were abated. The following January 1, the client switched all workers to employees so as not to ever have to go through such an ordeal again.

Paying an Independent Contractor

Paying an independent contractor is pretty simple. You can pay by the hour or by the job. In most situations, no income tax is withheld, no FICA taxes (Social Security and Medicare) need to be withheld, and no other employment taxes must be paid. However, if you are served with a child support order, you will have to withhold and submit child support payments. (See the section in chapter 8 titled "New Hire Reporting.")

STATUTORY EMPLOYEES AND STATUTORY NONEMPLOYEES

If a worker isn't an independent contractor, they are an employee, right? Actually, it is not that simple. We need to talk about statutory employees and nonstatutory employees. The government, has decided that some workers will be employees regardless of what the determination would be under the common law test or any other test. These are called statutory employees. The government has also decided that some workers will not be employees regardless (again) of how any determination test would turn out.

Statutory Employees

Statutory employees are independent contractors who do not necessarily meet the common law tests as an employee but, who have been deemed employees for federal law purposes by the federal government. They are employees for employment tax purposes. Wages paid to statutory employees are not subject to income tax withholding on the federal level. Wages are, however, subject to withholding for FICA purposes. In some instances, they will also be subject to federal unemployment taxes as well.

There are four groups of statutory employees.

Agent-Drivers or Commission-Drivers

The worker must be working in the distribution of vegetables or fruit, meat, beverages other than milk, baked goods, or in driving for a dry cleaning/laundry business. They also must be generating income on a commission basis or on a difference in price between the sales price of the goods and the price that the drivers pays his employer for the goods. Many vending machine drivers are paid this way.

Full-Time Life Insurance Salespersons

The worker's business activity must be principally marketing life insurance and/or annuity contracts. He or she works for just one insurance agency or company. The worker may have facilities including space, phone, computer systems, and clerical staff, along with marketing materials provided by the employer.

Homeworkers

The worker works away from the employer's premises. They work to the specifications that the employer creates. They work with material made available by the employer. The materials will be delivered per the employer's instructions. The homeworker must make and be paid at least $100 in wages a calendar year before their earnings become taxable for FICA purposes.

The earnings of a homeworker who does not qualify as an employee under the 20 common law rules are not subject to federal unemployment tax. The homeworker definition does not mean a domestic worker who works in an employer's house.

Traveling or City Salespersons

The salesperson must be a full-time worker. Their main job has to be seeking orders from organizations who either are wholesaling in the products offered for resale or who use the products of the employer in their own establishments. A salesperson who casually sells orders for another employer can still be a statutory employee of the full-time employer only.

General Requirements

Workers who qualify as one of the above types of workers have to meet the following conditions to qualify as a statutory employees.

1. Services will be performed by themselves personally.
2. They cannot have made a large investment in equipment or accommodations for the actual work.
3. There must be an ongoing relationship with the employer rather than a single occurrence.

Statutory Nonemployees

Some types of workers who would clearly be employees under the 20 common law tests are treated as independent contractors because Congress chose to categorize them as independent contractors instead of employees. They are looked at by the IRS as independent contractors for income tax, FICA taxes, and FUTA taxes, as long as clear circumstances are met. There are two types of these statutory nonemployees.

Qualified Real Estate Agents

This category applies to salespeople who are licensed by the appropriate licensing authority to operate as real estate agents in their state. Their duties are performed in the process of the sale of real estate including showing prospective buyers properties and advertising properties for sale.

Direct Sellers

Applies to workers who sell consumer goods on a resale basis or for commission. They normally sell in the client's home, or possibly their own, but not in an established retail sales location. Think Mary Kay or Fuller Brush (for the older generation). The exemption applies to newspaper delivery people or related products such as buying guides like the *Greensheet*. This also includes people who put on box shows for clothing companies.

General Requirements

These two types of nonemployees must meet the following requirements before they are exempt from payroll tax withholding requirements:

1. Their compensation mainly has to depend on their sales or production and not on how long they work.
2. They must have a contract in writing agreeing that they will not be treated as an employee for federal employment taxes.

CHILDREN

Children under the age of 18 are subject to all kinds of restrictions on employment. The details are in chapter 8 in the "Federal Child Labor Laws" section.

VOLUNTEERS

The Fair Labor Standards Act (FLSA) defines employment very broadly, i.e., "to suffer or permit to work."

The Supreme Court of the United States ruled and the Department of Labor has regulated that in the case of individuals serving as unpaid volunteers in various.community services, "Individuals who volunteer or donate their services, usually on a part-time basis, for public service, religious, or human-itarian objectives, not as employees and without contemplation of pay, are not considered employees of the religious, charitable, or similar non-profit organizations that receive their service." (Government-speak at its finest!)

Members of civic organizations may help at shelter workrooms or may send members or students into hospices, hospitals, nursing facilities, assisted living homes, and the like to provide personal services for the infirm or elderly. Parents of students may volunteer in a school library or lunch room as a civic activity to help keep up standards of services for their children; they may volunteer to chaperone or to drive a school vehicle for a drama camp or band trip.

In the same vein, people may volunteer to do things like driving, helping with a blood drive for the local blood bank, mentoring underserved populations, or acting as counselors, scoutmasters, and so on.

Under FLSA, workers cannot volunteer services to for-profit private sector employers. However, normally, individuals can volunteer services to public sec-tor employers.

In 1985, the amendments to the FLSA were clear that individuals are allowed to volunteer their services to public agencies or within their commu-nity. The exception is public sector employers, who may not allow or require their employees to do the same work both for pay and as a volunteer as well. There is no prohibition on employees in private businesses from volunteering in any way in the public employment sector of the economy.

If you are in business you probably don't have volunteers doing work for you.

If you do, don't push it too far. AOL got into trouble for using their members as unpaid moderators and the like in the late 1990s and was sued by vari-ous members of the AOL community for violation of labor laws. The Depart-ment of Labor never charged AOL with any legal violations; nevertheless, this cost AOL a lot of time and money. It also led to a number of changes in its policies.

 ## INTERNS

Interns in the "for-profit" business sector of the economy, who are classified as employees, are subject to FLSA and state minimum wage and overtime stan-dards, similar to any other employee.

There can be situations where individuals who work in "for-profit" busi-ness sector internships or training programs may not be paid to do so. The

Supreme Court definition of "suffer or permit to work" should not be held so as to make an individual who works for their own education an employee under certain circumstances.

These six principles must be looked at when making this decision.

1. For the intern who is actually performing work, the work is the equivalent to the same training that would be given in an educational setting.
2. The experience the intern receives accrues to the benefit of the individual intern.
3. The individual intern is not used to replace other workers and the intern works under the close direction of current employees.
4. The employer who employs the intern receives no apparent current return from the work of the intern, and, in fact, the internship may cause the employer additional costs or reduced efficiency.
5. The individual is not promised a position at the end of the internship.
6. The employer and the individual intern have a mutual understanding that there is no compensation for the labor or time expended by the intern.

If all of the criteria are in place, an employer-employee bond is not forged under the FLSA and standards in place for overtime and minimum wages do not apply.

This exclusion is designed to be very restrictive and hard to meet. It has been tested in the courts recently and a number of decisions have been in favor of the interns being employees and not unpaid interns, particularly for overtime.

Basically, the more an internship is structured around an academic experience rather than an employer's actual operations, the more likely it is to survive litigation as an unpaid internship. The broader the applicability of the skills learned, the more likely the internship will be viewed as education, as opposed to skills only applicable to the employer. The fact that the work assists the employer does not disqualify the work because, as well as benefiting the employer, it is providing new skillsets or better working habits to the intern.

If the employer would have had to hire additional employees if the interns were not there to do the work, the internship will not survive scrutiny to remain as excluded from FLSA. Neither will it if the intern is used to replace workers who were previously employed there. Also, it is expected that the intern would need more supervision than a standard worker; otherwise it suggests work, not training.

If an individual is placed with an employer as an unpaid intern for a probationary period of time with the justifiable expectation that they would then be placed in a permanent position, then the intern will be viewed as an employee under FLSA, not as an unpaid intern.

 ## RELIGIOUS WORKERS

If you are a religious institution there are numerous and complex rules. Please download www.irs.gov/pub/irs-pdf/p517.pdf (Publication 517 Cat. No. 15021X, Social Security and Other Information for Members of the Clergy and Religious Workers) or employ a local CPA who handles religious institutions for payroll purposes.

CHAPTER THREE

Earnings

W e are now going to move into the heart of payroll, earnings. The first thing you have to do, now that you know who is an employee and who is not, is to make a further distinction.

Who earns a salary and who is paid hourly?

We will cover commissions, piecework tips, and the rest a little later. You don't get to choose who is a salaried worker and who is an hourly worker, nor do the employees get to choose. It comes down to a provision of the Fair Labor Standards Act (FLSA), which is the federal law that governs much of wages and employment. FLSA sets out the rules on who is entitled to overtime pay if they work more than 40 hours in a work week. Those who are entitled to overtime are referred to as "nonexempt" (from overtime rules) and they are paid by the hour. Those who are not subject to overtime rules are referred to as "exempt" and they are normally paid a salary. Let's dive in.

SALARY

 If you are a small business owner and you are hiring only labor and clerical help, this is simple. You are paid a salary and are exempt and everybody else is hourly and nonexempt. The labor department has statistics that show that as many as 70% of employers misclassify employees. The cost can be staggering, as you and your company may be liable for all unpaid overtime and taxes going back for years.

We are going to lay out some fairly specific criteria for determining exempt versus nonexempt employees. If you have any doubt about the correct calculation, the federal Department of Labor has a series of fact sheets that give more details and references. Or you may choose to consult with a local CPA who is an employment tax expert.

Exceptions to the Rule: Who Is Exempt?

While the FLSA applies to the majority of employees in the United States, it does allow employers to claim exemptions from its requirements for certain employees whose jobs meet specific criteria.

Section 13(a)(1) of the FLSA provides an exemption from both minimum wage and overtime requirements for employees employed in bona fide executive, administrative, professional, and outside sales positions. Section 13(a)(1) and Section 13(a)(17) also exempt certain employees in computer-related occupations. These exemptions are defined in the department's regulations located at 29 CFR Part 541 (hereafter the "Part 541 exemptions").

To qualify for one of these exemptions, employees generally must meet certain tests regarding their job duties and be paid a certain minimum salary. Job titles alone do not determine exempt status, and neither does the receipt of a particular salary. In order for an exemption to apply, an employee's specific job duties *and* earnings must meet all of the applicable requirements. It is important to note that simply paying an employee a salary does not relieve an employer of minimum wage and overtime obligations to that employee. Unless they meet the criteria of a specific exemption, employees covered by FLSA protections who are paid a salary are still due overtime if they work more than 40 hours in a week.

This guide provides an overview of each of the Part 541 exemptions, and describes the basic tests and requirements to qualify for each. The specific salary levels listed below apply beginning on January 1, 2020, which is the effective date of the revised regulations implementing the exemptions.

If you have specific questions about any of these exemptions, please contact the Wage and Hour Division (WHD) at 866-4US-WAGE for assistance, or visit them online at www.dol.gov/whd.

Claiming an Exemption

For an employer to claim an exemption for a particular employee the following three conditions generally need to be satisfied:

1. Payment on a salary basis: the employee must be paid a predetermined and fixed salary that is not subject to reduction because of variations in the quality or quantity of work performed.
2. Payment of a minimum salary level: the amount of salary paid must meet a specified minimum amount.
3. A duties test: the employee's job duties must primarily involve those associated with exempt executive, administrative, professional, outside sales, or computer positions.

Basic Requirements for Exemption

Exemption	Salary Level Test	Salary Basis Test	Duties Test
Executive	▪ At least $684 per week ($35,568 per year)	▪ At least 90% of the salary level ($616 per week) must be paid on a "salary" basis ▪ Up to 10% ($68 per week) may be satisfied with nondiscretionary bonuses or incentive payments	▪ The employee's "primary duty" must be that of an exempt executive employee, as described in the "Duties Tests" section of this guide
Administrative	▪ At least $684 per week ($35,568 per year) ▪ "Academic administrative personnel" may qualify with a salary at least equal to the entry salary for teachers at their educational establishment.	▪ At least 90% of the salary level ($616 per week) must be paid on a "salary" or "fee" basis ▪ Up to 10% of the salary level ($68 per week) may be satisfied with nondiscretionary bonuses or incentive payments	▪ The employee's "primary duty" must be that of an exempt administrative employee, as described in the "Duties Tests" section of this guide

Exemption	Salary Level Test	Salary Basis Test[1]	Duties Test
Professional	▪ At least $684 per week ($35,568 per year); ▪ Salary level test does *not* apply to doctors, lawyers, or teachers	▪ At least 90% of the salary level ($616 per week) must be paid on a "salary" or "fee" basis ▪ Up to 10% of the salary level ($68 per week) may be satisfied with nondiscretionary bonuses or incentive payments ▪ These requirements do *not* apply for doctors, lawyers, and teachers	▪ The employee's "primary duty" must be that of an exempt professional employee, as described in the "Duties Tests" section of this guide
Outside Sales	▪ Does not apply	▪ Does not apply	▪ The employee's "primary duty" must be that of an exempt outside sales employee, as described in the "Duties Tests" section of this guide
Computer	▪ At least $684 per week ($35,568 per year), *or* at least $27.63 per hour	▪ At least 90% of the salary level ($616 per week) must be paid on a "salary" or "fee" basis unless the employee is paid on an hourly basis and receives at least $27.63 per hour ▪ Up to 10% of the salary level ($68 per week) may be satisfied with nondiscretionary bonuses or incentive payments	▪ The employee's "primary duty" must be that of an exempt computer employee, as described in the "Duties Tests" section of this guide

Exemption	Salary Level Test	Salary Basis Test	Duties Test
Highly Compensated Employees	▪ $107,432 per year in total compensation, including payment of at least $684 per week	▪ 100% of the standard salary level ($684 per week) must be paid on a "salary" or "fee" basis ▪ The remainder of the total annual compensation requirement may be paid in nondiscretionary bonuses or incentive payments (including commissions)	▪ The employee's "primary duty" must be office or nonmanual work ▪ Must "customarily and regularly" perform any one or more of the exempt duties or responsibilities of an executive, administrative or professional employee, as described in the "Duties Tests" section of this guide

[1] This chart does not include the special salary levels applicable to US territories or the special "base rate" for the motion picture producing industry.

The Salary Basis Test

Generally, for an employer to claim a Part 541 exemption from minimum wage and overtime requirements for an employee, that employee must be paid on a salary basis.

Being paid on a "salary basis" means an employee regularly receives a predetermined amount of money each pay period on a weekly, or less frequent, basis. The predetermined amount cannot be reduced because of variations in the quality or quantity of the employee's work. Generally, an exempt employee must receive at least the required weekly salary amount (discussed in more detail in the section titled "The Salary Level Test") for any week in which the employee performs any work, regardless of the number of days or hours worked. Exempt employees do not need to be paid for any workweek in which they perform no work. Deductions from pay are permissible only:

- When an exempt employee is absent from work for one or more full days for personal reasons other than sickness or disability.
- When an exempt employee is absent from work for absences of one or more full days due to sickness or disability if the deduction is made in accordance with a bona fide plan, policy, or practice of providing paid sick leave.

- To offset amounts employees receive as jury or witness fees, or for military pay.
- For penalties imposed in good faith for infractions of safety rules of major significance.
- For unpaid disciplinary suspensions of one or more full days imposed in good faith for workplace conduct rule infractions.

See 29 CFR 541.602.

An employer is not required to pay the full salary in the initial or final week of employment, or for weeks in which an exempt employee takes unpaid leave under the Family and Medical Leave Act. If the employer makes improper deductions from an employee's predetermined salary, that employee is not paid on a "salary basis." If the employee is ready, willing, and able to work, deductions may not be made for times when work is not available.

The salary basis test does not apply to outside sales employees, teachers, and employees practicing law or medicine.

Fee Basis

Administrative, professional, and computer employees may be paid on a "fee basis" rather than on a salary basis. If the employee is paid an agreed sum for a single job, regardless of the time required for its completion, the employee will be considered to be paid on a "fee basis." A fee payment is generally paid for a unique job rather than for a series of jobs repeated a number of times and for which identical payments are repeatedly made. To determine whether the fee payment meets the minimum salary level requirement, the test is to consider the time worked on the job and determine whether the payment is at a rate that would amount to at least $684 per week if the employee worked 40 hours. For example, an artist paid $500 for a picture that took 20 hours to complete meets the minimum salary requirement since the rate would result in $1,000 if 40 hours were worked.

The Salary Level Test

Standard Salary Level

Generally, an employee must be paid at least $684 per week to qualify for one of the Part 541 exemptions. Exempt computer employees may be paid at least $684 per week, *or* on an hourly basis of at least $27.63 an hour.

The salary level test does not apply to outside sales employees, teachers, and employees practicing law or medicine. Academic administrative employees may qualify for exemptions either by satisfying the standard salary level test or, alternatively, by being paid on a salary basis at a rate at least equal to the entrance salary for teachers in the educational establishment by which the employee is employed.

Special Salary Levels

The regulations provide for special salary levels for certain U.S. territories and an updated base rate for employees in the motion picture producing industry. A special salary level of $455 per week applies to Puerto Rico, the US Virgin Islands, Guam, and the Commonwealth of the Northern Mariana Islands. A special salary level of $380 per week applies to American Samoa.

The regulations also establish a special "base rate" threshold for employees in the motion picture producing industry. The base rate is $1,043 per week, or a prorated amount based on the number of days worked.

Total Annual Compensation Requirement for Highly Compensated Employees

Employees who receive total annual compensation of at least $107,432, referred to as "highly compensated employees" (HCEs), are exempt from the minimum wage and overtime requirements of the FLSA if they meet a more relaxed duties test than is required for employees paid the standard or special salary levels (the HCEs duties test is discussed below in the "Duties Tests" section of this guide). Nondiscretionary bonuses and incentive payments (including commissions) may be counted toward the $107,432 HCEs total annual compensation requirement, but the employer must pay at least the full standard salary level of $684 per week on a salary or fee basis to qualify for this exemption. If an employee's total compensation in a given annual period fails to meet the $107,432 threshold, an employer may make a "catch-up" payment within one month of the end of the annual period. Any such catch-up payment counts only toward the prior year's total annual compensation. If such a catch-up payment is not made within the timeframe allotted, the exemption is lost and overtime premium pay must be paid in any week the employee worked more than 40 hours.

Nondiscretionary Bonuses and Incentive Payments

Employers may use nondiscretionary bonuses and incentive payments (including commissions) to satisfy up to 10% of the standard or special salary levels. Thus, for the standard salary level, employers may use such payments to satisfy up to $68 of the $684 per week threshold, but must still pay at least $616 per week on a salary basis.

For employers to credit these payments toward the salary level test, they must be paid on an annual or more frequent basis. The employer may use any 52-week period, such as a calendar year, a fiscal year, or an anniversary of the hire year. If, by the end of the 52-week period, the sum of the salary paid plus the nondiscretionary bonuses and incentive payments (including commissions) paid does not equal the required salary level for the 52-week period ($35,568 for the standard salary level for a full-year worker), the employer may make a "catch-up" payment to achieve the required level within one pay period of the end of the 52-week period. Any such "catch-up" payment counts only toward the prior year's salary, not toward the salary amount during the 52-week period in which it was paid. If such a catch-up payment is not made within the timeframe allotted, the exemption is lost and overtime premium pay must be paid for any week the employee worked more than 40 hours.

Nondiscretionary bonuses and incentive payments (including commissions) are forms of compensation promised to employees to induce them to work more efficiently or to remain with the company. Examples may include individual or group production bonuses and bonuses for quality and accuracy of work. Incentive payments, including commissions, are also considered nondiscretionary, as such payments are generally based on a prior contract or understanding, and employees generally have a contract right to the commission promised.

By contrast, discretionary bonuses are generally paid without prior contract, promise, or announcement, and the decision to provide the bonus and the payment amount is at the employer's sole discretion. An example would be an "on-the-spot" award made without announcement and at the employer's sole discretion (e.g., an unannounced year-end bonus). Discretionary bonuses cannot be used to satisfy any part of the salary level requirement.

As noted above, employees who are exempt under the HCEs test must receive at least the standard salary amount ($684 per week) on a salary or fee basis. The HCEs test does not permit any portion of this amount to be satisfied by nondiscretionary bonuses or incentive payments. Thus, HCEs must receive the full standard salary amount each week on a salary or fee basis.

The Duties Test

To qualify for any of the Part 541 exemptions, employees must meet certain tests regarding their job duties. The regulations establish separate duties requirements for executive, administrative, professional, outside sales, and computer employees, respectively.

Most employees who are exempt under the white collar exemptions are subject to the standard duties test. Under the standard duties test, an employee's primary duty must be that of an exempt executive, administrative, or professional employee. "Primary duty" means the principal, main, major, or most important duty that the employee performs. Determination of an employee's primary duty must be based on all the facts in a particular case, with the major emphasis on the character of the employee's job as a whole.

Certain employees can also qualify for exemption under the special test for HCEs. As discussed above, this test applies only to employees who receive total annual compensation of $107,432, including at least $684 per week on a salary or fee basis. Under the HCEs duties test, the employee's primary duty must still consist of office or nonmanual work, but the employee need only "customarily and regularly" perform one of the exempt duties of a bona fide executive, administrative, or professional employee, as described in the regulations.

The duties requirements for each of the exemptions are described below in greater detail.

 ## EXECUTIVE EXEMPTION

To qualify for the executive employee exemption under the standard test, all of the following job duties requirements must be satisfied:

- The employee's primary duty must be managing the enterprise in which the employee is employed, or managing a customarily recognized department or subdivision of the enterprise.
- The employee must customarily and regularly direct the work of at least two or more other full-time employees or their equivalent (for example, one full-time and two half-time employees are equivalent to two full-time employees).
- The employee must have the authority to hire or fire other employees, or the employee's suggestions and recommendations as to the hiring, firing, promotion, or any other change of status of other employees must be given particular weight.

 ## ADMINISTRATIVE EXEMPTION

To qualify for the administrative employee exemption under the standard test, all of the following duties requirements must be satisfied:

- The employee's primary duty must be the performance of office or nonmanual work directly related to the management or general business operations of the employer or the employer's customers.
- The employee's primary duty must include the exercise of discretion and independent judgment with respect to matters of significance.

Academic administrative personnel whose primary duty is performing administrative functions directly related to academic instruction or training in an educational institution, such as principals and vice-principals responsible for the operation of an elementary or secondary school; department heads at institutions of higher education; academic counselors who perform work such as administering school testing programs, assisting students with academic problems, and advising students concerning degree requirements; and others with similar responsibilities are eligible for a special alternative salary level that does not apply to employees outside of an educational institution. These academic administrative personnel are exempt from the FLSA's minimum wage and overtime requirements if they are paid at least as much as the entrance salary for teachers at their educational establishment.

 ## PROFESSIONAL EXEMPTION

Several different kinds of "professional" employees may qualify for the professional employee exemption. These include "learned professionals," "creative professionals," teachers, and employees practicing law or medicine.

Learned Professionals

To qualify as a "learned professional" under the standard test, all of the following duties requirements must be satisfied:

- The employee's primary duty must be the performance of work requiring advanced knowledge, defined as work which is predominantly intellectual in character and which includes work requiring the consistent exercise of discretion and judgment.
- The advanced knowledge must be in a field of science or learning, including law, medicine, theology, accounting, actuarial computation, engineering, architecture, teaching, various types of physical, chemical, and biological sciences, pharmacy, and other occupations that have a recognized

professional status and are distinguishable from the mechanical arts or skilled trades, where the knowledge could be of a fairly advanced type, but is not in a field of science or learning.

- The advanced knowledge must be customarily acquired by a prolonged course of specialized intellectual instruction, which means specialized academic training is a standard prerequisite for entry into the profession.

Creative Professionals

To qualify for the creative professional employee exemption under the standard test, the employee's primary duty must be the performance of work requiring invention, imagination, originality, or talent in a recognized field of artistic or creative endeavor. This includes such fields as music, writing, acting, and the graphic arts.

Teachers

Teachers are exempt if their primary duty is teaching, tutoring, instructing, or lecturing in the activity of imparting knowledge, and if they are employed and engaged in this activity as a teacher in an educational establishment. Exempt teachers include, but are not limited to, regular academic teachers, kindergarten or nursery school teachers, teachers of gifted or disabled children, teachers of skilled and semi-skilled trades and occupations, teachers engaged in automobile driving instruction, aircraft flight instructors, home economics teachers, and vocal or instrumental music teachers.

Employees Practicing Law or Medicine

An employee holding a valid license or certificate permitting the practice of law or medicine is exempt if the employee is actually engaged in such a practice. An employee who holds an academic degree for the general practice of medicine is also exempt if they are engaged in an internship or resident program for the profession.

Outside Sales Exemption

To qualify for the outside sales employee exemption, all of the following duties requirements must be satisfied:

- The employee's primary duty must be making sales or obtaining orders or contracts for services or for the use of facilities for which a consideration will be paid by the client or customer. "Sales" includes any sale, exchange, contract to sell, consignment for sale, shipment for sale, or other disposition. It includes the transfer of title to tangible property, and in certain cases, of tangible and valuable evidences of intangible property.

- The employee must be customarily and regularly engaged away from the employer's place or places of business.

Computer Employee Exemption

To qualify for the computer employee exemption, the following duties requirements must be satisfied:

- The employee must be employed as a computer systems analyst, computer programmer, software engineer, or other similarly skilled worker in the computer field.
- The employee's primary duty must consist of:
  1. The application of systems analysis techniques and procedures, including consulting with users, to determine hardware, software, or system functional specifications.
  2. The design, development, documentation, analysis, creation, testing or modification of computer systems or programs, including prototypes, based on and related to user or system design specifications.
  3. The design, documentation, testing, creation or modification of computer programs related to machine operating systems.
  4. A combination of the aforementioned duties, the performance of which requires the same level of skills.

 ## HIGHLY COMPENSATED EMPLOYEES

An employee with a primary duty of office or nonmanual work who meets the HCEs compensation requirements ($107,432 per year in total annual compensation, with at least $684 per week on a salary or fee basis) is exempt if the employee customarily and regularly performs at least one of the exempt duties of a bona fide executive, administrative, or professional employee, as described in the regulations. An employee who performs such exempt duties only on an isolated or occasional basis will not satisfy this duties requirement.

ADDITIONAL GUIDANCE

The Department of Labor has issued additional compliance assistance materials to help employers, including small businesses understand the changes to the Part 541 exemption regulations. This includes detailed guidance for specific sectors, including higher education and nonprofit organizations. These materials are available at www.dol.gov/whd.

WHEN AN EMPLOYER MAY MAKE DEDUCTIONS FROM SALARY PAYROLL

 A well-written employee handbook/policy manual is necessary if you have exempt employees besides yourself and want time-off policies in place. See chapter 17.

Deductions from an exempt employee's pay are permissible:

- When the employee is absent from work for one or more full days for personal reasons other than sickness or disability.
- For absences of one or more full days due to sickness or disability.
- If the deduction is made in accordance with a bona fide plan, policy, or practice of providing compensation for salary lost due to illness.
- To offset amounts employees receive as jury or witness fees, or for military pay.
- For penalties imposed in good faith for infractions of safety rules of major significance.
- For unpaid disciplinary suspensions of one or more full days imposed in good faith for workplace conduct rule infractions.

Also, an employer is not required to pay the full salary in the initial or terminal week of employment, or for weeks in which an exempt employee takes unpaid leave, under the Family and Medical Leave Act.

HOURLY WAGE

The Fair Labor Standards Act (FLSA or Act) is administered by the Wage and Hour Division (WHD) of the US Department of Labor. The Act establishes standards for minimum wages, overtime pay, recordkeeping, and child labor. These standards affect more than 135 million workers, both full-time and part-time, in the private and public sectors.

The Act covers enterprises with employees who engage in interstate commerce; produce goods for interstate commerce; or handle, sell, or work on goods or materials that have been moved in or produced for interstate commerce. For most firms, a threshold of $500,000 in annual dollar volume of business even if the company is not in interstate commerce creates a presumption (refutable) that the company is covered by FLSA (i.e., the Act does not cover enterprises with less than this amount of business).

In addition, the Act covers the following regardless of their dollar volume of business:

- Hospitals
- Institutions primarily engaged in the care of the sick, aged, mentally ill, or disabled who reside on the premises
- Schools for children who are mentally or physically disabled or gifted
- Preschools, elementary and secondary schools, and institutions of higher education
- Federal, state, and local government agencies

Employees of firms that do not meet the $500,000 annual dollar volume threshold may be covered in any workweek when they are individually engaged in interstate commerce, the production of goods for interstate commerce, or an activity that is closely related and directly essential to the production of such goods.

In addition, the Act covers domestic service employees, such as housekeepers, cooks, gardeners, nurses, or home health aides, if they receive at least $2,200 in 2020 from one employer in a calendar year, or if they work a total of more than eight hours a week for one or more employers. (This calendar year wage threshold is set by the Social Security Administration each year.) For additional coverage information, see the Wage and Hour Division Fact Sheet #14: Coverage under the FLSA.

The Act exempts some employees from its overtime pay and minimum wage provisions, and it also exempts certain employees from the overtime pay provisions only. Because the exemptions are narrowly defined, employers should check the exact terms and conditions for any applicable exemption by contacting their local Wage and Hour Division office.

BASIC PROVISIONS/REQUIREMENTS

The Act requires employers of covered employees who are not otherwise exempt to pay these employees a minimum wage of not less than $7.25 per hour. Youths under 20 years of age may be paid a minimum wage of not less than $4.25 per hour during the first 90 consecutive calendar days of employment with an employer. Employers may not displace any employee to hire someone at the youth minimum wage. For additional information regarding the use of the youth minimum wage provisions, see the Wage and Hour Division Fact Sheet #32: Youth. Youth wages are covered later in this chapter.

Minimum Wage – FLSA

Employers may pay employees on a piece rate basis (see below for a full explanation of piecework), as long as they receive at least the equivalent of the required minimum hourly wage rate and overtime for hours worked in excess of 40 hours in a workweek. Employers of tipped employees (i.e., those who customarily and regularly receive more than $30 a month in tips) may consider such tips as part of their wages, but employers must pay a direct wage of at least $2.13 per hour if they claim a tip credit. They must also meet certain other requirements. For a full listing of the requirements an employer must meet to use the tip credit provision, see the Wage and Hour Division Fact Sheet #15: Tipped Employees Under the FLSA.

The Act also permits the employment of certain individuals at wage rates below the statutory minimum wage under certificates issued by the Department of Labor:

- Student learners (vocational education students)
- Full-time students in retail or service establishments, agriculture, or institutions of higher education
- Individuals whose earning or productive capacities for the work to be performed are impaired by physical or mental disabilities, including those related to age or injury

The Act does not limit either the number of hours in a day or the number of days in a week that an employer may require an employee to work, as long as the employee is at least 16 years old. Similarly, the Act does not limit the number of hours of overtime that may be scheduled. However, the Act requires employers to pay covered employees not less than one and one half times their regular rate of pay for all hours worked in excess of 40 in a workweek, unless the employees are otherwise exempt. For additional information regarding overtime pay requirements, see the Wage and Hour Division Fact Sheet #23: Overtime Pay Requirements of the FLSA.

The Act prohibits performance of certain types of work in an employee's home unless the employer has obtained prior certification from the Department of Labor. Restrictions apply in the manufacture of knitted outerwear, gloves and mittens, buttons and buckles, handkerchiefs, embroideries, and jewelry (where safety and health hazards are not involved). Employers wishing to employ homeworkers in these industries are required to provide written assurances to the Department of Labor that they will comply with the Act's wage and hour requirements, among other things.

The Act generally prohibits manufacture of women's apparel (and jewelry under hazardous conditions) in the home except under special certificates that may be issued when the employee cannot adjust to factory work because of age or disability (physical or mental), or must care for a disabled individual in the home.

State Minimum Wage

 Minimum wage has become a political topic in recent years and state and local minimum wage rate increases have proliferated. You are required to use the state or local minimum wage when you are paying employees if it exceeds federal minimum wage, regardless of whether you participate in interstate commerce or not.

Check to see if state minimum wage rates apply to you at https://www.dol.gov/agencies/whd/minimum-wage/state. For local minimum wage levels you should be able to google "minimum wage" and the city or locality you're concerned with if it is different from the state or federal minimum wage.

Overtime

The federal law governing overtime is contained in the FLSA. The overview of overtime is directly from the Department of Labor website.

> Covered nonexempt employees must receive overtime pay for hours worked over 40 per workweek (any fixed and regularly recurring period of 168 hours – seven consecutive 24-hour periods) at a rate not less than one and one-half times the regular rate of pay. There is no limit on the number of hours employees 16 years or older may work in any workweek. The FLSA does not require overtime pay for work on weekends, holidays, or regular days of rest, unless overtime is worked on such days.

A covered employee is one whose employer is subject to FLSA.

An exempt employee is not subject to the overtime rules, basically those employees on salary or nonemployees.

There is no federal provision for double-time, triple-pay, or anything of the sort. There are many union contracts that specify double- and triple-time, and the State of California, among others, also mandates double-time pay in certain instances.

Many states follow the federal guidelines on overtime pay and if an employer is not subject to FLSA they are still responsible to paying overtime under appropriate state laws. Not all states have overtime laws and if the employer is not subject to FLSA and they are in a state with no overtime law they do not have to pay overtime. Employers in those states may choose to pay overtime to keep workers happy but may not be required to do so.

If you are audited by the US Department of Labor (DOL), typically for a complaint filed by an employee or ex-employee, the assumption is that the DOL has jurisdiction and that you are subject to Federal Labor Laws, particularly FLSA for overtime, because you are in business. If you feel you are not subject to FLSA because you are not in interstate commerce, you need to fight it. The DOL with come up with arguments that may not hold up under scrutiny.

We had a small local restaurant. The DOL in an audit made the argument that, because a patron's credit card was processed in

South Dakota, the waiter who carried it to the cashier was involved in interstate commerce and was subject to FLSA. We refused to pay the fines and take the action the DOL suggested. The DOL dropped the case.

Commission

A commission is a sum of money that is paid to a worker upon completion of a task, often the task of selling a certain amount of goods or services.

Commission can be paid to an employee, or nonemployee.

If commission is paid to an employee the employee must still make at least minimum wage in each pay period. If the commission is paid to a nonemployee, say an independent contractor or statutory nonemployee, the minimum wage and FLSA do not come into play.

Types of Commission Schemes

There are multiple ways to compensate workers with commission; here are a few.

Base Salary Plus Commission An employee has a guaranteed base salary, plus a compensation for sales they make. The employee can rely on their salary during periods of time when it may be tough to earn commissions. The employer can set a lower salary base because the employee has the opportunity to earn a commission based on their performance and ability to sell.

Straight Commission This means that the worker earns their entire compensation based on the sales they produce. The commissions per sale will tend to be higher than those paid to an employee with a base salary. The employer pays less employment taxes on nonemployee workers (independent contractors) who earn straight commissions and the worker pays more in employment taxes. The nonemployee worker also gains tax advantages in being able to deduct all of his work-associated expenses where an employee's deductions are much more limited.

Draw against Commission Some workers on straight commission are able to receive a draw against their commission. This means they are given a certain amount of compensation each pay period. When a commission is earned, the draw is subtracted from the commission and only the remainder, if any, is paid to the worker. However, the entire commission including any previous draws is taxable income in the year earned. Should the worker never make enough commissions to pay back the draw the company should issue a Form 1099-C (Cancellation of Debt) at the end of their association. The unearned draw the worker receives is seen as a loan and is not taxable to the worker when received. The amount on the Form 1099-C is also taxable income to the worker in the year the 1099-C is issued for unless the taxpayer is insolvent. This is done to make all of the unpaid back draws deductible to the business as a bad debt.

Residual Commission   Some commissioned workers can earn a residual commission on the sales they produce. This is common in insurance companies, where the salesperson will continue to receive a part of the premiums paid in to the insurance company by the policyholder every year that the policy the worker sold remains in effect.

Tips

Tips are discretionary (optional or extra) payments determined by a customer that employees receive from customers.

Tips include:

- Cash tips received directly from customers.
- Tips from customers who leave a tip through electronic settlement or payment. This includes a credit card, debit card, gift card, or any other electronic payment method.
- The value of any noncash tips, such as tickets or other items of value.
- Tip amounts received from other employees paid out through tip pools or tip splitting, or other formal or informal tip-sharing arrangement.

All cash and noncash tips an employee receives are income and are subject to federal income taxes. All cash tips received by an employee in any calendar month are subject to Social Security and Medicare taxes, and must be reported to the employer, unless the tips received by the employee during a single calendar month, while working for the employer, total less than $20. Cash tips include tips received from customers, charged tips (e.g., credit and debit card charges) distributed to the employee by his or her employer, and tips received from other employees under any tip-sharing arrangement.

Employee Responsibilities

As an employee who receives tips, you must do three things:

1. Keep a daily tip record.
2. Report tips to the employer, unless they amount to less than $20 in a month.
3. Report all tips on an individual income tax return.

Keep a Daily Tip Record Employees must keep a daily record of tips received. You can use Form 4070A, Employee's Daily Record of Tips, included in Publication 1244. In addition to the information asked for on Form 4070A, you also need to keep a record of the date and value of any noncash tips you get, such as tickets, passes, or other items of value. Although you do not report these tips to your employer, you must report them on your tax return.

Report Tips to the Employer, Unless Less Than $20 The Internal Revenue Code requires employees to report to their employer in a written statement all cash tips received except for the tips from any month that do not total at least $20. Cash tips include tips received from customers, charged tips (e.g., credit and debit card charges) distributed to the employee by his or her employer, and tips received from other employees under any tip-sharing arrangement. No particular form must be used. The statement must be signed by the employee and must include:

- Employee's name, address, and Social Security number
- Employer's name and address (establishment name, if different)
- Month or period the report covers
- Total of tips received during the month or period

The employee may use Form 4070, Employee's Report of Tips to Employer, (available only in Pub. 1244, Employee's Daily Record of Tips and Report to Employer), unless some other form is provided by the employer. You can use an electronic system provided by your employer to report your tips.

Both directly and indirectly tipped employees must report tips to the employer.

Report All Tips on an Individual Income Tax Return An employee must use Form 4137, Social Security and Medicare Tax on Unreported Tip Income, to report the amount of any unreported tip income to include as additional wages on their Form 1040, U.S. Individual Income Tax Return, and the employee share of Social Security and Medicare tax owed on those tips.

When to Report Tips to Your Employer Employees must report tips to the employer by the 10th of the month after the month the tips are received. For example, tips received by an employee in August are required to be reported by the employee to the employer on or before September 10. If the 10th falls on a Saturday, Sunday, or legal holiday, an employee may give the report to the employer by the next day that is not a Saturday, Sunday, or legal holiday.

An employer may require employees to report tips more than once a month. However, the statement cannot cover a period of more than one calendar month.

 The employer may wish to have employees report tips for every pay period of work to make administration easier.

Do Not Include Service Charges in Your Daily Tip Record Charges added to a customer's check, such as for large parties, by your employer and distributed to you should not be added to your daily tip record. These additional charges your employer adds to a customer's bill do not constitute tips. They are service charges. These distributed payments are nontip wages and are subject to Social Security tax, Medicare tax, and federal income tax withholding.

An employer's or employee's characterization of a payment as a "tip" is not the last word. Distributed service charges, often referred to as "auto-gratuities" by service industries, should be recorded as nontip wages. Revenue Ruling 2012-18 lists the factors that determine whether such payments are tips or service charges.

Revenue Ruling 2012-18 provides that the absence of any of the following factors creates a doubt as to whether a payment is a tip, and indicates that the payment may be a service charge:

- The payment must be made free from compulsion.
- The customer must have the unrestricted right to determine the amount.

- The payment should not be the subject of negotiation or dictated by employer policy.
- Generally, the customer has the right to determine who receives the payment.

The example from the Revenue Ruling is:

Restaurant's menu lists a 15% charge apply to all parties of six or more customers. The customer's bill for food and beverages for the party of six includes an amount listed as "Tip" equal to 15% of the charges for food and beverages, and is included in the total charges. The restaurant pays out this amount to the serving staff and tip pool. The patron did not have the unconstrained right to determine the amount of the "Tip" because it was automatically calculated under the restaurant's policy. The client did not make the payment free from compulsion. The 15% charge is not reported as a tip. Instead, the amount is not reported as tip income to the staff to whom it was distributed.

Allocated Tips   If the total tips reported to the employer by all employees at a large food or beverage establishment are less than 8% of the gross receipts (or a lower rate approved by the IRS), the employer must allocate the amount less than the 8% among the employees who receive tips. If your employer allocates tips, they are shown separately in Box 8 of the employee's Form W-2. They are not included in Box 1 (Wages, tips, other compensation), Box 5 (Medicare wages and tips), or Box 7 (Social Security tips) of your Form W-2.

You must report the tips allocated to you by your employer on your income tax return. Attach Form 4137, Social Security and Medicare Tax on Unreported Tip Income, to Form 1040, U.S. Individual Income Tax Return, to report tips allocated by your employer (Box 8 of Form W-2). Any tips not reported to the employer must also be reported on Form 4137. The employee does not need to report tips allocated to the employee on their federal income tax return if the employee has records to show that the employee received fewer tips in that reporting year than the allocated amount.

Employer Responsibilities

The employer has several responsibilities regarding tips including recordkeeping, reporting, collecting taxes on tips, filling and filing forms as well as depositing taxes.

- Employers must retain employee-created tip reports and withhold federal income tax and the employee share of FICA taxes based on wages paid and tips reported to the employer. The employer reports this information and deposits taxes along with all other employment tax obligations the employer has. Of course, employers must calculate and pay the employer portion of FICA taxes as well. This is calculated on the total wages paid and the tips reported to the employer by tipped employees.
- Tips reported to the employer by the employee are to be included in Box 1 (Wages, tips, other compensation), Box 5 (Medicare wages and tips), and Box 7 (Social Security tips) of the employee's Form W-2. Enter the amount of any uncollected Social Security tax and Medicare tax in Box 12 of Form W-2. For more information, see the General Instructions for Forms W-2 and W-3.
- Employers report FIT and FICA taxes withheld from employees' wages and the employer calculated portion of FICA taxes on Form 941, Employer's Quarterly Federal Tax Return. The taxes are deposited according to current federal tax deposit requirement for the employer.
- Employers are also required to file Form 940, Employer's Annual Federal Unemployment (FUTA) Tax Return, and deposit the calculated taxes as well. The employee pays no FUTA tax; it is levied only on the employer. See chapter 5 for more on FIT, FICA, Medicare and FUTA taxes.

Employer Share Taxes on Unreported Tips   When employees do not report some of their tips to their employer, the employer is not liable for the employer share of Social Security and Medicare taxes on the unreported tips until notice and demand for the taxes is made to the employer by the IRS. The employer is not liable to withhold and pay the employee share of Social Security and Medicare taxes on the unreported tips.

For more information on Section 3121(q) Notice and Demand, see Revenue Ruling 2012-18, which sets forth guidance on Social Security and Medicare taxes on tips.

Distributed Service Charges   Service charges distributed to employees must be treated as wages to those employees. The employer must keep a record of the name, address, and Social Security number of the employee, the amount and date of each payment, and the amount of income, Social Security, and Medicare taxes collected with respect to the payment.

In an audit, the IRS may ask the employer to show how sales subject to service charges are kept separate from sales subject to tipping. Agent examiners may ask for point-of-sale (POS) records and other such data to verify the reported amounts. To further confirm the employer's processes, agents may sample various reports throughout the year. They may ask for complete explanation of the procedures and policies of the employer to validate how the distributed service charges were calculated, reported, and paid to the employee.

Service Charges Retained by Employer Are Income to the Employer   Service charges as we have discussed above are fees the establishment imposes on the customer by policy, not by the customer's choice. Service charges are always income to the employer. When and if the employer distributes some or all of the service charges to employees, that amount becomes income to the employee and a payroll cost to the employer. This is to separate out monies from "tips," which are freely paid by customers to employees.

Tips are not income to the employer, only to the employee. The employer can distribute service charges collected from customers as the employer chooses and to any employee it chooses. The employer also may retain some or all of the service charges. Notwithstanding whether the service charges are distributed to employees, the amount of the collected service charge is gross income to the employer. The employer may well be entitled to a business deduction, as payroll expense, for the service charges paid out to employees. All of the standard rules concerning business deduction under section 162 of the Internal Revenue Code apply.

Voluntary Tip Compliance Agreements   "Voluntary tip compliance agreements have been established by the IRS for industries where tipping is customary, such as the restaurant industry and casinos. These agreements are designed to enhance tax compliance among tipped employees and their employers through taxpayer education instead of through traditional enforcement actions, such as tip examinations. In addition to helping taxpayers understand and meet their tip reporting responsibilities, these agreements offer many benefits for the employer and the employee."

The IRS currently offers employers the opportunity of entering into one of several types of voluntary tip compliance agreements.

- TRAC: Tip Reporting Alternative Commitment
- TRDA: Tip Rate Determination Agreement
- GITCA: Gaming Industry Tip Compliance Agreement

Employers Who Operate Large Food or Beverage Establishments An employer who runs a large food or beverage establishment must file Form 8027, Employer's Annual Information Return of Tip Income and Allocated Tips. This is an annual report to the IRS for the revenue from food and beverage sales and the tips employees reported to the employer. Form 8027 is also used to calculate allocated tips for tipped employees. Employers must file a separate Form 8027 for each large food or beverage establishment.

A business is considered a large food or beverage establishment if all of the following apply.

- Food or beverage operation is located in the 50 states or in the District of Columbia.
- Food or beverages are provided for consumption on the premises (other than fast food operations).
- Tipping of food or beverage employees by customers is a customary practice.
- Employer normally employed more than 10 employees on a typical business day during the preceding calendar year. See the Instructions for Form 8027, to determine if you had more than 10 employees on a typical business day.

Tip Credit Under the Fair Labor Standards Act (FLSA), employers are required to pay tipped employees only $2.13 per hour in wages, so long as the employee's tips are enough to make up the remainder of the minimum hourly wage then in effect ($7.25 per hour). This is a tip credit against wages. Under federal law, if you have tipped employees you can pay tipped employees as little as $2.13 an hour in cash wages as long as the employees make at least $5.12 an hour in tips.

The employer may pay tipped employees more than the $2.13 per hour if the employer so chooses.

If the employee's tips do not bring the employee's total wages up to the current minimum wage of $7.25, then the employer must pay the difference as cash wages to the employee.

Tipped employees are those who work in a job where they ordinarily and regularly receive tips that exceed $30 per month. There are rules to which the employer is subject to be able to take the tip credit against wages.

- Tipped employees must actually receive the tips that equal or exceed the tip credit taken by their employer.

- Employees must be educated about the tip credit law and how it will affect their wages and net pay before the employer can use the tip credit.
- All tips that the employee receives are to be kept by the employee. Tip pooling is allowed among employees who regularly receive tips.
- Any tips paid by credit card must be paid to the employee no later than the next payday. The employer may withhold the amount charged by the credit card company to process the charges on the credit card.
- The tip credit remains the same even if the employee is working overtime hours at time and one half under FLSA overtime requirements.

Service charges paid to an employee will count as wages paid toward satisfying the $2.13 per hour, the federal minimum wage currently $7.25 per hour.

Many states do not follow federal law in regards to tip credits. Some states prohibit them entirely. The laws most favorable to the employee must be used. The employer needs to figure out which way provides the highest cash payout to the employee and use it in calculating wages. Your state labor department will have brochures detailing any state tip credit or denial of tip credit.

FICA Tip Credit

As an employer you have to collect the employee share of FICA taxes on tips that the employee reports to you. You also have to pay the employer matching amount. However, if you operate a food and/or beverage operation, and, quoting the IRS Form 8846 instructions, "You had employees who received tips from customers for providing, delivering, or serving food or beverages for consumption if tipping of employees for delivering or serving food or beverages is customary," there is a credit available. You take all of the tips that were reported to you by employees during the year. From that you subtract all the tips that were used as a tip credit. These tips are referred to as "tips deemed wages."

You take the rest of "tips deemed wages" and multiply it by .0765. That is your credit. This credit is a general business credit and can offset other taxes that the reporting entity has. It is not a refundable credit, however. If you owe no taxes you can't use the credit. It does carry backward and forward to other periods. This can amount to thousands of dollars a year in tax credits, especially in states that don't allow tip credits.

PIECEWORK

When paying a worker, employers can use various methods including "paid by the piece." That is the number of things a worker makes or tasks they complete.

Some industries where piece-rate-pay jobs are common are agricultural work, cable installation, call centers, writing, editing, translation, truck driving, data entry, carpet cleaning, craftwork, and manufacturing. Working for a piece rate does not mean that employers are exempt from paying minimum wage or overtime requirements under FLSA and/or state or local minimum wage or overtime rule.

FLSA requires that all employees, including piecework employees, earn at least the minimum wage. In calculating an appropriate piecework rate, employers must keep track of average productivity rates for specific activities, and set a piecework rate that ensures that all workers are able to earn minimum wage. If a worker earns less than the minimum wage, the employer has to pay the difference. There are exceptions:

- If the worker is a family member of the employer.
- Any employer in agriculture who did not utilize more than 500 "man-days" of agricultural labor in any calendar quarter of the preceding calendar year is exempt from the minimum wage and overtime pay provisions of the FLSA for the current calendar year. A man-day is defined as any day during which an employee performs agricultural work for at least one hour.
- In agricultural businesses, if a worker primarily takes care of livestock on the range.
- If nonlocal hand-harvesting workers are under 16 years of age, are employed on the same farm as their parent, and receive the piecework rate for those over 16 years of age.

TRAINING WAGE

The FLSA establishes minimum wage, overtime pay, recordkeeping, and youth employment standards affecting full-time and part-time workers in the private sector and in federal, state, and local governments. The FLSA requires payment of the federal minimum wage to all covered and nonexempt employees. Overtime pay at a rate of not less than one and one-half times the regular rate of pay is required for all hours worked over 40 in a workweek.

The 1996 Amendments to the FLSA allow employers to pay a youth minimum wage of not less than $4.25 an hour to employees who are under 20 years of age during the first 90 consecutive calendar days after initial employment. The law contains certain protections for employees that prohibit employers from displacing any employee in order to hire someone at the youth minimum wage. The fact sheet at www.dol.gov/whd/regs/compliance/whdfs32 .pdf provides general answers to questions that may arise about the youth wage provisions.

All employers covered by the FLSA may pay eligible employees the youth minimum wage, unless prohibited by state or local law. Where a state or local law requires payment of a minimum wage higher than $4.25 an hour and makes no exception for employees under age 20 years of age, the higher state or local minimum wage standard would apply.

The eligibility period runs for 90 consecutive calendar days beginning with the first day of work for an employer. It does not matter when the job offer was made or accepted, or when the employee started work. The 90-day period starts with the first day of work for the employer. The 90-day period is counted as consecutive days on the calendar, not days of work. It does not matter how many days during this period the youth actually performs any work.

If an employee reaches 20 years of age before he or she has worked the full 90-day eligibility period for the employer their pay must be raised to the minimum wage starting as of their birthday.

A break in service does not affect the calculation of the 90-day period of eligibility. In other words, the 90-calendar -day period continues to run even if the employee comes off the payroll during the 90 days. For example, if a student initially works for an employer over a 60-calendar-day period in the summer and then quits to return to school, the 90-day eligibility period ends for this employee with this employer 30 days after he/she quits; i.e., 90 consecutive calendar days after initial employment.

The law contains specific protections for employees that make it illegal for employers to terminate employees to hire someone at the youth wage. Employers may not take any action to displace any employee (including partial displacements such as a reduction in hours, wages, or employment benefits) for employing someone at the youth wage. Violation of this antidisplacement provision is a violation of the FLSA's Section 15(a)(3) antidiscrimination provision.

IF an employer hires only employees under 20 years of age at the youth wage, and employs them serially for 90 days each, it would be a violation of the antidisplacement provisions.

Displacement includes discharge, or any reduction in an employee's hours, wages, or employment benefits. Employees who are illegally displaced are entitled to "make whole" relief, such as reinstatement to their previous or an equivalent position of employment, payment of lost wages or benefits, etc.

For additional information, visit the DOL Wage and Hour Division website: www.wagehour.dol.gov.

 ## SUBMINIMUM WAGE PROVISIONS

The FLSA provides for the employment of certain individuals at wage rates below the statutory minimum. Such individuals include student learners (vocational education students), as well as full-time students employed in retail or service establishments, agriculture, or institutions of higher education. Also included are individuals whose earning or productive capacities are impaired by a physical or mental disability, including those related to age or injury. Employment at less than the minimum wage is authorized to prevent curtailment of opportunities for employment. Such employment is permitted only under certificates issued by the Wage and Hour Division.

- Employment of Workers with Disabilities: Section 14(c) of the Fair Labor Standards Act authorizes employers, after receiving a certificate from the Wage and Hour Division, to pay special minimum wages – wages less than the federal minimum wage – to workers who have disabilities for the work being performed.
- Industrial Homework: Homeworkers must be paid at a rate of not less than the minimum wage provided in the Act for all hours worked unless a lower rate is permitted under a special certificate for an individual homeworker in accordance with Regulations, 29 CFR 525.
- Student Learners: Section 14(a) of the FLSA authorizes the payment of subminimum wages – at rates not less than 75% of the applicable minimum wage under section 6(a) of the FLSA – to a student-learner after the employer has applied for an authorizing certificate from the DOL.

OTHER PAYROLL CATEGORIES

There are an unlimited number of other types of pay that the employer can provide. We list some of them, but by no means all, below. They are all taxable unless otherwise noted but are usually exempt from FLSA provisions because they are not mentioned in Federal Law.

Holiday Pay

Holiday pay is pay for holidays that are not worked by an employee. This may be recognized Federal Reserve banking holidays. It can be a religious holiday or any holiday that the employer chooses to recognize and pay the employee for, without the employee working that day. It is normally paid at the normal rate of hourly pay but that again is at the discretion of the employer. Holiday pay is fully taxable as if it was normal pay, but is not included in overtime calculations.

Many employers recognize the basic six holidays:

- New Year's Day
- Memorial Day
- Independence Day
- Labor Day
- Thanksgiving Day
- Christmas

Other employers such as banks recognize all 11 federal holidays, adding:

- Martin Luther King Jr. Day
- Presidents Day
- Columbus Day
- Veterans Day
- Inauguration Day (for federal employees in the Washington area every fourth year)

Bereavement Pay

This pays the employee even though they are not working as the result of a death of a select group of people. It may cover:

- Immediate family

- The death of close or related family both by birth and marriage
- Close friends

Again, it is at the discretion of the employer. It can be for as much or as little time as the employer feels appropriate, and the length of time covered can be varied by the relationship of the employee to the person who died. What you don't want to do is vary the period of time based on the employee or you are courting a discrimination suit. I have written on this subject elsewhere and feel that the bereavement pay needs to be what the employee requires. That may be a day or a month. As long as you don't change the time based on an attribute that is subject to discrimination claims (i.e. race, religion, gender, etc.) you should be okay.

Bereavement pay may or may not be considered paid time off (PTO) (see below) or for purposes of using accrued PTO hours. It is instead often considered a separate category of time off solely in consideration for the suffering of the employee. Bereavement pay is fully taxable as if it were normal payroll, but is not included in overtime calculations.

Jury Duty

Some employers pay an employee that is called to do jury duty. This is for time taken off to serve on a jury in the local court system. Jury duty is a public service that takes citizens to perform. Not all companies pay for the time taken from the business. It is at the discretion of the company. Jury duty may or may not be considered PTO (see later section) for purposes of using accrued PTO hours, it is treated as a way to not penalize employees for doing their civic duty as a juror. Some companies will pay the employee's regular pay less what the court pays the employee for serving. However, that is solely at the discretion of the company. Such pay is fully taxable as if it was normal payroll, but is not included in overtime calculations.

Bonuses

A bonus is compensation paid to an employee or contractor above and beyond their normal pay. It can be for achieving specific goals. It can be for providing service above and beyond the normal expectation. It can for anything the employer wants to pay a bonus. Many times, the bonuses are quantified in a document that sets out the terms under which a bonus is earned, i.e., a percentage of sales above a set quota, miles driven without an accident, number of new clients signed up, etc. Bonuses are fully taxable as payroll.

Allowances

Allowances may be taxable or not taxable depending on circumstances and whether they are paid under an accountable plan or not.

Allowances paid under an accountable plan are not taxed to the employee. Under an accountable plan the employee reports expenses that the employee incurred, and they are reimbursed for those expenses. Also, per diem amounts paid to employees who travel are not taxed for income tax purposes as long as the amounts do not exceed the approved IRS per diem rates, as published and updated regularly by the IRS. Amounts paid as per diem in excess of the IRS approved rate are taxable. Under the plan, any amounts paid in excess of the IRS approved rate must be returned to the employer or it is taxable income.

Allowances paid under a nonaccountable plan, which does not meet the IRS requirements for business connection, substantiation, and return of excess are fully taxable to the employee and employer as regular wages.

Uniform Allowance

If the employer provides, or otherwise pays, for a uniform for the employee it is not taxable wages, as long as it the uniform is required as a condition of employment and cannot be worn as ordinary streetwear. If paid as an advance, the employee must account to the employer for the amount spent and return any excess monies received above the actual cost.

Reimbursements

Reimbursements are payments to an employee for payments the employee has made out-of-pocket for business-related expenses accruing to the benefit to the employer. These are not normally considered payroll and are not taxed.

Don't include expenses that have tax implications, such as moving expenses. Typically, this includes expenses incurred for limited items. This includes mileage driven for:

- Company business.
- Miscellaneous items picked up for work.
- Professional memberships that are work related.
- Seminars that are work related, and so on.

For guidelines on reimbursements, check the employee business expense reimbursements section of IRS Publication 15 (Circular E): Employer's Tax Guide.

Paid Time Off

This is time for which workers get paid by their companies when they aren't actually working. On average, employers in the United States offer 10 paid holidays, two weeks of vacation, two personal days, and eight sick days per year. A new trend at some companies allows workers to take unlimited paid time off (PTO). PTO is normally fully taxable as payroll but not included in calculating overtime.

How PTO Works

PTO is often accrued over time, with hours earned and put into a bank based on hours already worked. Some companies accrue a year's worth of PTO on the first day of the year. Many companies allow more PTO for long-term employees as a benefit. PTO can be calculated in any way the employer chooses.

Using PTO

To use PTO, you essentially take away hours from your accrued hours of PTO. These hours of PTO are added to an employee's check as if they worked the hours. They do not figure into calculation for overtime nor do they accrue PTO as if they were worked hours. To use your PTO for one regular working day, you would use eight hours of PTO. Many companies allow you to take a partial day of PTO for numerous reasons. Companies can dictate the PTO policy as they wish. Some states and municipalities are beginning to mandate "sick pay," a type of PTO for employees in their jurisdictions.

Vacation versus PTO

Most of the time, you'll hear the phrases PTO and vacation time interchangeably, but they are not, in fact, the exact same thing. All vacation time is PTO but not all PTO is vacation time. Many companies are getting away from specifically designating vacation and just going with a generic PTO hours-per-year. This includes all PTO taken for whatever reason.

Types of PTO

PTO can be used for a variety of different reasons other than for taking a vacation; the following lists several reasons but the number is limited only by the imagination and the willingness of the company.

- Holiday pay
- Sick pay
- Vacation pay
- Birthday pay
- Flexible days off
- Personal days off
- Parental leave
- Time for voting

PTO versus FMLA

In Chapter 8, we will talk in detail about Family Medical Leave Act. FMLA mandates that an employee be given time off but does not mandate that the employee be paid for the time off. Several jurisdictions have begun to enact programs where the employee can take FMLA time off, and be paid for it under certain state mandated programs.

 Review the section on IRS code section 45S in Chapter 8 under the FMLA. It concerns tax credits for certain types of PTO.

Personal Use of Company Automobiles

Do your employees use company-owned or company-leased vehicles?

When an employee uses a company vehicle for business purposes, the vehicle use is a working condition fringe benefit. This means the value of using the vehicle isn't included in the employee's income, nor is it taxed.

But when an employee uses a company vehicle for personal reasons, you generally must include the value of using the vehicle in the employee's income. And you must withhold taxes on the value of the benefit.

Personal use of a company vehicle is a taxable noncash fringe benefit. Fringe benefits are benefits you provide to employees in addition to their wages.

Personal use of a company car (PUCC) includes:

- Commuting to and from work.
- Running a personal errand.

- Vacation or weekend use.
- Use by a spouse or dependent.

This company car fringe benefit is considered part of the employee's compensation for tax purposes. You must determine its value, include it in employee wages, and withhold taxes on it.

Exceptions to the Personal Use Rule

In some cases, personal use of a company vehicle is exempt from inclusion in employee wages and taxes.

De Minimis Fringe Benefits

"De minimis" means too small for consideration. Personal use of a company vehicle is a de minimis fringe benefit if the employee uses the vehicle mainly for business purposes. Infrequent and brief side trips for personal reasons are excluded from the employee's income.

Qualified Nonpersonal Use Vehicle

If a company vehicle has a special design that makes personal use unlikely, any personal use is excluded from employee wages.

Vehicles in this category include:

- Marked police, fire, and public safety officer vehicles.
- Unmarked vehicles used by law enforcement officers, if the use is officially authorized.
- Ambulances.
- Hearses.
- Delivery trucks with only a driver's seat, or the driver plus a folding jump seat.
- Moving vans.
- School buses.
- Passenger buses seating at least 20 people.
- Animal control vehicles.
- Construction or specially designed work vehicles (e.g., dump trucks, cement mixers, forklifts, garbage trucks).
- Refrigerated trucks.
- Qualified utility repair vehicles.

- Trucks with a loaded weight over 14,000 pounds.
- Tractors and other special-purpose farm vehicles.

Valuing Personal Use

You need to include the fair market value of the employee's personal use of the company vehicle in their wages. To determine the fair market value of the personal use, you can use a general valuation method or one of three special valuation rules to do a personal use of company vehicle calculation.

Apply the rules on a vehicle-by-vehicle basis. You can use different rules for different vehicles.

General Valuation Rule

With the general valuation rule, the fair market value is the price the employee would pay to lease the same or a comparable vehicle in the same geographic area for the same length of time. You cannot use a cents-per-mile rate unless you can show that a lease was available for the type of vehicle in the same area at the same time.

The general valuation rule does not account for mixed use. It assumes the vehicle is used only for personal reasons. Because an employee will likely use the vehicle for both business and personal reasons, it may be advantageous to use a special valuation rule.

Group-Term Life Insurance

The amount of the premium that provides coverage up to $50,000 is considered a nontaxable fringe benefit, and is not taxable to the employee.

Compensatory Time Off

Compensatory time off is the idea that instead of paying an employee overtime you grant them the number of hours times worked in an overtime situation as additional hours of paid time off at a normal rate of pay. This saves the employer the overtime premium and at the same time gives the employee more time off, allowing the employee more flexibility.

Compensatory time off is allowed if the employer is the government. It is not available to private employers. If you are a private employer you are not allowed to set up a compensatory time-off program for your employees, even if they want it. There are very limited exceptions in having to giving one and one-half the numbers of hours off that were worked as overtime within the same pay period.

Other Earnings

"Other earnings" is a catchall heading for everything not itemized into a specific payroll category. They are normally fully taxable. Pay that was missed, retroactive pay, and severance pay are all fully taxable and considered gross income and income for child support purposes.

CHAPTER FOUR

Deductions

VOLUNTARY DEDUCTIONS

An employee can voluntarily agree to wage deductions that must be implemented by the payroll department. These deductions may include wage assignments to repay a debt, charitable deductions, wages withheld to purchase US savings bonds, credit union loan repayments, and so forth.

Wage Assignments

A wage assignment is a voluntary agreement by an employee (assignor) to have a portion of the employee's wages assigned to a third party (assignee). Generally, employees assign wages to secure a debt. The assignment gives the creditor an opportunity to recover the unpaid amount if the employee fails to repay the debt.

A wage assignment also allows both the third party and the employee to avoid the time and expense connected with court-run garnishment proceedings. Wholesale or retail outlets that allow customers to pay for merchandise in installments will sometimes ask the customer to enter into a wage assignment agreement as a manner of guaranteeing payment. Assignments are also used to secure loans from financial institutions.

Sometimes an assignment will be used to pay the debt directly rather than waiting for the employee to default. And in some cases, noncustodial parents may be allowed to voluntarily assign a portion of their wages to pay child support rather than having to submit to a child support withholding order.

Garnishment Limits Do Not Apply

Voluntary wage assignments are not covered by the Consumer Credit Protection Act (CCPA), which sets the maximum amounts that can be deducted from an employee's pay to satisfy creditor garnishments and child support withholding orders. But if the debt secured by the assignment remains unpaid and becomes the subject of a court-ordered garnishment, the resulting garnishment is governed by the CCPA.

State Law Governs Wage Assignments

While wage assignments are not subject to Federal law restrictions, the States regulate them to varying degrees. Where they do not, wage assignments are governed by the general law of contracts as developed by state courts. Wage assignments that are generally regulated by the states are described in the following sections.

Validity of Wage Assignments   Some states do not allow voluntary wage assignments of any kind. Most allow employees to agree to an assignment of wages that have already been earned, although not yet paid, while some prohibit the assignment of future wages (i.e., wages not yet earned). This also is one area where the federal government has become involved. Federal Trade Commission regulations prohibit loan companies and retail installment sellers from securing payment with a wage assignment unless:

- The assignment can be revoked at any time by the employee.
- The assignment is a payroll deduction plan starting at the time of the transaction.
- The assignment applies only to wages already earned when the assignment is made.

Several states have passed laws incorporating similar restrictions on assignments arising out of consumer credit transactions or prohibiting such assignments altogether.

Maximum Amount That Can Be Assigned   Those states that allow assignment of future wages often restrict the amount of an employee's wages that can be assigned in the form of a maximum percentage or a dollar amount. They also may put a limit on how long into the future an assignment can be enforced.

Priorities Where more than one wage assignment is presented to the employer, generally the one received first must be given priority if the full amount for both cannot be withheld. In those states that require wage assignments to be registered with a local court or municipal clerk, priority must be given to the assignment filed earlier. In such a state, an employer that has been withholding to satisfy an assignment that has not been properly registered may have to give priority to a subsequent assignment for which the proper procedures have been followed.

Small Loan Restrictions Many states have special laws regarding wage assignments to secure small loans provided by finance companies. These laws usually limit the amount of the loan that can be secured by a wage assignment and attach several procedural requirements, including:

- The assignment must be in writing.
- The assignment must be signed by the employee and his or her spouse.
- The amount borrowed must be given to the employee when the assignment is signed.
- The employer must receive a copy of the loan agreement, the assignment, and the state laws regulating the assignment.

Notice Requirements In several states, creditors holding a wage assignment cannot collect from the employer without providing notice to the employer and/or the employee either before or at the time the wage assignment is presented to the employer. In states where an assignment is not binding on the employer unless the employee has received notice of its pending execution, the employer should check with the employee once an assignment is received to make sure the notice requirement has been met. If the employee claims that no notice was given, the employer should contact the creditor for a copy of the notice for proof that it was served on the employee.

Federal, State, and Local Employees

As with garnishments, wage assignments cannot be enforced against a public sector employer unless a law allows public employees to assign their wages. Some states have enacted laws that treat government employees the same as private sector employees where wage assignments are concerned, while others place more restrictions on the public sector.

State Laws

Because of the different treatment of wage assignments provided by different states, employers must be sure to check their own state's laws when faced with a wage assignment. Notifying legal counsel might also be a good idea, at least where there are questions regarding the validity of a wage assignment, or its priority, if the employee involved has any other proceedings against their wages.

Union Dues

In addition to mandatory deductions for union dues required by a collective bargaining agreement, in some situations, employees have the option of paying union dues on their own or having them deducted from their wages by their employer. This voluntary check-off procedure is authorized by federal labor law, so long as the amount withheld is for union dues, initiation fees, and assessments only. The federal law also requires the employer to get a written, signed authorization from each employee allowing wages to be deducted. Once signed, the authorization cannot be revoked for one year or until the union contract expires. To be irrevocable beyond that point, the employee would have to sign another authorization.

Credit Union Deductions

Many employees save money with or borrow money from a credit union, an organization formed by employees (often in conjunction with their collective bargaining representative) that serves as a savings and loan company. When it is time to repay a credit union loan or place funds in a savings account, the employee may wish to have a portion of his or her wages deducted by the employer and paid over to the credit union. Employers often encourage the formation and use of credit unions by agreeing to the payroll deductions. Before deducting any wages, however, employers should get written, signed authorizations from employees that detail the amount to be withheld, the duration of the withholding, and the party to whom the withheld wages will be paid.

US Savings Bonds

Another type of voluntary payroll deduction allows employees to purchase Series EE US Savings Bonds in denominations beginning at $100. The purchase price of the bond is one-half of the bond's denomination, or face value. Therefore, the purchase price of a $500 bond is $250.

Employer Responsibilities

Other than providing enrollment cards and making the deductions and payments, employers also must make sure the proper amounts have been deducted and remitted by reconciling the deductions and the bonds purchased. And they must return any excess amounts deducted to the employees or use them toward the purchase of more bonds. When employees leave the job, they must receive any amounts that have been deducted but have not yet been used to purchase a bond.

Charitable Contributions

Many employers work with local and national charities to provide their employees with the opportunity to make voluntary donations to those charities through payroll deductions. The payroll department makes the deductions and processes their remittance to the appropriate charitable organizations.

This process became somewhat more complicated in 1994, when Section 13172 of the Omnibus Budget Reconciliation Act of 1993 went into effect. That section created IRC §170(f)(8), which prohibits taxpayers from deducting charitable contributions of $250 or more without substantiation of the gift, and any substantial goods or services received in return. The required substantiation is a contemporaneous written acknowledgment (before the taxpayer files his or her personal tax return for the year of the contribution) from the charitable organization that includes the following information:

- The amount of cash and a description of any noncash property contributed.
- Whether the charitable organization provided any goods or services in return for the contribution.
- A description and good faith estimate of the value of these goods or services.

Payroll Problems Recognized

In issuing regulations to deal with the new law, the IRS recognized that, in a payroll deduction situation, the charitable organization will generally not know the names of the contributing employees or the amounts they contributed during a given year, since employers do not pay over the withheld amounts in separate checks for each employee, but in one lump sum. This makes it difficult for charities to provide, and for employees to obtain, the acknowledgment required to substantiate the contributions.

Employer and Charity Share Reporting burden.

To make it feasible for employees to obtain the required acknowledgment, the regulations allow them to substantiate contributions by a combination of two documents:

- A pay stub, Form W-2, or other document provided by the employer that shows the amount withheld for payment to a charitable organization
- A pledge card or other document prepared by the charitable organization or another party (e.g., the employer) at the direction of the charitable organization that includes a statement that no goods or services are provided in return for Employee contributions made by payroll deduction.

 ## INVOLUNTARY DEDUCTIONS

Involuntary payroll deductions are those over which an employer or employee has little or no control. The employer is required by law to deduct a specific dollar amount of the employee's pay and remit it to a person or agency to satisfy the law. If the employer fails to deduct and remit that amount, the employer will generally be subject to a penalty equal to the amount required plus possible fines and interest.

A common problem for employers is determining deduction amounts when several orders for involuntary deductions are received against an employee's wages. If there is not enough pay left in the employee's wages, after any exempt amounts have been taken into consideration, to pay all the orders, the employer must decide which order has the highest priority.

Tax Levy

Employees who fail to pay their taxes may become subject to a federal or state tax levy. The levy requires their employer to deduct the amount claimed from their wages and remit it to the proper government agency. The employer is faced with the task of determining the amount of the employee's wages that is subject to the levy; and whether there are other claims on the Employee's wages that take priority over the levy.

Federal Tax Levy

A federal tax levy is accomplished by garnishing an employee's wages to the extent that they are not exempt from levy. The employee's employer receives notice of the levy when the IRS sends Form 668-W, Notice of Levy on Wages, Salary, and Other Income, informing the employer of the amount of the levy and the employer's obligation to withhold and remit the levy amount. This form is in six parts.

- Parts 2 through 5 must be given to the employee.
- Part 2 is the employee's copy of the levy notice.
- Parts 3 through 5 require the employee to provide information to the employer and the IRS regarding his or her tax filing status and any dependents who can be claimed as personal exemptions.
- Parts 3 and 4 must be returned to the employer within three days of the date the employer receives the form. The employer then sends Part 3 to the IRS after completion and keeps Part 4.
- Part 5 is the employee's copy of the tax filing status and exemption information.
- Part 6 is retained by the IRS.

Priority Versus Other Attachment Orders

Tax levies must be satisfied before all other garnishments or attachment orders, except for child support withholding orders that are in effect before the date of the levy. Where more than one entity has levied an employee's wages, and there are insufficient nonexempt funds to satisfy all of them, the one received first by the employer must be satisfied before any others, unless the IRS instructs otherwise.

Figuring the Amount to Deduct and Remit

All amounts paid to an employee are subject to levy unless specifically exempt under the Internal Revenue Code or IRS regulations. Federal tax levies are not governed by the exemption rules that apply to garnishments or child support withholding orders under the Consumer Credit Protection Act. These are the payments that are exempt from a federal tax levy:

- Unemployment compensation benefits
- Workers' compensation benefits
- Annuity and pension payments under the Railroad Retirement Tax Act and to certain armed services personnel
- Certain armed service–connected disability payments
- Certain public assistance payments (welfare and supplemental Social Security benefits)

- Amounts ordered withheld under a previously issued court order for child support

Some Payments Are No Longer Exempt

Under the Taxpayer Relief Act of 1997, the IRS can attach a continuing levy on up to 15% of certain payments that had been totally exempt from levy, including:

- Federal payments not based on income or assets of the payee
- Unemployment compensation benefits
- Workers' compensation benefits
- Annuity and pension payments under the Railroad Retirement Tax Act
- Federal Employee wage and salary payments up to the exempt amount
- Supplemental Social Security benefits
- State or local public assistance payments

In addition, each employee is entitled to an amount exempt from levy equal to the employee's standard deduction and personal exemptions including one for the employee divided by the number of pay periods in the year. Employees paid on a daily basis have their standard deduction and personal exemption amounts divided by 260, the number of workdays in a year (52 weeks × 5 workdays per week). Employees who are paid on a one-time or recurrent basis, but irregular basis are entitled to the weekly exempt amount for each week to which the payment is attributable. The value of the employee's standard deduction and personal exemptions is determined for the year the levy is received. If the employee does not submit a verified, written statement regarding the employee's tax filing status and personal exemptions (Parts 3 and 4 of Form 668-W serve this purpose), the employer must figure the exempt amount as if the Employee's filing status is married filing separately with one personal exemption. *Employers cannot rely on the employee's Form W-4 to determine the filing status and number of exemptions on a pre 2020 Form W-4.* The IRS issues tables for figuring the exempt amount each year as IRS Publication 1494.

Withholding Payroll Deduction Levy

According to Form 668-W, the employer must continue to withhold and make levy payments until it receives Form 668-D, Release of Levy/Release of Property from levy. This means the employer may not stop withholding when the payments match the total due that the IRS stated on the front of Part 1 of Form 668-W. Withholding must continue because interest and possible penalties continue to accumulate on the amount remaining due after each levy payment is made. Form 668-D will contain the final amount due and release the Employee's wages from levy after that amount is paid.

If the Employee Is Terminated

If the employee named on the Notice of Levy is no longer employed by the employer when the form is received, the employer must note that on the reverse side of Part 3 and return it to the IRS, along with the employee's last known address.

If employment terminates while the levy is in effect, the employer should notify the IRS office where payments have been sent of the termination and the name and address of the employee's new employer, if known. The employer must deduct and remit any nonexempt amounts contained in severance or dismissal pay provided the employee. The employer is not liable to the employee for amounts withheld. If an employer honors a Notice of Levy from the IRS and withholds and pays over nonexempt amounts as instructed, the employer is not liable to the employee for the amount of wages paid to the IRS.

Penalties for Failing to Withhold and Remit

Employers failing to withhold and pay over amounts not exempt from levy after receiving Form 668-W are liable for the full amount required to be withheld, plus interest from the wage payment date. Any amount paid by the employer as a penalty will be credited against the taxes owed by the employee. In addition, the employer is liable for a penalty equal to 50% of the amount recoverable by the IRS after the failure to withhold and remit. This penalty is not applicable where there is a genuine dispute as to the amount to be withheld and paid over or the legal sufficiency of the levy.

Withholding for Child Support

Child support order collection is a combined federal/state program, with federal laws providing standard state laws must meet or exceed in order to qualify for federal funding of state child support enforcement. Title IV of the Social

Security Act and the Consumer Credit Protection Act (CCPA) provide the legal framework around which State Child Support Withholding laws are constructed. The maximum that can be withheld from an employee's wages for spousal or child support is:

- 50% of the employee's disposable earnings if the Employee is supporting another spouse and/or children.
- 60% if the employee is not supporting another spouse and/or children.

These amounts increase to 55% and 65%, respectively, if the employee is at least 12 weeks late (i.e., in arrears) in making support payments. If arrearages are being paid, the total of the current support and the arrearages cannot exceed the applicable maximum amount. State child support withholding laws may impose lower limits on the amount that may be withheld, but may not exceed the limits imposed by the CCPA. Correct limits for any child support withholding order will be contained in the court order you receive.

Calculating Disposable Earnings

Disposable earnings are determined by subtracting all deductions required by law from an employee's gross earnings. Deductions required by law include withholding for federal, state, or local income tax, Social Security or Medicare tax, state unemployment or disability tax, and mandated payments for state employee retirement systems. Voluntary deductions, such as health and life insurance premiums, union dues, and retirement plan contributions, are not subtracted from earnings to calculate disposable earnings.

Some states allow health insurance premiums to be deducted when calculating disposable earnings. Wages already subject to withholding for tax levies, bankruptcy orders, other child support withholding orders, or wage garnishments are not considered deductions required by law. Therefore, they should not be subtracted from gross earnings when determining the maximum amount subject to child support withholding. However, if the tax levy, bankruptcy order, etc., has priority over the current child support withholding order, the amount required to be deducted under the order having priority must be taken into account when determining whether the CCPA maximum has been reached.

One-Time Payments

The CCPA definition of earnings subject to the limits on child support withholding includes all compensation paid or payable for personal services.

Tips

Tips given directly to employees by customers are not considered earnings for the purpose of determining disposable earnings, whereas service charges added to the bill that are later given to the employee by the employer are considered earnings. Employers should check the state laws in the states where they operate regarding the inclusion of tips as earnings.

Priority of Orders

Orders to withhold wages for child support take priority over all other garnishments or attachments issued against the employee's wages except for tax levies received by the employer before the child support withholding order or bankruptcy court orders. Under the Federal Bankruptcy Code, debts due for child support are nondischargeable debts.

When Order Takes Effect

The employer must put the wage withholding order into effect no later than the first pay period beginning after 14 working days following the mailing of the notice to withhold to the employer. States may require that the order take effect sooner. The employer must continue to withhold until notified otherwise in writing by the court or agency involved.

Remittance

The employer must send payment of the withheld wages to the party noted on the order *within seven business days of the date wages are paid to the employee.* State law may set a shorter time limit for making payment. Timeliness is determined by the postmark if the payment is mailed, or if the payment is transmitted electronically, by the date the transmission is proven to have been initiated by the employer.

Firing an Employee Who Has a Withholding Order

The employer is prohibited from discharging, disciplining, or otherwise discriminating against an employee because the employee receives a withholding order for child support. Violators can be fined an amount set by state law.

Fees

Employers may charge the employee an administrative fee for processing the wage withholding order each pay period.

The maximum amount is set by state law, and the fee must be withheld from the employee's other wages, not the child support payment.

Employee Terminates

If an employee whose wages are subject to a child support withholding order separates his/her employment, the employer has a certain amount of time set by state law to notify the child support enforcement agency of the employee's last known address and, if known, the name and address of the employee's new employer. If the employee has been injured or is ill and cannot work, the employer should notify the court or agency that sent the withholding notice and provide the employee's name, and the name and address of the entity paying workers' compensation or disability benefits. If the benefits are not being paid by the employer, the employer is not responsible for withholding.

⚠ If the employer fails to withhold the amount required, the employer is liable for the full amount not withheld and any fine set by state law. The employer need not alter its pay periods to comply with the law. It can contact the agency administering the order to arrange a revision of the amount to withhold that fits the employer's pay cycle. Please beware! These penalties may apply to independent contractors who are required to be reported as "newly hired employees" in certain states. Many employers are unaware of the provisions that force them to report independent contractors as new hires so that child support orders can be served on the employer to withhold from payments to independent contractors.

Out-of-State Orders

A problem for employers is handling child support withholding orders issued by a court or agency in a state other than the state where the employee works. Under the Uniform Interstate Family Support Act (UIFSA) an employer must put into effect a child support withholding order that it receives directly from another state's child support enforcement agency so long as the order appears "regular on its face." Registration of the order with the child support enforcement agency in the employee's work state is not necessary under UIFSA. Under UIFSA, employers must follow the rules as stated on the order that specify:

- The duration and amount of periodic payments of current child support, stated as a specific amount.
- The person or agency designated to receive payments and the address to which the payments are to be forwarded.
- Medical support, whether in the form of periodic cash payments, stated as a specific amount, or ordering the noncustodial parent to provide health insurance coverage for the child under a policy available through the parent's employer.
- The amount of periodic payment of fees and costs for a support enforcement agency, the issuing court, and/or the custodial parent's attorney, stated as specific amounts.
- The amount of periodic payments of arrears and interest on arrears, stated as specific amounts.

Employee's work state laws rule when determining:

- The employer's administrative fee for processing an income withholding order.
- The maximum amount permitted to be withheld from the noncustodial parent's income.
- The time periods within which the employer must implement the withholding order and forward the amount withheld.
- The priorities for withholding and allocating income withheld for multiple withholding orders.

States and UIFSA

All the states adopted UIFSA and Personal Responsibility and Work Opportunity Reconciliation Act (PRWORA) before 1/1/99. The PRWORA also specifically addressed several out-of-state order issues by requiring state laws to mandate that employers follow the income withholding law of the noncustodial parents work state in determining:

- The employer's administrative fee.
- The maximum amount permitted to be withheld for child support.
- The time period for implementing the withholding order and remitting withheld amounts.
- The priorities for withholding and allocating income withheld for multiple withholding orders.
- Any withholding terms or conditions not specified in the order.

State laws must also provide that employers who comply with an out-of-state income withholding order that is "regular on its face" are not liable to any person or agency for withholding or making payments in compliance with the order.

Multiple Orders

If an employer receives more than one child support withholding order for an employee, state law governs how they must be handled. If the orders are from different states, the law in the state where the employee works applies. These considerations generally come into play when the total withholding amount required under all orders exceeds the maximum allowed under the applicable state law. States handle this problem in one of several ways. The first method is to allocate the available wages to each order depending on its percentage in relation to the total amount required to be withheld. Another method is to allocate the available wages equally toward each order until each order is individually complied with or the maximum amount of allowable withholding is reached. The final method (currently used only in Montana) is to give the orders priority depending on when they were received by the employer.

Employee Complaints

Sometimes the employer is confronted by an employee whose wages have been withheld to pay child support and who claims either that the amount withheld was wrong or that the employee received no notice before withholding began. In either situation, the employer is obligated to continue withholding according to a valid withholding order unless it receives notification in writing from the agency or court issuing the order that a change is necessary. The employee should be told to contact the agency or court issuing the order if a mistake has allegedly been made.

Orders for Military Reservists

According to the Office of Child Support Enforcement (OCSE), the employer should notify the state child support agency either by calling, writing, or faxing when it is notified by an employee/reservist subject to a child support withholding order that he or she is being mobilized. Child support agencies around the country have been asked to give the highest priority to reviewing cases involving military personnel who are being activated, and to redirect income withholding notices from the civilian employers involved to the appropriate office of the Department of Defense so that the child support payments would not be interrupted.

As reservists return home, the Department of Defense will notify the child support agencies when an individual transfers from military status to civilian status. Once an employee returns to work, the employer should reactivate the income withholding order it has on file. Some states may send a letter or issue a new income withholding order, but most of them will expect the employer simply to reinstitute existing orders. If an employer has any questions, it should contact the state agency involved.

Independent Contractors

 Payments to be made to independent contractors who perform services for a business constitute property that is subject to a child support withholding order. In numerous states, employers are required to report independent contractors as new hires, under the New Hire Reporting System (see chapter 8) and are subject to penalties for not doing so, which may be the entire amount not withheld, plus penalties and interest.

Medical Orders

All the states have passed laws allowing courts to require medical child support as part of a child support order, and requiring employers to enroll children and withhold premiums from the employee's pay to the same extent as other employees with similar coverage. New child support orders issued by a state child support agency must include a medical support provision. All employer-sponsored group health plans are required to comply with state laws regulating medical child support and to honor "qualified medical child support orders." However, the plans cannot be forced to offer any new or different benefits. "Qualified medical child support orders" are judgments or orders issued by a court or an administrative agency, including those approving settlement agreements, which recognize the right of a child to be covered under the same group health plan for which the noncustodial parent is eligible. They also must specify:

- The name and address of the noncustodial parent.
- The name and address of any children to be covered by the order.
- A description of the coverage each child must be provided, or the way in which it will be determined.

- The length of time coverage must be provided.
- Each plan governed by the order.

Addresses of Each State Child Support Agency

 The following link from the US Department of Health and Human Services lists all state and tribal child support agencies and their contact information:

www.acf.hhs.gov/css/resource/state-and-tribal-child-support-agency-contacts

Creditor Garnishments

When an employee has a debt that remains unpaid, a wage garnishment is one legal means by which the person who is owed the money can obtain payment. This method requires that the employee's employer withhold the unpaid amount from the employee's wages. In some states, a wage garnishment is known as a "wage attachment" or "income execution." The employer can be required to withhold a portion of the employee's wages for a wage garnishment only if the creditor first brings a court proceeding where proof of the debt is offered and the employee has a chance to respond. Not all states allow creditor garnishments.

Federal Garnishment Limits

Creditor garnishments are also governed by a joint federal/state system of laws and regulations. The federal Consumer Credit Protection Act (CCPA) places restrictions on states in their regulation of creditor garnishments, both on the amount that may be garnished; and on the freedom to discharge an employee because the employee's wages have been garnished.

Garnish Limits

The CCPA states that the maximum amount of an employee's disposable earnings that can be garnished to repay a debt is the lesser of:

- Twenty-five percent of the employee's disposable earnings for the week.
- The amount by which the employee's disposable earnings for the week exceed 30 times the federal minimum hourly wage then in effect.

State Laws May Still Apply

The garnishment limits in the CCPA preempt state laws to the extent the state laws allow greater amounts to be garnished. But state law will apply if the maximum amount subject to garnishment is lower than the federal maximum or if the state does not allow creditor garnishments at all.

Disposable earnings are determined by subtracting all deductions required by law from an employee's gross earnings (wages, commissions, bonuses, sick pay, and periodic pension payments). Deductions required by law include withholding for federal, state, or local income tax, Social Security or Medicare tax, state unemployment or disability tax, and mandated payments for state employee retirement systems (but not amounts designated for direct deposit into an employee's bank account). Voluntary deductions, such as health and life insurance premiums, union dues, and retirement plan contributions, are generally not subtracted from earnings to calculate disposable earnings. In some states, health insurance contributions may be included in the calculation of disposable pay, especially if the contributions are mandated under a child support order.

Tips May or May Not Be Earnings

Tips given directly to employees by customers are not considered earnings for the purpose of determining disposable earnings, whereas service charges added to the bill that are later given to the employee by the employer are earnings. Employers should check the state laws in the states where they operate.

Limits on Multiple Orders

The federal garnishment maximum applies no matter how many garnishments are received for an employee. If the maximum is already being withheld when a second garnishment is received, nothing may be withheld for the second garnishment. If more than the maximum is withheld and the employee receives less than the required minimum wage because of the excess withholding, the employer may be subject to penalties for violating the Fair Labor Standards Act.

Exception for Other Types of Garnishments

The general limit on garnishments under the CCPA does not apply to certain types of garnishments. An exception in the law itself allows for higher maximums for child support withholding orders. The limit does not apply to tax levies, which are governed by the Internal Revenue Code, or to bankruptcy orders. Special provisions are also applicable to garnishments for delinquent student loans and other federal agency debt collections.

In determining an employee's disposable earnings, wages already subject to withholding for child support, tax levies, or bankruptcy orders are not considered deductions required by law. Therefore, they should not be subtracted from gross earnings when determining the maximum amount subject to garnishment. However, if the child support withholding order, tax levy, or bankruptcy order has priority over the creditor garnishment and constitutes at least 25% of the employee's disposable wages, no amount can be withheld for the creditor.

Termination

Employers are prohibited by the CCPA from terminating an employee because the employee's earnings have been subjected to garnishment for any one debt.

Employers that violate this provision can be fined up to $1,000 and/or imprisoned for up to one year. This prohibition applies to all garnishments, including tax levies, bankruptcy orders, and child support withholding orders.

Watch Out for Employee State Laws

While the CCPA provides a minimum standard of employee protection, it does not preempt state laws that provide greater protection for employees by increasing the number of garnishments that can serve as the basis for termination or by prohibiting all terminations because of garnishment. Some states also protect employees from discipline by employers that is short of discharge.

Out-of-State Orders

Generally, employers must comply with a garnishment order issued by a court in another state for an employee in the employer's state. The procedure and applicable exemptions are those of the state issuing the garnishment order, not the employee's home state. However, most states have laws prohibiting creditors from deliberately going outside the state to get a judgment and garnishment order and avoid the garnishment limits of the state where the employee lives and the underlying debt was incurred.

Employer's Responsibilities

When an employer receives a garnishment order from a court or government agency, it is bound to comply with the order to withhold and remit the amount demanded, up to the maximum allowed by law. While preparing to comply, the employer should do the following:

- Check to make sure the underlying claim is valid and the amount stated on the order is correct by contacting the agency or court issuing the order.
- Tell the employee about the garnishment order to make sure the employee has received a notice that garnishment would be taking place and has had the chance to object.
- Tell the employee about any exemptions that might apply under state or federal law.
- Tell the employee how the garnishment will affect his or her wages and net pay.
- Determine whether the amount demanded in the garnishment exceeds the maximum allowed by federal or state law.
- If the employee is already subject to one or more garnishment orders, determine their order of priority and how the available disposable earnings must be allocated.
- Contact legal counsel to review the garnishment order and answer any outstanding questions regarding validity, disposable earnings determinations, complying with out-of-state orders, priorities, and allocation, etc.

Bankruptcy Orders

Bankruptcy is governed by the Federal Bankruptcy Act. Once an employee voluntarily declares bankruptcy or is found to be bankrupt by a court, the satisfaction of the employee's creditors is handled by the "Bankruptcy Trustee" appointed by the court.

Once the employee's employer receives a bankruptcy order from the trustee under a court-approved plan requiring a certain amount of the employee's wages to be paid to the trustee to satisfy the employee's creditors, the employer must stop withholding on any other garnishments against the employee. Bankruptcy orders issued under Chapter XIII of the Bankruptcy Act take priority over any other claim against the employee's wages, including federal and state tax levies and child support withholding orders received before the bankruptcy order. The reasoning behind ceasing all other withholding for garnishments once a bankruptcy order is received is that the debts underlying those garnishments will be paid by the trustee out of the money withheld under the bankruptcy order.

If an employer continues to withhold and remit in satisfaction of other withholding orders, creditors may receive double payments and the employer may open itself to a lawsuit brought by the employee for the withheld wages. The only time an employer should continue to withhold for other garnishments is if the trustee specifically provides instructions to do so. If the creditor is not listed in the bankruptcy order, verify with the trustee before stopping the garnishment.

Termination

Federal bankruptcy law prohibits employers from terminating employees because they become the subject of a bankruptcy proceeding.

Student Loan Collections

Because of the high percentage of students who were failing to repay loans for education granted under the Federal Family Education Loan Program in 1991, Congress amended the Higher Education Act to allow for garnishment of employees' wages to repay delinquent loans. Student loan garnishments are subject to the following restrictions.

Maximum

If the garnishment is issued by a state guarantee agency, no more than the lesser of 10% of an employee's disposable earnings or the excess of the employee's disposable earnings over 30 times the federal hourly minimum wage then in effect may be garnished to satisfy a delinquent student loan, unless the employee consents in writing to a higher percentage. Even though the Higher Education Act limits garnishments to 10% of an employee's wages, this limit applies to each individual holder of a student loan. Where an employee faces multiple student loan garnishments, the maximum amount that can be garnished in total is the CCPA limit of 25% of disposable earnings or the excess of the employee's weekly disposable earnings above 30 times the federal minimum hourly wage, whichever is less.

Penalties

If an employer fails to comply with a lawful student loan garnishment order, it is liable for the amount not withheld from wages, as well as punitive damages, court costs, and attorneys' fees. Employers that unlawfully terminate employees because of a student loan garnishment may be ordered to reinstate the employee with backpay and to pay punitive damages and attorneys' fees.

Federal Agency Debt Collections

Because student loans aren't the only type of federal government debts that have been subject to a high percentage of nonpayment, Congress enacted the Debt Collection Improvement Act of 1996. Part of this law allows federal government agencies, which administer a program under which they provide money to individuals, to garnish the wages of individuals who fail to repay their debt according to their agreement with the agency. These garnishments can be applied only to nontax debts, since tax debts are collected through tax levies issued by the IRS. This law preempts state laws governing garnishments.

Maximum Amount

The amount of a federal agency loan garnishment is limited by the Consumer Credit Protection Act as well as the Debt Collection Improvement Act. The amount to be garnished is the lesser of:

- The amount indicated on the garnishment order up to 15% of the employee's disposable pay.
- The amount by which the employee's disposable pay exceeds 30 times the federal minimum hourly wage then in effect.

Where an employee owes multiple debts to one federal agency, the agency may issue multiple withholding orders for the debts, so long as the total amount garnished does not exceed the limit for one garnishment. Under rules issued by the Financial Management Service to implement federal agency wage garnishments, employers are required to certify information about the employee's employment status and disposable pay (defined as amounts required to be deducted by law and to pay for health insurance) on a form accompanying the withholding order and to pay over amounts withheld promptly after payday. The employer must begin withholding within the reasonable period of time indicated in the withholding order. The employer must continue withholding until notified to stop by the agency.

Termination of Employees

Employees may not be discharged, disciplined, or otherwise discriminated against because of a garnishment order to repay a federal agency loan.

Priority

Unless otherwise provided by federal law, federal agency wage garnishments have priority over other types of withholding orders served on the employer after the federal agency wage garnishment, except for family support orders. If an employee's pay is already subject to another type of withholding order when the employer receives a federal agency wage garnishment, or if a family support withholding order is served on the employer at any time, the amount subject to the federal agency wage garnishment is the lesser of:

- The amount of the order up to 15% of the employee's disposable pay or the amount of the employee's disposable pay in excess of 30 times the federal minimum wage then in effect.
- Twenty-five percent of the employee's disposable pay minus the amounts withheld under the withholding orders with priority.

Wage assignments by an employee that would interfere with or prevent the collection of the debt owed to the agency through a federal agency wage garnishment are void unless the employee makes the assignment under a family support judgment or order.

Penalties

If an employer fails to comply with a lawful federal agency loan garnishment order, it is liable for the amount not withheld from wages, as well as punitive damages, court costs, and attorneys' fees. The agency can sue the employer for amounts not withheld. Employers that unlawfully terminate or otherwise discriminate against employees because of a federal agency loan garnishment may be ordered to reinstate the employee with back pay and to pay punitive damages and attorneys' fees.

Federal Wage Law Restrictions on Deductions

The Consumer Credit Protection Act and the Debt Collection Improvement Act are not the only federal laws regulating the types and amounts of deductions that may be made from an employee's wages. The Fair Labor Standards Act, also known as the Federal Wage-Hour Law, places its own restrictions on such deductions when they bring an employee's wages below the minimum wage and overtime pay guaranteed by the Act.

Board, Lodging, Employee Meals and Other Facilities

Where an employee voluntarily accepts meals, lodging, or other facilities provided by an employer primarily for the employee's benefit, the reasonable cost of the facilities may be deducted from wages paid to the employee, even if the deduction results in the employee receiving less than the required minimum wage or overtime pay. Goods and services connected with employment, such as tools, required uniforms, and company-provided security, are not facilities, and deductions for providing them may be taken only if they do not bring the employee's wages below the minimum. If the employer makes a profit from providing the facilities, deductions for providing them are unlawful only if the profit reduces the employee's wages (including the reasonable cost of the facilities) below the minimum. If the deductions do not reduce the employee's wages below the minimum, none of the conditions above have to be considered.

Uniforms

If an employee is required to wear a uniform while at work that cannot be used as ordinary streetwear and the employer picks up the cost of the uniform and/or its maintenance, the employer cannot deduct any amount of such cost that brings the employee's wages below the minimum required by the FLSA.

Loans to Employees

Employers can deduct amounts equal to the principal of loans made to employees from their wages, even if the deduction reduces the employee's wages below the required minimum under the FLSA. Deductions for interest on the loan or administrative costs associated with the loan are allowed only if they do not bring the employee's wages below the required minimum.

Salary Advances and Overpayments

Deductions to recover salary advances or overpayments due to bookkeeping errors may be taken by the employer even if they reduce the employee's current wage below the required minimum, but employers should consider spreading out the recovery of amounts overpaid or advanced to reduce the economic hardship on the employee.

Docking or reducing an employee's pay because the employee misses work due to lateness can cause special problems where the employee earns an amount that is close to the minimum wage and is penalized beyond an amount that equals the time actually lost. If the employee is docked the same amount of pay as time lost, there is no FLSA violation. However, if the employee is docked an additional amount as a penalty, the employer acts unlawfully if the additional reduction brings the employee's wages below the minimum required for the hours actually worked.

Deductions for Taxes

Amounts withheld from an employee's pay for federal, state, and local income taxes, as well as the employee's share of Social Security and Medicare taxes, are considered wages paid to the Employee. The fact the employee may receive net pay below the FLSA-required minimum does not make these deductions unlawful. However, the employer may not deduct any amount from an employee's wages to pay for the employer's share of any tax, including Social Security, Medicare, federal unemployment, and state unemployment and disability taxes.

Garnishments and Wage Assignments

Employers can deduct amounts from an employee's wages to satisfy garnishment orders from a court or government agency or to satisfy a voluntary assignment of wages by an employee to some third party, even if the deduction reduces the employee's wages below the minimum required by the FLSA. The payment of the deducted amounts to the third party is considered the same as payment to the employee, so long as the employer derives no profit or other benefit from making the deduction. Also, any amount deducted in excess of the limits on garnishment contained in the CCPA is not considered wages paid to the employee and may not reduce the employee's wages below the required minimum.

Union Dues

If required by a union contract, an employer can deduct union dues from an employee's wages and pay that amount to the union even if the deduction reduces the employee's wages below the FLSA minimum. But if the deduction (or "check-off") is unlawful under a law other than the FLSA (e.g., a federal or state labor relations law), it cannot reduce the employee's wages below the minimum wage or overtime required by the FLSA.

Cash Shortages, Bad Checks

Generally, employers may not deduct amounts from an employee's wages to make up for cash shortages, bounced checks, or customers who fail to pay their bills if the deductions would reduce the employee's wages below the minimum wage or overtime required under the FLSA. There is an exception to this general rule where the employee has stolen the amount involved, but only if the employee's guilt has been decided by a court, either after a trial or upon a plea of guilty.

Employer Insurance Bonds

An employer that bonds an employee by buying insurance to protect against fraud or negligence attributed to the employee may not require the employee to pay for the bond before starting work. The cost of the bond may be spread out and deducted from the employee's subsequent wages, but only to the extent that the deductions do not reduce the employee's wages below the FLSA minimum. These bonds may be desirable when employing ex-convicts or workers on client premises.

PRE-TAX DEDUCTIONS

Pre-tax deductions are deductions that are applied to an individual's gross income rather than their net pay. This decreases the wages that are subject to federal, state, and local taxes. Since they reduce the taxable income they also reduce the required contribution the employee and employer must make to Social Security and Medicare. Also most states that have a state income tax start with adjusted gross income as a point for calculating state income tax. Adjusted gross income is the amount of wages after pre-tax deductions are taken out, thereby reducing state income tax withholding.

All the laws and regulations around pre-tax deductions are subject to change on an ongoing basis. This includes particular deductions, limits, and maximums rules. Make sure that you have the most recent information if you provide any of these pre-tax deductions for your employees.

Common Pre-Tax Deductions

- Retirement savings
- 401(k) contributions
- HSA
- Flexible savings accounts
- Group insurance plans

Cafeteria Plans (Section 125)

A cafeteria plan is like an employee benefit buffet that allows an employee to select their benefits from a buffet of a variety of pre-tax benefits as if in a benefit cafeteria. It is also known as a flexible benefit plan that was established under IRS Code Section 125. Sometimes it is referred to as a Section 125 plan as well. The plans have become more desirable as employees seek to customize their benefits for their individual needs and wants.

Section 125 of the Internal Revenue Code says that cafeteria plans under Section 125 are not to be used in calculating gross income for federal income tax purposes. An employee's taxable income for federal income tax, Social Security, and Medicare purposes do not include any amounts withheld under a Section 125 plan. Also, many states eliminate pre-tax benefits from calculation for state income tax. This saves an employee and an employer taxes.

Cafeteria plan selections can include:

- Insurance options.
- Contributions to health savings accounts.
- Group term life insurance.
- Disability insurance.
- Retirement plan contributions.
- Flexible spending accounts for medical purposes.
- Adoption assistance plans.
- Flexible spending accounts.
- Commuting expenses.
- Child care expenses.

Cafeteria Plan Limitations

The variety of benefits available can make the plans difficult and time-consuming to administer. However, cafeteria plans can be as simple as only medical insurance and nothing else. The plans are determined by the employer. Many small business plans include only the medical insurance, this is referred to a POP (premium-only plan).

Premium-Only Plans

 If you have group insurance for your employees, you want to make sure that it qualifies under Section 125 as a POP. This will save you money as the employer by reducing the taxable income for the participants, which reduces the employment taxes (FICA and Medicare) paid by the employer. It also reduces the employment taxes withheld from the employees, increasing their net pay. Your agent should be able to provide you with the plan at no charge, but if not they are available on the web, inexpensively. You need a new plan document in your file every year with all of the changes that have been made in the plan and the law.

Some of the administration problems in a Section 125 Plan can be eliminated by allowing only periodic – i.e., annual – changes to an employee's selections.

HSA (Health Savings Account)

A health savings account (HSA) is a tax-advantaged account created for individuals who are covered under a high-deductible health plan. This allows an employee to save on a pre-tax basis for medical expenses that may not be covered by their high deductible medical insurance.

Contributions are added into an HSA account by the employee or directly by the employer. There is a maximum allowed contribution into the account by the individual or the individual's employer and are limited to a maximum amount each year. The contributions are invested and can be used to pay for qualified medical expenses, which include most medical care such as dental, vision, and over-the-counter drugs.

Insurance Deductibles and Total Costs

An HSA is a way for an individual to pay for costs with a high deductible health policy. The deductible is the part of a medical bill that is not paid when filed as a claim with the insurance company. A high-deductible health insurance plan has a substantially higher annual deductible than typical health plans.

To qualify as a high deductible health policy the deductible as of 2020 has to be a minimum of $1,400 for individual policies and $2800 for family policies. This is subject to annual change.

The maximum out-of-pocket costs on a high deductible health policy, which includes deductibles, copayments, and coinsurance, cannot exceed $6900 for individual policies and $13,800 for family policies for 2020.

Qualifying for an HSA

An employee who is insured under a high deductible health policy may qualify for an HSA. HSAs are offered by some insurance companies that offer high deductible policies. They can also be set up at a number of financial institutions and banks.

To qualify for an HSA, the taxpayer must be eligible per IRS regulations, have no other health care coverage, not be on Medicare, and not be a dependent on another's federal tax return.

An eligible individual contributing to an HSA must do so with cash. An HSA owned by an employee can be funded by the employee and/or his employer. Any other person, such as a family member, can also contribute to the HSA of an eligible individual. Individuals who are self-employed or unemployed may also contribute to an HSA, provided they meet the qualifications of owning a Health Savings Account in the first place.

For 2020, the contribution limit to an HSA is $3,550 for individuals and those with families can contribute up to $7,100. Individuals who are 55 years or older by the end of the tax year can contribute an additional $1,000 to their HSAs. Contributions are subject to the maximum limits above whether made by the employee the employer or both. If an individual contributes $1,500 the maximum his employer can contribute is $2,050.

Tax Advantages of an HSA

Taxpayers benefit from using an HSA because contributions are made pre-tax, meaning that the contribution is removed from gross pay before federal income tax and Social Security and Medicare taxes are calculated. Therefore, their taxable income and actual taxes are lower than they would otherwise be. Additionally, not only are contributions made to an HSA pre-tax, any interest or investment gains are not taxable when earned. Excess contributions above the annual limits are subject to a 6% tax and are not pre-tax for tax purposes.

If the HSA owner uses the funds, either contributed or earned, for qualified medical expenses that are not covered under their high deductible medical plan, those funds withdrawn and used are not taxed to the HSA owner.

Qualified medical expenses include insurance deductibles and copays, dental and vison care, prescription drugs, psychiatric treatments, and other qualified medical expenses that the High Deductible Medical Plan does not cover. Most medical insurance premiums are not considered qualified medical expenses. Premiums for Medicare or other health care coverage for those over 65 are considered qualified medical expenses. Health care insurance when one is unemployed and receiving unemployment compensation and long-term care insurance are also considered qualified medical expenses. Distributions from an HSA that are not for qualified medical expenses are subject to tax as ordinary income and incur a 20% penalty of the amount withdrawn as well.

Individuals who are 65 years old or older will no longer be able to contribute to an HSA. They can withdraw funds for qualified medical expenses with no tax effect. If they withdraw funds for other reasons the withdrawal will be taxable but not subject to the 20% penalty.

The contributions to the HSA belong to the owner. It is not tied to an employer who might have made the contributions. The contributions do not have to be used in the year made. The made contributions can be left in the HSA and continue to grow indefinitely. In fact, many use the HSA as an additional retirement savings vehicle to increase the pre-tax amounts that an individual can sock away. If they have adequate funds, they pay uncovered medical expenses with taxed funds and allow the HSA continue to grow and compound untouched. The HSA is literally a way to make part of your income tax exempt forever.

In addition, an HSA plan can be transferred to a surviving spouse tax-free upon the death of the account holder.

Though similar to an HSA the FSA has major difference which we explore in the next section.

FSA

A health flexible spending account (FSA) allows employees to be reimbursed for medical expenses. FSAs are usually funded through voluntary salary reduction agreements with your employer. No employment or federal income taxes are deducted from your contribution. The employer also may contribute. Note: Unlike HSAs, which must be reported on Form 1040 or Form 1040NR, there are no reporting requirements for FSAs on your income tax return.

Contributions to an FSA

You contribute to your FSA by electing an amount to be voluntarily withheld from your pay by your employer. This is sometimes called a salary reduction agreement. The employer also may contribute to your FSA if specified in the plan. You don't pay federal income tax or employment taxes on the salary you contribute or the amounts your employer contributes to the FSA. However, contributions made by your employer to provide coverage for long-term care insurance must be included in income.

When to Contribute At the beginning of the plan year, employees must designate how much they want to contribute. Then, the employer will deduct amounts periodically (generally, every payday) in accordance with the employee's annual election. They can change or revoke their election only if there is a change in their employment or family status that is specified by the plan.

Amount of Contribution For 2020, salary reduction contributions to a health FSA cannot be more than $2,750 a year (or any lower amount set by the plan). This amount is indexed for inflation and may change from year to year. Generally, contributed amounts that aren't spent by the end of the plan year are forfeited. However, see the section "Balance in an FSA" further on, for possible exceptions. For this reason, it is important to base your contribution on an estimate of the qualifying expenses you will have during the year.

Distributions

Generally, distributions from a health FSA must be paid only to reimburse an employee for qualified medical expenses the employee incurred during the period of coverage. The employee must be able to receive the maximum amount of reimbursement (the amount they have elected to contribute for the year) at any time during the coverage period, regardless of the amount they have actually contributed. The maximum amount you can receive tax free is the total amount you elected to contribute to the health FSA for the year. They must provide the health FSA with a written statement from an independent third party stating that the medical expense has been incurred and the amount of the expense. They also must provide a written statement that the expense hasn't been paid or reimbursed under any other health plan coverage. The FSA can't make advance reimbursements of future or projected expenses. Debit cards, credit cards, and stored value cards given to them by the employer can be used to reimburse participants in a health FSA. If the use of these cards meets certain substantiation methods, the employee may not have to provide additional information to the health FSA.

Qualified Medical Expenses

Qualified medical expenses are those specified in the plan that generally would qualify for the medical and dental expenses deduction. These are explained in IRS Pub. 502. Also, nonprescription medicines (other than insulin) aren't considered qualified medical expenses for FSA purposes. A medicine or drug will be a qualified medical expense for FSA purposes only if the medicine or drug:

- Requires a prescription.

- Is available without a prescription (an over-the-counter medicine or drug) and you get a prescription for it.
- Is insulin.

Qualified medical expenses are those incurred by the following persons:

- The employee and their spouse
- All dependents they claim on their tax return
- Any person they could have claimed as a dependent on their return except that:
  - The person filed a joint return.
  - The person had gross income of $4,050 or more.
  - The employee, or their spouse if filing jointly, could be claimed as a dependent on someone else's income tax return.
  - The employee's child is under age 27 at the end of your tax year.

The employee can't receive distributions from their FSA for the following expenses:

- Amounts paid for health insurance premiums.
- Amounts paid for long-term care coverage or expenses.
- Amounts that are covered under another health plan.
- If they are covered under both a health FSA and an a Health Reimbursement Arrangement (HRA), see Notice 2002-45, Part V, 2002-28 I.R.B. 93, available at IRS.gov/pub/irs-drop/n-02-45.pdf. They can't deduct qualified medical expenses as an itemized deduction on Schedule A (Form 1040).

Balance in an FSA

Flexible spending accounts are generally "use-it-or-lose-it" plans. This means that amounts in the account at the end of the plan year generally can't be carried over to the next year. However, the plan can provide for either a grace period or a carryover. The plan can provide for a grace period of up to 2 1/2 months after the end of the plan year. If there is a grace period, any qualified medical expenses incurred in that period can be paid from any amounts left in the account at the end of the previous year.

The employer isn't permitted to refund any part of the balance to the employee. Plans may allow up to $500 of unused amounts remaining at the end of the plan year to be paid or reimbursed for qualified medical expenses the employee incurs in the following plan year. The plan may specify a lower dollar amount as the maximum carryover amount. If the plan permits a carryover, any unused amounts in excess of the carryover amount are forfeited. The carryover doesn't affect the maximum amount of salary reduction contributions that the employee is permitted to make.

A plan may allow either the grace period or a carryover, but it may not allow both.

Employer Participation

For the health FSA to maintain tax-qualified status, employers must comply with certain requirements that apply to cafeteria plans. For example, there are restrictions for plans that cover highly compensated employees and key employees. The plans also must comply with rules applicable to other accident and health plans. Chapters 1 and 2 of IRS Pub. 15-B, Employer's Tax Guide to Fringe Benefits, explain these requirements.

CHAPTER FIVE

Taxes

Alert

As of the editing of this book, the CARES Act (Coronavirus Aid, Relief, and Economic Security Act) (government acronyms are thought of first and then words found to match) is in discussion. There is a general outline but the details will take weeks, if not months, to sort out, even after it is passed. Forms and procedures will have to be created. Regulations will have to be written. The Bill itself will have to be interpreted and parsed before we know exactly what it means. Some parts of the law may be temporary and some may be permanent or made permanent later.

Please go to www.ThePayrollBook.com/resources/Covid-19 for all the details of the various legislative acts as they bear on payroll. We will be keeping this page up to date for all of our readers and interested parties.

Let's take up the subject of taxes. There are taxes that the employer withholds from the employee and pays to the appropriate governmental agency for the employee. There are taxes that the employer pays based on having and paying employees. This is also where it is important to understand the difference between employees and nonemployees (see Chapter 1).

We are going to explore all of the taxes that you as an employer and your employees may be subject to because of their employment and you paying them. We are not going to look at income taxes on your company, either federal, state, or local; excise taxes; sales taxes; or other numerous ways that businesses get taxed in this country. Nor, other than for withholding purposes, are we going to go into personal income tax law. We are just going to deal with payroll-related taxes.

TAX NUMBERS

 These are identification numbers that you will need to get to be able to properly and correctly report the taxes you withhold from your employees, the employment taxes imposed on you as the employer. It is best to get these as early on as possible.

Federal Employment Identification Number (EIN)

Employer identification numbers are issued for the purpose of tax administration and are not intended for participation in any other activities (e.g., tax lien auction or sales, lotteries, etc.) You will need it to make your deposits and for all the federal forms you are required to file. Your federal EIN works for federal unemployment purposes as well.

To get a Federal EIN you need to file a Form SS4. This can also be done online at www.irs.gov/businesses/small-businesses-self-employed/apply-for-an-employer-identification-number-ein-online, which is an IRS website. Issuance online is immediate and free. There are other sites that will charge you for this service – beware.

State Revenue Tax Number

Unless you are in one of the nine states that don't tax wages you will need to obtain a state identification number from your state revenue department. This department is called by different names. The website www.irs.gov/businesses/small-businesses-self-employed/state-government-websites lists all of the various state taxing agencies. Find your state agency that collects withheld state income tax. It will have the forms that you need to fill out. You will need to do this in every state where you have employees.

State Unemployment Tax Number

Every state has unemployment taxes. You will be required to get a state unemployment identification number. Sometimes it is the same as your income tax withholding number but usually not. The website www.irs.gov/ businesses/small-businesses-self-employed/state-government-websites lists all of the various state taxing agencies. Find your state agency that collects state unemployment taxes. It will have the forms that you need to fill out. You will need to do this in every state where you have employees.

EMPLOYEE TAXES

No matter what form of business you choose, if you have any employees, payroll taxes will be something you must contend with. Following is a summary to offer guidance regarding the rules and regulations from a variety of taxing authorities.

Publication 15

 Publication 15 from the Internal Revenue Service is the base guide for federal payroll taxes. It has additional names such as Circular E but you will be able to find it as Publication 15 on the Internal Revenue website, www.IRS.gov. Don't be confused by a private site like www.IRS .com. It is *not* the same. This manual is issued at least once a year by the IRS with updated tax tables and rules. If you are doing payroll in-house, it is your first and most-used reference guide.

Current Federal Tax Rates

Following is a chart that contains the taxable wage basis and tax rates for employers and employees. The 2019 maximum contributions and limits are given per employee.

FICA
On wages of $137,700 (2020), the employee rate is 6.20%.
On wages of $137,700 (2020), the employer rate 6.20%.

Medicare

On **ALL** wages, the employee rate is 1.45%.
On **ALL** wages, the employer rate is 1.45%.

For wages above $200,000 for an individual or $250,000 for joint filers there is an additional surcharge of 0.9% on the employee only.

Federal Unemployment

The employer rate is 0.6%, after credit for paid SUI (state unemployment insurance) on wages up to $7,000.

Federal (Social Security, Medicare, and Income Tax) Depositing

Generally, you must deposit federal income tax withheld and both the employer and employee Social Security and Medicare taxes. You must use EFT to make all federal tax deposits, except you may make a payment with a timely filed Form 941 or Form 944 instead of depositing, without incurring a penalty, if one of the following applies. (See "Electronic Deposit Requirements" further on.)

- Your Form 941 total tax liability for either the current quarter or the prior quarter is less than $2,500.
- You didn't incur a $100,000 next-day deposit obligation during the current quarter.

When to Deposit

There are two standard deposit schedules – monthly and semi-weekly – for determining when you deposit Social Security, Medicare, and withheld federal income. These schedules tell you when a deposit is due after your payday. In addition, "If you accumulate $100,000 or more in taxes on any day during a monthly or semiweekly deposit period … you must deposit the tax by the next business day, whether you're a monthly or semiweekly schedule depositor."

Your deposit schedule isn't determined by how often you pay your employees or make deposits. The deposit schedule you must use is based on the total tax liability you reported on Form 941 during a lookback period.

One of the few penalties we were not able to have abated was for a client who came to us with a monthly payroll. One of the questions we ask is "What is your deposit schedule?" The client told us monthly. He was wrong. He was a semi-weekly depositor even though he only deposited taxes once a month for his only payroll.

Lookback Period

If you're a Form 941 filer, your deposit schedule for a calendar year is determined from the total taxes reported on Forms 941, line 12, in a four-quarter lookback period. The lookback period begins July 1 and ends June 30 for the previous two calendar years. If you reported $50,000 or less of taxes for the lookback period, you're a monthly schedule depositor; if you reported more than $50,000, you're a semiweekly schedule depositor. For example: The lookback period for 2020 deposits is July 1, 2018 through June 30, 2019.

 You should receive an IRS Form CP136 if you deposit period changes, but the IRS is going to hold you liable for knowing your deposit schedule regardless of the notice. The IRS does not always send them to a payroll provider who has filed an IRS Form 2848 Limited Power of Attorney, even though they are required to. So if you get an IRS Form CP 136 or CP 236, make sure you forward it to your payroll provider.

Deposit Period

The term "deposit period" refers to the period during which tax liabilities are accumulated for each required deposit due date. For monthly schedule depositors, the deposit period is a calendar month. The deposit periods for semiweekly schedule depositors are Wednesday through Friday and Saturday through Tuesday.

Monthly Deposit Schedule If you are on a monthly deposit schedule deposit employment taxes, on payments made during a month, by the 15th day of the following month.

If you are a new employer with a zero lookback period, you are a monthly schedule depositor for the first two calendar years of your business unless you exceed $100,000 tax deposit liability in a single month. See "$100,000 Next-Day Deposit Rule" further on.

Semiweekly Deposit Schedule If you are on a semi-weekly deposit schedule, deposit employment taxes for payroll paid made on Wednesday, Thursday, and/or Friday by the following Wednesday. Deposit taxes for payroll paid on Saturday, Sunday, Monday, and/or Tuesday by the following Friday.

Semiweekly schedule depositors must complete Schedule B (Form 941) and submit it with Form 941 semiweekly deposit schedule. If you have more than one pay date during a semiweekly period and the pay dates fall in different calendar quarters, you'll need to make separate deposits for the separate liabilities. The one before the quarter end goes on the current Form 941 and Form 941 Schedule B, and the deposit after the quarter end goes on the next quarter Form 941 and Form 941 Schedule B.

Deposits Due on Business Days Only If a deposit is required to be made on a day that isn't a business day, the deposit is considered timely if it is made by the close of the next business day. A business day is any day other than a Saturday, Sunday, or legal holiday.

For example, if a deposit is required to be made on a Friday and Friday is a legal holiday, the deposit will be considered timely if it is made by the following Monday (if that Monday is a business day). Semiweekly schedule depositors have at least three business days following the close of the semiweekly period to make a deposit. If any of the three weekdays after the end of a semiweekly period is a legal holiday, you'll have an additional day for each day that is a legal holiday to make the required deposit.

Legal holidays for 2020 are listed next.

- January 1 – New Year's Day
- January 20 – Birthday of Martin Luther King, Jr.
- February 17 – Washington's Birthday
- April 16 – Emancipation Day (District of Columbia only)
- May 25 – Memorial Day
- July 3 – Independence Day

- September 7 – Labor Day
- October 12 – Columbus Day
- November 11 – Veterans Day
- November 26 – Thanksgiving Day
- December 25 – Christmas Day

Year to year, the dates may change.

$100,000 Next-Day Deposit Rule   If you accumulate $100,000 or more in taxes on any day during a monthly or semiweekly deposit period you must deposit the tax by the next business day, whether you're a monthly or semi-weekly schedule depositor. For purposes of the $100,000 rule, don't continue accumulating a tax liability after the end of a deposit period. For example, if a semiweekly schedule depositor has accumulated a liability of $95,000 on a Tuesday (of a Saturday-through-Tuesday deposit period) and accumulated a $10,000 liability on Wednesday, the $100,000 next-day deposit rule doesn't apply because the $10,000 is accumulated in the next deposit period. Thus, $95,000 must be deposited by Friday and $10,000 must be deposited by the following Wednesday. However, once you accumulate at least $100,000 in a deposit period, stop accumulating at the end of that day and begin to accumulate anew on the next day.

If you're a monthly schedule depositor and accumulate a $100,000 tax liability on any day during the deposit period, you become a semiweekly schedule depositor on the next day and remain so for at least the rest of the calendar year and for the following calendar year.

Accuracy of Deposits Rule   You're required to deposit 100% of your tax liability on or before the deposit due date. However, penalties won't be applied for depositing less than 100% if both of the following conditions are met.

- Any deposit shortfall doesn't exceed the greater of $100 or 2% of the amount of taxes otherwise required to be deposited.
- The deposit shortfall is paid or deposited by the shortfall makeup date as described next.

Makeup Date for Deposit Shortfall
1. Monthly schedule depositor. Deposit the shortfall or pay it with your return by the due date of your return for the return period in which the shortfall occurred. You may pay the shortfall with your return even if the amount is $2,500 or more.

2. Semiweekly schedule depositor. Deposit by the earlier of:
   a. The first Wednesday or Friday (whichever comes first) that falls on or after the 15th day of the month following the month in which the shortfall occurred.
   b. The due date of your return (for the return period of the tax liability).

Electronic Deposit Requirements   You must deposit employment taxes by EFT except under "Payment with Return" (see above). Generally, an EFT is made using EFTPS. If you don't want to use EFTPS, you can arrange for your tax professional, financial institution, payroll service, or other trusted third party to make electronic deposits on your behalf. EFTPS is a free service. To get more information about EFTPS or to enroll in EFTPS, visit EFTPS.gov, or call 800-555-4477. Additional information about EFTPS is also available in IRS Publication 966.

When you receive your EIN.

If you're a new employer that indicated a federal tax obligation when requesting an EIN, you'll be pre-enrolled in EFTPS. You'll receive information about Express Enrollment in your Employer Identification Number (EIN) Package and an additional mailing containing your EFTPS personal identification number (PIN) and instructions for activating your PIN. Call the toll-free number located in your "How to Activate Your Enrollment" brochure to activate your enrollment and begin making your payroll tax deposits. If you outsource any of your payroll and related tax duties to a third-party payer, such as a payroll service provider (PSP) or reporting agent, they should make all of your deposits for you using their batch processing functions. They will need to set an individual PIN for you through their system, however, for the IRS to properly apply the payment to your account.

Deposit Record

For your records, an EFT Trace Number will be provided with each successful payment. The number can be used as a receipt or to trace the payment. If your payroll provider makes your deposit they will have the EFT trace number in their files if there is a problem.

Depositing on Time   For deposits made by EFTPS to be on time, you must submit the deposit by 8 p.m. Eastern Time the day before the date that the deposit is due.

Same-Day Wire Payment Option   If you fail to submit a deposit transaction on EFTPS by 8 p.m. Eastern Time the day before the date that a deposit is due, you can still make your deposit on time by using the Federal Tax Collection Service (FTCS) to make a same-day wire payment. To use the same-day wire payment method you will need to work with a bank that can make wire transfers for you. It will not be free but will probably cost less than the penalty for a late deposit. To learn more about the information that you'll need to give to your financial institution to make a same-day wire payment, go to IRS.gov/SameDayWire.

You may want to set the process for same-day wire payments in advance with your financial institution. They may be unable to accommodate you within a single day when a problem occurs with depositing via EFTPS.

How to Claim Credit for Overpayments   If you deposited more than the right amount of taxes for a quarter, you can choose on Form 941 for that quarter to have the overpayment refunded or applied as a credit to your next return. You may also lower a later payment within the quarter by the over deposited amount. As long as you over deposit for a payroll and then underdeposit by the same amount for a later payroll in the quarter there is no penalty. If you underdeposit in the quarter and then in a later deposit overdeposit by the same amount there will be a penalty for under depositing the taxes.

Deposit Penalties

Penalties may apply if you don't make required deposits on time or if you make deposits for less than the required amount. The IRS may waive deposit penalties if you inadvertently failed to deposit and it was the first quarter that you were required to deposit any employment tax, or if you inadvertently failed to deposit the first time after your deposit frequency changed. See Chapter 6, "Tax Penalties," to learn how to fight any penalty.

For amounts not properly or timely deposited, the penalty rates are as follows.

Deposits made 1 to 5 days late: 2%

Deposits made 6 to 15 days late: 5%

Deposits made 16 or more days late, but before 10 days from the date of the first notice the IRS sent asking for the tax due: 10%

Amounts that should have been deposited, but instead were paid directly to the IRS, or paid with your tax return: 10% (see "Payment with Return," earlier in this section, for exceptions)

Amounts still unpaid more than 10 days after the date of the first notice the IRS sent asking for the tax due or the day on which you received notice and demand for immediate payment, whichever is earlier: 15%

Late deposit penalty amounts are determined using calendar days, starting from the due date of the liability.

Order in Which Deposits Are Applied. Deposits generally are applied to the most recent tax liability within the quarter. If you receive an FTD penalty notice, you may designate how your deposits are to be applied in order to minimize the amount of the penalty if you do so within 90 days of the date of the notice. Follow the instructions on the penalty notice you received. For more information on designating deposits, see IRS Revenue Procedure 2001-58.

Trust Fund Recovery Penalty

If federal income, Social Security, or Medicare taxes that must be withheld (that is, trust fund taxes) aren't withheld or aren't deposited or paid to the US Treasury, the trust fund recovery penalty may apply. The penalty is 100% of the unpaid trust fund tax.

If these unpaid taxes can't be immediately collected from the employer or business, the trust fund recovery penalty may be imposed on all persons who are determined by the IRS to be responsible for collecting, accounting for, or paying over these taxes, and who acted willfully in not doing so. A responsible person can be an officer or employee of a corporation, a partner or employee of a partnership, an accountant, a volunteer director/trustee, an employee of a sole proprietorship, or any other person or entity who is responsible for collecting, accounting for, or paying over trust fund taxes. A responsible person also may include one who signs checks for the business or otherwise has authority to cause the spending of business funds.

Willfully means voluntarily, consciously, and intentionally. A responsible person acts willfully if the person knows the required actions of collecting, accounting for, or paying over trust fund taxes aren't taking place, or recklessly disregards obvious and known risks to the government's right to receive trust fund taxes.

Separate Accounting

Separate accounting may be required if you don't pay over withheld employee Social Security, Medicare, or income taxes; deposit required taxes; make required payments; or file tax returns. In this case, you would receive a written notice from the IRS requiring you to deposit taxes into a special trust account for the US government. You may be charged with criminal penalties if you don't comply with the special bank deposit requirements for the special trust account for the US government.

Federal (Social Security, Medicare and Income Tax) Filing

Filing Form 941

Each quarter, if you pay wages subject to income tax withholding (including withholding on sick pay and supplemental unemployment benefits) or Social Security and Medicare taxes, you must file Form 941 unless you receive an IRS notification that you're eligible to file Form 944 (see Chapter 15 Form 944) or the exceptions discussed later apply.

Form 941 must be filed by the last day of the month that follows the end of the quarter.

The following exceptions apply to the filing requirements for Forms 941.

- Seasonal employers don't have to file a Form 941 for quarters when they have no tax liability because they have paid no wages. To alert the IRS you won't have to file a return for one or more quarters during the year, check the "seasonal employer" box on Form 941, line 18. When you fill out Form 941, be sure to check the box on the top of the form that corresponds to the quarter reported. Generally, the IRS won't inquire about unfiled returns if at least one taxable return is filed each year. However, you must check the "seasonal employer" box on every Form 941 you file. Otherwise, the IRS will expect a return to be filed for each quarter.

- Household employers reporting Social Security and Medicare taxes and/or withheld income tax. If you're a sole proprietor and file Form 941 or Form 944 for business employees, you may include taxes for household employees on your Form 941 or Form 944. Otherwise, report Social Security and Medicare taxes and income tax withholding for household employees on Schedule H (Form 1040). See Publication 926 for more information.
- For employers reporting wages for employees in American Samoa, Guam, the Commonwealth of the Northern Mariana Islands, the US Virgin Islands, or Puerto Rico, if your employees aren't subject to US income tax withholding, use Forms 941-SS. Employers in Puerto Rico use Formularios 941-PR. If you have both employees who are subject to US income tax withholding and employees who aren't subject to US income tax withholding, you must file only Form 941 and include all of your employees' wages on that form. For more information, see Publication 80, Federal Tax Guide for Employers in US Virgin Islands, Guam, American Samoa, and the Commonwealth of the Northern Mariana Islands, or Publication 179, Guía Contributiva Federal para Patronos Puertorriqueños for Puerto Rico.
- Agricultural employers reporting Social Security, Medicare, and withheld income taxes. Report these taxes on Form 943. For more information, see IRS Publication 51.

Form 941 E-file

The Form 941 e-file program allows a taxpayer to electronically file Form 941 or Form 944 using a computer with an Internet connection and commercial tax preparation software. For more information, go to IRS.gov/EmploymentE-file, or call 866-255-0654.

Penalties For each whole or part month a return isn't filed when required there is a failure-to-file (FTF) penalty of 5% of the unpaid tax due with that return. The maximum penalty is generally 25% of the tax due. Also, for each whole or part month the tax is paid late there is a failure-to-pay (FTP) penalty of 0.5% per month of the amount of tax. The maximum amount of the FTP penalty is also 25% of the tax due. If both penalties apply in any month, the FTF penalty is reduced by the amount of the FTP penalty.

See Chapter 6, "Tax Penalties," for how to fight tax penalties.

In addition to any penalties, interest accrues from the due date of the tax on any unpaid balance. If income, Social Security, or Medicare taxes that must be withheld aren't withheld or aren't paid, you may be personally liable for the trust fund recovery penalty. See the section "Trust Fund Recovery Penalty: earlier in this chapter.

Generally, the use of a third-party payer, such as a payroll service provider (PSP) or reporting agent, doesn't relieve an employer of the responsibility to ensure tax returns are filed and all taxes are paid or deposited correctly and on time. However, an exception is mentioned in Chapter 17,which discusses the certified professional employer organization (CPEO).

Don't file more than one Form 941 per quarter. Employers with multiple locations or divisions must file only one Form 941 per quarter. Filing more than one return may result in processing delays and may require correspondence between you and the IRS. For information on making adjustments to previously filed returns, see below.

Final Return   If you go out of business, you must file a final return for the last quarter (last year for Form 944) in which wages are paid. If you continue to pay wages or other compensation for periods following termination of your business, you must file returns for those periods. See the Instructions for Form 941 or the Instructions for Form 944 for details on how to file a final return.

Reporting Current Period Adjustments to Form 941

Publication 15 goes into adjustments in Section 13. You will normally not be making adjustments to your Form 941s. If you have unusual items that need to affect the current 941 such as third party sick pay or tip income adjustments or excess group insurance, go to that section of Pub 15 for details.

Prior Period Adjustments

Use Form 941-X to make a correction after you discover an error on a previously filed Form 941.

If you find an under-reporting error on a 941, and you report it and make the deposit before the IRS finds it, it is a no harm, no foul situation. Let's say you find you did not make and report a payroll on the 941 for the last quarter. You can make the deposit for the taxes and file a 941-X. There should be no penalties or interest assessed on anything to do with the 941-X. If the IRS has found a problem and notified you of it, then they can assess penalties and interest. But if you find it first and fix it there should be no penalties. If the service disagrees refer to the Revenue Ruling 2009-39, 2009-52 I.R.B. 951, for examples of how the interest-free adjustment and claim for refund rules apply in 10 different situations.

You will use the Form 941-X if you over-reported employment taxes and are requesting a refund of the over-reported and paid amount. When you discover an error on a previously filed Form 941 you must:

- Correct that error using Form 941-X.
- File a separate Form 941-X for each Form 941 you're correcting.
- File each Form 941-X separately.

Don't file current quarter adjustments with a Form 941X. Continue to report current quarter adjustments for fractions of cents, third-party sick pay, tips, and group-term life insurance on Form 941.

Check this Box 1 if you underreported amounts. Also check this Box 1 if you overreported amounts and you would like to use the adjustment process to correct the errors. You must check this box if you're correcting both under- and overreported amounts on Form 941-X.

Check Box 2 if you overreported amounts only and you would like to use the claim process to ask for a refund or abatement of the amount shown on line 21. Don't check this Box 2 if you're correcting *any* underreported amounts on the 941-X.

See the chart on the page 4 Form 941-X or Form 944-X for help in choosing whether to use the adjustment process or the claim process.

Federal Unemployment Depositing and Filing

The Federal Unemployment Tax Act (FUTA), with state unemployment systems, provides for payments of unemployment compensation to workers who have lost their jobs. Most employers pay both a federal and a state unemployment tax. For a list of state unemployment agencies, visit the US Department of Labor's website at oui.doleta.gov/unemploy/agencies.asp. Only the employer pays FUTA tax; it isn't withheld from the employee's wages.

Who Must Pay?

In general, if you have paid employees more than $1,500.00 in a calendar quarter, and you had employees for some part of a day in each of 20 weeks for this year or last year, you will be subject to FUTA. That is basically everyone who has an employee.

There are special rules for a household employee or farm workers.

Figuring FUTA Tax

For 2019, the FUTA tax rate is 6.0%. The tax applies to the first $7,000 you pay to each employee as wages during the year. The $7,000 is the federal wage base. Your state wage base may be different.

Generally, you can take a credit against your FUTA tax for amounts you paid into state unemployment funds. The credit may be as much as 5.4% of FUTA taxable wages. If you're entitled to the maximum 5.4% credit, the FUTA tax rate after credit is 0.6%. You're entitled to the maximum credit if you paid your state unemployment taxes in full, on time, and on all the same wages that are subject to FUTA tax. In some states, the wages subject to state unemployment tax are the same as the wages subject to FUTA tax.

However, certain states exclude some types of wages from state unemployment tax, even though they're subject to FUTA tax (for example, wages paid to corporate officers, certain payments of sick pay by unions, and certain fringe benefits). In such a case, you may be required to deposit more than 0.6% FUTA tax on those wages. See the instructions for Form 940 for further guidance.

Successor Employer

If you acquired a business from an employer who was liable for FUTA tax, you may be able to count the wages that employer paid to the employees who continue to work for you when you figure the $7,000.00 FUTA tax wage base. See the Instructions for Form 940 for more information.

Depositing FUTA Tax

For deposit purposes, figure FUTA tax quarterly. Determine your FUTA tax liability by multiplying the amount of taxable wages paid during the quarter by 0.6%. Stop depositing FUTA tax on an employee's wages when he or she reaches $7,000 in taxable wages for the calendar year.

If your FUTA tax liability for any calendar quarter is $500 or less, you don't have to deposit the tax. Instead, you may carry it forward and add it to the liability figured in the next quarter to see if you must make a deposit. If your FUTA tax liability for any calendar quarter is over $500 (including any FUTA tax carried forward from an earlier quarter), you must deposit the tax by EFT.

Deposit the FUTA tax by the last day of the first month that follows the end of the quarter. If the due date for making your deposit falls on a Saturday, Sunday, or legal holiday, you may make your deposit on the next business day.

If your liability for the fourth quarter (plus any undeposited amount from any earlier quarter) is over $500, deposit the entire amount by the due date of Form 940 (January 31). If it is $500 or less, you can make a deposit, pay the tax with a credit or debit card, or pay the tax with your 2020 Form 940 by January 31, 2021. If you file Form 940 electronically, you can efile and use EFT to pay the balance due. For more information on paying your taxes with a credit or debit card or using EFT, go to IRS.gov/Payments.

Reporting FUTA Tax

Use Form 940 to report FUTA tax. File your Form 940 by January 31 of the year following your payroll calendar year (i.e. for 2020 payroll, the Form 940 must be filed by January 31, 2021).

Form 940 E-file

The Form 940 e-file program allows a taxpayer to electronically file Form 940 using a computer with an Internet connection and commercial tax preparation software. For more information, visit the IRS website at IRS.gov/EmploymentE-file, or call 866-255-0654.

Current Federal Tax Rates

Following is a chart that contains the taxable wage basis and tax rates for employers and employees. The 2019 maximum contributions and limits are given per employee.

FICA

On wages of $137,700 (2020), the employee rate is 6.20%.
On wages of $137,700 (2020), the employer rate 6.20%.

Medicare

On unlimited wages, the employee rate is 1.45%.
On unlimited wages, the employer rate is 1.45%.
For wages of more than $200,000 for an individual or $250,000 for joint filers there is a additional surcharge of 0.9% on the employee's wages only.

Federal Unemployment

The employer rate is 0.6% (after credit for paid SUI) on wages of $7,000.

Backup Withholding

If you are a taxpayer receiving certain types of income payments, the IRS requires the employer to report these payments on an information return (see types of payments further on). The person or business paying doesn't generally withhold taxes from these types of payments. It is assumed that the recipient will report and pay taxes on this income when they file their federal income tax return.

What Is Backup Withholding?

There are situations when the employer is required to withhold at the current rate of 24%. This 24% tax is taken from any future payments to ensure the IRS receives the tax due on this income.

This is known as backup withholding (BWH) and may be required by the IRS:

- Under the BWH-B program, because the employee failed to provide a correct taxpayer identification number (TIN) to the payer for reporting on the required information return. A TIN can be either a Social Security number (SSN), employer identification number (EIN), or individual taxpayer identification number (ITIN).
- Under the BWH-C program because the employee failed to report or underreported interest and dividend income they received on their federal income tax return; or they failed to certify that you're not subject to BWH for underreporting of interest and dividends.

Types of Payments Subject to Backup Withholding

BWH can apply to most kinds of payments reported on Forms 1099 and W-2G, including:

- Interest payments (Form 1099-INT).
- Dividends (Form 1099-DIV).
- Payment card and third-party network transactions (Form 1099-K).
- Patronage dividends, but only if at least half the payment is in money (Form 1099-PATR).

- Rents, profits, or other gains (Form 1099-MISC).
- Commissions, fees, or other payments for work as an independent contractor (Form 1099-MISC).
- Payments by brokers/barter exchanges (Form 1099-B).
- Payments by fishing boat operators, but only the part that is in money and that represents a share of the proceeds of the catch (Form 1099-MISC).
- Royalty payments (Form 1099-MISC).
- Gambling winnings (Form W-2G), which may also be subject to backup withholding.
- Original issue discount reportable on (Form 1099-OID), original issue discount, if the payment is in cash.
- Certain government payments (Form 1099-G).

How to Prevent or Stop Backup Withholding

To stop backup withholding, the employee will need to correct the reason they became subject to backup withholding. This can include providing the correct TIN to the employer, resolving the underreported income, and paying the amount owed, or filing the missing return(s), as appropriate.

Credit for Backup Withholding

If the employee had income tax withheld under the backup withholding rule, report the federal income tax withholding (shown on Form 1099 or W-2G) on the employee's return for the year they received the income.

Lock-In Letter from IRS

 Recently, I received an inquiry from a client's employee, who wanted to submit a new W-4 to her employer. Her employer would not accept it because the employer had a lock-in letter from the IRS on file specifying how much to withhold (based on setting the withholding status) from the employee's payroll. That lock-in letter mandates what the employer must withhold from the employee regardless of the employee's wishes.

I told the employee she should have received a letter from the IRS telling her how to refute the amount that the government was requiring her employer to withhold because the employer is required to maintain that withholding status until the IRS changes or releases the lock-in letter – if ever.

Here's what the IRS has to say in regard to lock-in letters and employees' rights:

The IRS will tell the employer to withhold tax at a higher rate to insure enough withholding by sending a lock-in letter to the employer. The employer must ignore any W4 the employee file that would lower that withholding. The employee should get a copy of the letter from the IRS. They will have a grace period before it goes into effect. The employee can send a new Form W4 and a statement to the IRS supporting their position on the withholding status they want to claim. The employee should send everything to the address on the letter they received from the IRS. Once the lock-in letter goes into effect the employee can't change their withholding status without the IRS saying that he or she can.

Employees researching lock-in letters online will probably find sites insisting that the IRS can't send lock-in letters, that the IRS does not have the right. These sites will also say that you can sue your employer and other silly things. But in truth, the IRS does have the right to set an increased withholding rate – and employees also have the right to prove the case for a lower rate.

If the employee has a legitimate argument that taxes are being overwithheld, even after the grace period, the employee can send the information to the IRS, and ask for a change. Also, taxes that are over withheld will show up in a refund when the employee files that year's Form 1040 Individual Income Tax Return. And, there's nothing like a fat refund to prove to the IRS that a locked-in letter withholding amount needs to be changed.

State Income Tax Withholding, Depositing, and Filing

All but nine states have a state income tax on wages. They all require that the employer withhold from employee's checks the appropriate amount of taxes. These taxes are deposited with the state and reported by specific forms to the state. The employer will also report the amounts withheld on the employee's Form W-2 a copy of which is designed to be submitted with their state income tax return. The IRS lists all state tax agencies (www.irs.gov/businesses/small-businesses-self-employed/state-government-websites). This includes offices for state Income Tax, state unemployment tax, new hire reporting and more.

These sites will have the specific information on your state's procedures and requirements.

State Unemployment Calculating, Depositing, and Filing

State Unemployment Taxes (SUTA)

Depending on your state of residence, additional unemployment taxes may be due to a state unemployment agency. The Department of Labor, which funds them, maintains a list of all of the state unemployment agencies. You will normally pay a percentage of each employee's wages to a limit. The limit varies from state to state. The percentage for a new employer is higher than an existing employer with no claims.

Your SUTA rate will go up and down based on your experience – that is, the number of claims paid to former employees. It will also go up and down based on the status of the state fund, if the fund gets to low the state will kick up everybody's rate to make up the shortfall. If the state falls too low and has to borrow from the federal government there may be a surcharge to pay the loan back or the interest on the loan. You may not know about the surcharge until the end of the year.

A good plan for hiring and terminating employees is very important. You can pay over $500 per year per employee or less than $25 per year per employee depending on how employees are terminated and how many unemployment claims are filed, and the state you operate in.

 The employer SUTA rate is in a great part controllable by the employer. If you terminate employees properly, for cause, if you are careful in all your hiring and firing and have an employee handbook/policy manual that defines causes for termination, then you can keep your SUTA rate very low. If you fire employees willy-nilly and don't fight all unemployment claims, you may find yourself with a very high rate and expense for a number of years. See Chapter 17 for the employee handbook/policy manual.

Year-End Reporting of Wages Paid

Employee W-2/W-3

Who must file Form W-2?

You must file Form(s) W-2 if you have one or more employees to whom you made payments (including noncash payments) for the employees' services in your trade or business during the calendar year.

Complete and file Form W-2 for each employee for whom any of the following applies (even if the employee is related to you).

- You withheld any income, Social Security, or Medicare tax from wages regardless of the amount of wages.
- You would have had to withhold income tax if the employee based on their Form W-4 or as single with no allowances if they did not file a Form W-4.
- You paid $600.00 or more in wages even if you did not withhold any income, Social Security, or Medicare tax. Only in very limited situations will you not have to file Form W-2. This may occur if you were not required to withhold any income tax, Social Security tax, or Medicare tax and you paid the employee less than $600.00, such as for certain election workers and certain foreign agricultural workers.

Unless otherwise noted, references to Medicare tax include additional Medicare tax. If you are required to file 250 or more Forms W-2 or want to take advantage of the benefits of e-filing.

Who Must File Form W-3?   Anyone required to file Form W-2 must file Form W-3 to transmit Copy A of Forms W-2. Make a copy of Form W-3, keep it and Copy D (For Employer) of Forms W-2 with your records for 4 years. Be sure to use Form W-3 for the correct year. If you are filing forms you must have an employer identification number (EIN).

Who May Sign Form W-3?   A transmitter or sender (including a service bureau, reporting agent, paying agent, or disbursing agent) may sign Form W-3 (or use its PIN to e-file) for the employer or payer only if the sender satisfies both of the following:

- It is authorized to sign by an agency agreement (whether oral, written, or implied) that is valid under state law.
- It writes "For (name of payer)" next to the signature (paper Form W-3 only).

A payroll service provider with a signed Form 2848 Limited Power of Attorney may sign the Form W-3 for a client directly.

When to File   Mail or electronically file Copy A of Form(s) W-2 and Form W-3 with the SSA by January 31, of the following year.

Where to File Paper   Forms W-2 and W-3

File Copy A of Form(s) W-2 with Form W-3 at the following address:

Social Security Administration
Direct Operations Center
Wilkes-Barre, PA 18769-001

If you use certified mail to file, change the ZIP code to "18769-002."

If you use an IRS-approved private delivery service use the following address:

Social Security Administration
Direct Operations Center
Attn: W-2 Process
1150 E. Mountain Drive
Wilkes-Barre, PA 18702-7997

Go to IRS.gov/PDS for a list of IRS-approved private delivery services. Do not send cash, checks, money orders, or other forms of payment with the Forms W-2 and W-3 that you submit to the SSA.

Copy 1   Send Copy 1 of Form W-2, if required, to your state, city, or local tax department. For more information concerning Copy 1 (including how to complete boxes 15 through 20), contact your state, city, or local tax authority

Electronic Filing (E-Filing)   The SSA encourages all employers to e-file. E-filing can save you time and effort and helps ensure accuracy. You must e-file if you are required to file 250 or more Forms W-2 or W-2C. If you are required to e-file but fail to do so, you may incur a penalty.

The SSA's Business Services Online (BSO) website makes e-filing easy by providing two ways to submit your Forms W-2 or W-2C Copy A and Forms W-3 or W-3C information.

- If you need to file 50 or fewer Forms W-2 or 25 or fewer Forms W-2C at a time, you can use BSO to create them online. BSO guides you through the process of creating Forms W-2 or W-2C, saving and printing them, and submitting them to the SSA when you are ready. You do not have to wait until you have submitted Forms W-2 or W-2C to the SSA before printing copies for your employees. BSO generates Form W-3 or W-3C automatically based on your Forms W-2 or W-2C.

- If you need to file more than 50 Forms W-2 or more than 25 Forms W-2C, BSO's "file upload" feature might be the best e-filing method for your business or organization. To obtain file format specifications, visit the SSA's website at SSA.gov/employer/EFW2™EFW2C.htm, and select the appropriate document.

This information also is available by calling the SSA's Employer Reporting Service Center at 800-772-6270 (toll free).

Correcting W-2s Electronically   You can also use BSO to create, save, print, and submit Forms W-2C, Corrected Wage and Tax Statement, online for the current year as well as for prior years. After logging into BSO, navigate to the Electronic Wage Reporting home page and click on the "Forms W-2C/W-3C Online" tab. Also, see E-filing and E-filing Forms W-2C and W-3C.

Furnishing Copies B, C, and 2 to Employees   Generally, you must furnish Copies B, C, and 2 of Form W-2 to your employees by January 31 of the following year. You will meet the "furnish" requirement if the form is properly addressed and mailed on or before the due date.

If employment ends before December 31, you may furnish copies to the employee at any time after employment ends, but no later than January 31. If an employee asks for Form W-2, give him or her the completed copies within 30 days of the request or within 30 days of the final wage payment, whichever is later. These forms can also be furnished to the employee electronically which may save you time and effort. See Publication 15-A, Employer's Supplemental Tax Guide, Furnishing Form W-2 to employees electronically, for additional information.

Undeliverable Forms W-2

You have to keep for four years any employee copies of Forms W-2 that you tried to but could not deliver. However, if the undelivered Form W-2 can be produced electronically through April 15th of the fourth year after the year at issue, you do not need to keep undeliverable employee copies. Do not send undeliverable employee copies of Forms W-2 to the Social Security Administration (SSA).

Taxpayer Identification Numbers

Do not accept an IRS individual taxpayer identification number (ITIN) in place of an SSN for employee identification or for Form W-2 reporting. An ITIN is available only to resident and nonresident aliens who are not eligible for US employment and need identification for other tax purposes. You can identify an ITIN because it is a nine-digit number formatted like an SSN beginning with the number "9" and with a number in one of the following ranges in the fourth and fifth digit: 50–65, 70–88, 90–92, and 94–99 (for example, 9NN-70-NNNN

Electronic W-2/W-3 Filing

If you are interested in filing your W-2s/W-3s electronically the Social Security Administration has complete information at www.ssa.gov/employer/bsohbnew.htm.

If you use a payroll service provider, they should file all of your W-2s/W-3s and will probably do it electronically.

Special Reporting Situations for Form W-2

 Following are some special situations that may arise in relationship to your payroll that require special handling. For more information, see www.irs.gov/pub/irs-pdf/iW-2W-3.pdf.

- Adoption benefits
- Archer MSA
- Health Savings Accounts and other tax-favored health plans
- Clergy and religious workers
- Deceased employee's wages
- Designated Roth contributions
- Educational assistance programs
- Election workers
- Travel, gift, and car expenses
- Foreign agricultural workers
- Golden parachute payments
- Military differential pay
- Moving expenses
- Nonqualified deferred compensation plans
- Qualified equity grants under section 83(i)
- Qualified small employer health reimbursement arrangement
- Payroll repayments made in the current year, but related to a prior year
- Scholarship and fellowship grants

- Sick pay from an insurance company
- SIMPLE retirement account

Special W-2 boxes
For more information, see www.irs.gov/pub/irs-pdf/iW-2W-3.pdf.

Box 11 – Nonqualified Plans...
Box 12 – Codes

Code A – Uncollected Social Security or RRTA tax on tips.

Code B – Uncollected Medicare tax on tips.

Code C – Taxable cost of group-term life insurance over $50,000.

Codes D through H, S, Y, AA, BB, and EE. Use these codes to show elective deferrals and designated Roth contributions made to the plans.

Code J – Nontaxable sick pay.

Code K – 20% excise tax on excess golden parachute payments.

Code L – Substantiated employee business expense reimbursements.

Code M – Uncollected Social Security or RRTA tax on taxable cost of group-term life insurance over $50,000.

Code N – Uncollected Medicare tax on taxable cost of group-term life insurance over $50,000.

Code P – Excludable moving expense reimbursements paid directly to a member of the US Armed Forces.

Code R – Employer contributions to an Archer MSA.

Code S – Employee salary reduction contributions under a section 408(p) SIMPLE plan.

Code T – Adoption benefits.

Code V – Income from the exercise of non-statutory stock option(s).

Code W – Employer contributions to a health savings account (HSA).

Code AA – Designated Roth contributions under a section 401(k) plan.

Code BB – Designated Roth contributions under a section 403(b) plan

Code DD – Cost of employer-sponsored health coverage.

Code EE – Designated Roth contributions under a governmental section 457(b) plan.

Code FF – Permitted benefits under a qualified small employer health reimbursement arrangement.

Code GG – Income from qualified equity grants under section 83(i).

Code HH – Aggregate deferrals under section 83(i) elections.

Box 13 – Checkboxes. Check all boxes that apply.

Statutory Employee Box.

Retirement Plan Box:

Check this box if the employee was an "active participant" (for any part of the year) in any of the following:

- A qualified pension, profit-sharing, or stock-bonus plan described in section 401(a) (including a 401(k) plan).
- An annuity plan described in section 403(a).
- An annuity contract or custodial account described in section 403(b).
- A simplified employee pension (SEP) plan described in section 408(k).
- A SIMPLE retirement account described in section 408(p).
- A trust described in section 501(c)(18).
- A plan for federal, state, or local government employees or by an agency or instrumentality thereof (other than a section 457(b) plan).

Third-Party Sick Pay Box

Check this box only if you are a third-party sick pay payer filing a Form W-2 for an insured's employee, or are an employer reporting sick pay payments made by a third party.

Box 14 – Other.

If you included 100% of a vehicle's annual lease value in the employee's income, it also must be reported here or on a separate statement to your employee. You also may use this box for any other information that you want to give to your employee. Label each item. Examples include state disability insurance taxes withheld, union dues, uniform payments, health insurance premiums deducted, nontaxable income, educational assistance payments, or a minister's parsonage allowance and utilities.

In addition, you may enter the following contributions to a pension plan:

a. nonelective employer contributions made on behalf of an employee.
b. voluntary after-tax contributions (but not designated Roth contributions) that are deducted from an employee's pay.
c. required employee contributions.
d. employer matching contributions.

Boxes 15 through 20

State and local income tax information (not applicable to Forms W-2AS, W-2CM, W-2GU, or W-2VI). Use these boxes to report state and local income tax information. Enter the two-letter abbreviation for the name of the state. The employer's state ID numbers are assigned by the individual states. The state and local information boxes can be used to report wages and taxes for two states and two localities. Keep each state's and locality's information separated by the broken line. If you need to report information for more than two states or localities, prepare a second Form W-2.

 Technically, if an employee is terminated, the employee can ask for a Form W-2 in writing and you have to supply it to them within 30 days. Since Form W-2s are being changed each year now and some of the changes are made after the end of the year, this can be an impossible task. The lucky thing in all of the years I have been doing payroll for thousands of clients and hundreds of thousands of employees, I have never been asked to prepare a W-2 at other than year-end. If they insist, have your CPA or payroll processing company prepare one on last year's form or a substitute form, and if it changes send them a corrected one in January.

 The payroll tax requirements and the work related to compliance are quite burdensome and complex. Once a business is incorporated and the owner must take compensation or the business hires anyone, it is recommended to use a qualified payroll processing company. In our experience, the cost of the payroll service is minor compared to the cost of management and personnel time needed to run a payroll system in-house.

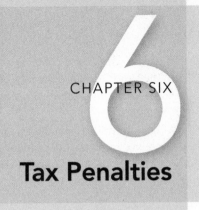

CHAPTER SIX

Tax Penalties

Penalties

 "PAYROLL TAXES ARE DUE, WITH PENALTIES AND INTEREST"

At least that is what the letter from the IRS says. First of all, don't panic.

Of the six billion dollars in employment tax penalties levied by the IRS in 2018, over half according to the "IRS Data Book" were abated after being questioned by taxpayers or their representatives. So the odds are good that the IRS is wrong or made a mistake. What do you do to get an abatement?

The normal problems with payroll taxes are:

- Failure to file or failure to file timely.
- Taxes underreported.
- Taxes underdeposited.
- Taxes deposited late.

Any of these can create a situation where the taxing agency charges penalties and interest against a business and then sucks up subsequent tax deposits, creating additional late and short payments and simply exacerbating the situation.

Read the notice from the IRS (we are just going to refer to the IRS but everything applies to state and local notices as well). It should tell you why they are charging a penalty and interest and how it is calculated. If the notice does not lay out that information, you may have well missed or not received the first notice from the IRS. That is not at all unusual. If you don't have the first notice, then call or write the IRS and get all the information from them. Also ask them to fax or send you a "Statement of Account" for the period and type of tax in question. This will show you what they have on the IRS file, without regard to whether it is correct or not.

Failure to File or Failure to File Timely

The IRS says you never filed a return. They will estimate taxes due in an amount they know exceeds what would be reasonably due based on your account. They do this to get your attention. Many people, if the estimated amount were too low, would just pay it. The IRS does not want that to happen so they always overestimate. They may in fact create a substitute return on their own volition and file it for you. Then they send you penalty and interest notices based on the fictional return they created. If they do so, get with your local CPA to file correct returns for reconsideration.

The answer to a failure-to-file penalty is to send a copy of the return. If you filed it by certified mail send a copy of the receipt when it was sent proving the date and a copy of the return receipt showing it was received.

One tip is to never send more than one return in an envelope. The clerk opening the envelope may staple them together and only the top return will ever be reported as being received.

If you didn't send you return by certified mail, then in your accompanying letter talk about your history of filing on time and explain that this return was surely just misrouted. If you have collateral proof of the filing date, like a cancelled check that was sent with the return, quote that information or even include copies. If the return was due on the 15th and the check attached cleared your bank on the 18th that is pretty convincing that the report was actually there by the 15th.

Underreported Taxes

Find out why they say that your taxes were underreported. Check your numbers against their numbers. Have they transposed a number when they hand-entered the return? That happens with manual entry on returns and even with computer scanning of handwritten returns or those with strange type fonts. Have they apparently pulled a number out of their hat? That has been known to happen. Mistakes happen on your part and on the part of the taxing agencies.

 Once we received two notices for two different customers on the same day saying they had overpaid their 940 taxes and offering them each a refund of over $36,000.00 each. The total 940 tax deposits for the two clients combined were less than $2,000.00. And no, I did not let them receive the refund!

Again send the IRS a copy of the return that you filed. If the return is wrong, then send the IRS a corrected form, such as a 941X, to correct the original filing. For instance, perhaps you put second-quarter figures on the third quarter report. There won't be a penalty for late filing if in fact you filed an original return on time, even if it was incorrect. See Chapter 5 for details on correct returns.

 If you cannot prepare the actual return on time, estimate it and file it and deposit taxes due. Then file a corrected return when you can. This avoids a late filing fee. You may have underpaid taxes and have underpayment penalties but not late filing penalties.

Underdeposited Taxes

They say you made fewer or smaller deposits than you reported. Check their list and dates of deposits against yours. Don't accept their word for when it was made. You have the proof in your files. We have noticed a real problem in the past; EFTPS payments are not being shown with the date in the electronic file the same as on the "IRS Statement of Account." How that got messed up is beyond me and we have not seen it recently. Prepare the data showing your proof that the payments were made on time, bank deposit slips, cancelled checks, EFTPS confirmations or whatever proof you have. Package up copies and send them to the IRS with a letter of explanation, and a request for them to update their records. If in fact you missed a deposit, it happens, make an immediate payment and then ask for an abatement anyway. Cite valid reasons why the deposit could have been inadvertently missed. Discuss steps you have taken to make sure it won't happen again. There is a first-time administrative abatement and if you have not has a penalty in three year or so they should abate the penalty automatically.

Late Deposit of Taxes

See the preceding "Underdeposited Taxes" section and do the same thing, only with dates. Document, document, and document; send letters. Don't give up. Just because the first person at the IRS turns you down, that literally means nothing and frankly it is expected. The IRS almost always turns down the first request for abatement of a penalty. Dealing with the IRS is a long series of no's followed by a single yes. When you do get the yes, shut up and walk away.

 One problem in the systems at the IRS involves a string of deposits. Let's say you were supposed to make 12 deposits of $1,000 each the 15th of each month, starting February 15 and ending January 15 for January through December. The second deposit is missing, and the check never got cashed. You don't know what happened. The IRS will take the third payment and apply it to the second month's taxes but it is late, so they charge a penalty. Now the fourth month's deposit gets applied to the third month's taxes, but it is also a month late so there is another late paying penalty. You will quickly have 10 late payment penalties and the 12th month penalized as not being paid at all. The penalties exceed the taxes missing. However, the service cannot do this. If you have specified what period the deposit is for, they must apply it there. If you do not specify, they will apply it to the oldest taxes due and the cascading penalties will occur. For example, If you designate the third deposit for the third month taxes, they must apply the payment there regardless. If they don't record them that way, you can insist that they do so; it is their regulations that say they must follow it. Accept the penalty only on the one month and then ask for an abatement anyway.

If you have a valid business reason that a penalty has occurred in spite of due diligence on your part the IRS is supposed to abate the penalty. There is no quota system that IRS employees have to meet for bringing in revenue but sometimes you may feel that way. You have what you think is a valid reason why you have not committed "gross negligence" or "willful neglect" and they don't agree with you. The IRS and other taxing agencies deal with people all the time who try to create "good cause" to get out of penalties. Some of these people lie to try to get out of penalties, others get abusive toward the agency employees. The men and women working for the IRS (and all other taxing authorities) are almost without exception trying to do their job as they are instructed to. If you think they are being unreasonable, you have avenues to appeal to higher authority. Feel free to do so. The employees should not make your life hard for doing so, in fact they may be happy to get the case off their desk and on to someone else's desk.

Don't yell at agency employees. Don't threaten them. Don't be stupid about what is going on. They are ordinary men and women trying to do a job in the way they are told to do it. They are trying to enforce the law that was passed by Congress or other legal authorities. If you disagree with the law, talk to your Congressperson or Legislator. If you disagree with how they are imposing the law, move up the chain. After you have exhausted all of the administrative options with the taxing authority you can always take your case to court and challenge it. This can be expensive but it is an option.

Another thing agency employees may do is to offer a reduced penalty. For example, some mitigating circumstances may be present. Or they will offer to abate penalties on two quarters if you pay the third. This allows the employee to clear the case. All of the employees at the taxing agencies are overworked and have large caseloads. They are constantly being pushed by their supervisors to clear cases. It may be tempting to accept an offer of a reduction, and if you are really in the wrong, take the offer. But it may not always be a good idea to accept. You may well be able to do better. Keep writing letters and filing documents at the higher and higher levels until one reasonable person say yes. Then, take that yes and run.

Can an ordinary citizen do this? Sure! Is it easier for a payroll tax professional? Sure! The IRS is far more likely to listen to a CPA than a citizen. The CPA knows the law and the agency procedures. He knows how to get to the next level of authority for an additional reconsideration. An ordinary citizen may not. The CPA is also far less likely to get emotionally involved than the citizen whose pocket is being emptied.

Your payroll service provider should have CPAs on staff to handle these situations for you. If not, seriously consider a payroll service provider that does. Because when, not if, the IRS, or you, make a mistake; your regular CPA will charge you his full rate to solve problems that should be solved by your payroll provider for little or nothing. Besides, if your regular CPA was an employment tax expert he would probably be doing your payroll already.

CHAPTER SEVEN

Workweek, Pay Period, Payday

 WORKWEEK

The federal government through the Fair Labor Standards Act (FLSA) sets the standard workweek at 168 continuous hours. Seven consecutive 24-hour periods. This is a predefined period, and the employer can set when it starts. It can be from midnight Saturday to midnight Saturday or it can be 9:15 Monday morning to 9:15 Monday morning, but it must be seven days straight. This is so you can figure overtime mandated under the FLSA. We discuss overtime in detail in chapter 3.

Even if you pay every two weeks, you have to figure overtime for both of the 168-hour weeks separately.

If you pay your employees semimonthly, you make figuring overtime more difficult because you will have periods of time that can overlap at the beginning or end of a regular workweek. Say your workweek is from Sunday through Saturday but your pay period is the first of the month through the 15th and the 16th through the last day of the month.

Let's take the month of March 2019 as an example. March 16 (a Saturday) falls into the workweek of March 10 through March 16. Then, the next seven days into the workweek of March 17 through March 23, the following seven days into the workweek of March 24 through March 30 and then the 31st falls into the next workweek of March 31 through April 6. This means you have to keep looking forward and backward to see if there are more than 40 hours in a workweek that have to be paid as overtime in a pay period.

If you use a biweekly schedule you can combine the two workweeks into one 14-day pay period. You still have to calculate the overtime for each workweek separately.

If you have a weekly pay period, and some states may still require some weekly payrolls, then your workweek and pay period should coincide and any overtime is very simple to figure.

Once the beginning time of an employee's workweek is established, it remains fixed regardless of the hours the employee is scheduled to work. However, the beginning time of the workweek may be changed if the change is intended to be permanent and is not designed to evade the overtime requirements.

 ## PAY FREQUENCY (PAY PERIOD)

The pay period is the period of time that you collect pay for or how often you pay your employees. The normal pay periods are:

- Monthly
- Semimonthly
- Biweekly
- Weekly
- Daily

Quarterly and annual pay periods are used occasionally in very special circumstances. In most cases you are required to pay at least monthly and, in some cases, more often than that. Here is a link to a chart showing the state-by-state requirements for pay frequency: www.dol.gov/whd/state/payday.htm.

 We recommend where possible that you pay on a biweekly basis. Monthly is not available in many cases for employees that are subject to overtime provisions of the FLSA or the states.

Semimonthly makes overtime difficult to calculate because the workweek for determining overtime does not coincide with the pay period, which may require you to go back and forth between pay periods to calculate overtime.

Biweekly should be two full workweeks. You can calculate any overtime in each workweek and include it all on the payment for that pay period. It cuts down the number of payrolls you have to run from 52 if weekly to 26. It may well cut down on the number of deposits you have to make to the government. It helps improve cash flow for the business. It is well accepted in most industries. It is a good balance between cost and convenience.

PAYDAY

Different states have different payday requirements. They are available on the same link as above for pay frequency requirements. FLSA requires that you pay your employees for work they have done but does not set when you must pay them; that is left to the states to determine.

 I suggest at least five days between the last day of the pay period and the actual payday. Seven is even better. I like to suggest to new clients that they consider a two-week pay period ending on Friday, with payday the following Friday. This eliminates a lot of problems. It gives you time to work around holidays without jumping through hoops. If the person doing payroll is sick for a day or two, it does not pose a problem. It just makes life easier than trying to figure payroll today for a check date of tomorrow.

In some states, you can go as long as 16 days between the end of the pay period and the payday. Almost no one tries to meet payroll on the last day of the pay period anymore. That forces an employer to make adjustments every pay period for what they think the employees would work, but for whatever reason they didn't work or worked beyond.

Remember: Every state has enforcement mechanisms on payroll, pay periods, paydays, and pay. There are fines and penalties for not paying people at the proper time or the proper amount. There are also different regulations on when you must pay people who terminate and that can vary whether the termination is voluntary or involuntary.

CHAPTER EIGHT

The Law

 **FEDERAL**

Fair Labor Standards Act

Perhaps the most basic of all payroll and employment laws is the Fair Labor Standards Act of 1938 (FLSA), also known as the Federal Wage-Hour Law. The FLSA does the following:

- Sets the minimum wage and overtime rates employees must receive for their work.
- Requires record-keeping by employers.
- Places restrictions on the types of work children can do and the hours they can work.
- Mandates equal pay for equal work.

Almost as important is what the FLSA does not do. The FLSA does not:

- Require employers to provide paid vacations, sick days, jury duty leave, holidays, lunch breaks, or coffee breaks.
- Regulate how often employees must be paid, or when they must be paid after termination of employment (either voluntarily or involuntarily).
- Restrict the hours that employees over 16 years of age may be required to work.

Another federal law or regulation may govern these areas, but in most instances, they are handled by the individual states. See the following note.

State Minimum Wage

Minimum wage has become a political topic in recent years and state and local minimum wage rates increase have proliferated. You are required to use the state or local minimum wage when you are paying employees if it exceeds federal minimum wage, regardless of whether you participate in interstate commerce or not.

Check here to see if state minimum wage rates apply to you: www.dol .gov/agencies/whd/minimum-wage/state. For local minimum wage levels you should be able to google "minimum wage" and the city or locality you're concerned with, if it is different from the state or federal minimum wage.

While the FLSA does not require that wages be paid within a certain amount of time after services are performed, federal courts have ruled that wages are unpaid unless they are paid on the employee's regular payday. Payment beyond that date violates the FLSA's minimum wage and overtime pay requirements, although overtime pay may lawfully be delayed until it can be correctly calculated.

On a related issue, a federal appeals court said that delaying payday by one day for each of five weeks while changing from a weekly current to a biweekly lagged pay schedule does not violate the FLSA's minimum wage and overtime provisions and may not violate the prompt payment requirement if the change is intended to be permanent, does not unreasonably delay payment, and is made for a legitimate business purpose.

DOL Enforcement

The Federal Wage-Hour Law (except for the equal pay provisions) is administered and enforced by the Wage and Hour Division of the US Department of Labor's Employment Standards Administration. The equal pay provisions are enforced by the Equal Employment Opportunity Commission. All employers and payroll practitioners must be aware not only of the FLSA but also of the state wage-hour laws in states where they operate. There are two reasons for this:

1. Areas left unregulated by the FLSA are most likely regulated by all states to one degree or another.
2. Even where the FLSA has an applicable provision, the employer must comply with a state law covering the same issue if the state law is more favorable to the employee. However, there are several states that exempt employers and employees covered by the FLSA from state law coverage.

There are two types of coverage under the FLSA – enterprise and individual employee coverage.

Enterprise Coverage

Under the enterprise coverage test, all the employees of a business are covered and protected by the FLSA if:

- At least two employees of the business are employed in jobs closely related and directly essential to interstate commerce or the production of goods for interstate commerce (including employees who handle, sell, or otherwise work on goods or materials that have been moved in or produced for interstate commerce).
- The business has annual gross sales of at least $500,000.
- Certain businesses (and all their employees) are specifically covered by the FLSA regardless of annual sales volume. They include:
  - Hospitals.
  - Nursing homes.
  - Elementary and secondary schools and colleges (public or private).
  - Public (government) agencies.

Individual Employee Coverage

Under the individual employee coverage test, an employee is covered by the FLSA if he or she is engaged in interstate commerce or in the production of goods for interstate commerce. It does not matter if the business is not a covered enterprise, so long as the employee's job is in interstate commerce.

Interstate Commerce Defined

Basically, interstate commerce is any trade, transportation, or communication between one state and another state (or states), or between a state and a foreign country. Both of these tests for FLSA coverage, as well as the definition of interstate commerce, have been interpreted very broadly by the Wage and Hour Division and the courts, so that nearly all businesses are covered by the FLSA unless a specific exemption applies.

One of the few remaining exemptions from the FLSA is for family-owned small businesses, where the only employees are the owner and immediate family members. Those employers that are not covered by the FLSA (e.g., their annual sales volume may be less than $500,000) may still be subject to state wage-hour requirements, which may be more generous to employees.

Federal Child Labor Laws

The Fair Labor Standards Act (FLSA) establishes child labor provisions. The FLSA's child labor provisions are designed to protect the educational opportunities of minors and prohibit their employment under conditions detrimental to their health or well-being.

Nonagricultural Employment

Minimum Age for Employment   The minimum age for employment is 14 years old. There are some exceptions such as newspaper delivery; performing in radio, television, movie, or theatrical productions; and work for parents in their solely owned nonfarm business (except in manufacturing or in hazardous jobs).

Hours of Employment   Fourteen- and 15-year-olds may be employed outside of school hours for a maximum of three hours per day and 18 hours per week when school is in session and a maximum of eight hours per day and 40 hours per week when school is not in session. This age group is prohibited from working before 7 a.m. and after 7 p.m., except during summers when they may work until 9 p.m. (from June 1 through Labor Day).

Sixteen- and 17-year olds may be employed for unlimited hours. There are no federal laws restricting the number of hours of work per day or per week.

Hazardous Employment   There are 17 prohibited jobs for youth under the age of 18. These include:

- Manufacturing or storing explosives.
- Driving a motor vehicle and being an outside helper on a motor vehicle.

- Coal mining.
- Logging and sawmilling.
- Power-driven woodworking machines.
- Exposure to radioactive substances and to ionizing radiations.
- Power-driven hoisting equipment.
- Power-driven metal-forming, punching, and shearing machines.
- Mining, other than coal mining.
- Meat-packing or processing (including power-driven meat slicing machines).
- Power-driven bakery machines.
- Power-driven paper-products machines.
- Manufacturing brick, tile, and related products.
- Power-driven circular saws, band saws, and guillotine shears.
- Wrecking, demolition, and ship-breaking operations.
- Roofing operations.
- Excavation operations.

There are additional prohibited occupations for 14- and 15-year-olds. Check with the US Department of Labor for more information.

Agricultural Employment

Minimum Age for Employment
- Ten- and 11-year-olds may perform jobs on farms owned or operated by parent(s), or with a parent's written consent, outside of school hours in nonhazardous jobs on farms not covered by minimum wage requirements.
- Twelve- and 13-year-olds may work outside of school hours in nonhazardous jobs, either with a parent's written consent or on the same farm as the parent(s).
- Fourteen- and 15-year-olds may perform any nonhazardous farm job outside of school hours.
- Sixteen-year-olds and older may perform any job, whether hazardous or not, for unlimited hours.

Hours of Employment   Youth under the age of 16 are restricted from employment during school hours.

Hazardous Employment   Eighteen is the minimum age for employment in nonagricultural occupations declared hazardous by the Secretary of Labor. The rules prohibiting working in hazardous occupations (HO) apply either on an industry basis, or on an occupational basis, no matter what industry the job is in. Parents employing their own children are subject to these same rules. General exemptions apply to all of these occupations, while limited apprentice/student-learner exemptions apply to those occupations marked with an asterisk(*).

These rules prohibit work in or with the following:

- Operating a tractor over 20 PTO horsepower or connecting or disconnecting its implements.
- Operating or assisting to operate a corn picker, cotton picker, grain combine, hay mower, forage harvester, hay baler, potato digger, mobile pea viner, feed grinder, crop dryer, forage blower, auger conveyor, unloading mechanism of a nongravity-type self-unloading wagon or trailer, power posthole digger, power post driver, or nonwalking-type rotary tiller.
- Operating or working with a trencher or earthmoving equipment, forklift, potato combine, or power-driven circular, band, or chain saw.
- Working in a yard, pen, or stall occupied by a bull, boar, or stud horse maintained for breeding purposes; a sow with suckling pigs; or a cow with a newborn calf (with umbilical cord present).
- Felling, buckling, skidding, loading, or unloading timber with a butt diameter of more than six inches.
- Working from a ladder or scaffold at a height of over 20 feet.
- Driving a bus, truck, or automobile to transport passengers, or riding on a tractor as a passenger or helper.
- Working inside a fruit, forage, or grain storage designed to retain an oxygen-deficient or toxic atmosphere; an upright silo within two weeks after silage has been added or when a top unloading device is in operating position; a manure pit; or a horizontal silo while operating a tractor for packing purposes.
- Handling or applying toxic agricultural chemicals identified by the words "danger," "poison," or "warning," or a skull-and-crossbones symbol on the label.
- Handling or using explosives.
- Transporting, transferring, or applying anhydrous ammonia.

* *These HOs provide limited exemptions for 16- and 17-year-olds who are bona-fide student-learners and apprentices.*

You can obtain more detail about any or all of the above listings by reviewing the child labor regulations.

Family Farms   The restrictions on Hazardous Occupations do not apply to youth who are employed by their parents on a farm owned or operated by their parents.

Child Labor Wages

The federal agricultural minimum wage is $7.25 per hour. Overtime pay at a rate of not less than one and one-half times their regular rates of pay is required after 40 hours of work in a workweek (except in some agricultural employment).

Youth Minimum Wage

A minimum wage of not less than $4.25 an hour is permitted for employees under 20 years of age during their first 90 consecutive calendar days of employment with an employer. Employers are prohibited from taking any action to displace employees in order to hire employees at the youth minimum wage.

Also prohibited are partial displacements, such as reducing employees' hours, wages, or employment benefits.

Subminimum Wage Provisions: The FLSA provides for the employment of certain individuals at wage rates below the statutory minimum. Individuals include student-learners (vocational education students). Such employment is permitted only under certificates issued by the US Department of Labor's Wage and Hour Division.

State Child Labor Laws

Most states have child labor laws. A few states solely rely on the federal laws found in the FLSA. State child labor laws may be more restrictive or less restrictive than the federal child labor laws (FLSA). In other words, states may have different minimum ages for employment, different hours of work restrictions, and additional occupations identified as hazardous. If the employment falls under FLSA jurisdiction, then both federal and state laws apply – and the most restrictive law (whether it is the state or the federal) is followed.

State Labor Laws

Every state has an "agency" that oversees state unemployment issues. Many, but not all, states also have a revenue department that oversees the collection of state income tax and the withholding and payment of those payments. Between the two possible agencies there is regulation of state tax and labor laws that fills the same position as the Federal Department of Labor and the FLSA laws that are promulgated by the US Department of Labor.

You need to be aware of your state agencies and the laws and regulations they issue. Remember if the state rules provide more protection or benefit to the employees then they are superior to federal rules. The employee gets the benefit of the most generous rules whether they be state or federal.

FMLA (FAMILY MEDICAL LEAVE ACT)

 At the time of editing this book, the Covid-19 pandemic crisis has started. There are a number of laws being passed and proposed laws concerning FMLA and other programs related to payroll. These may be short-term or long-term in duration, depending on the government. I will be posting full updates as they occur at www.ThePayrollBook.com/resources/Covid-19; please check the link if you have any questions.

The Family and Medical Leave Act (FMLA) is a federal statute requiring larger employers to provide their employees with unpaid time off in the case of serious family health issues. Issues that qualify include adoption, pregnancy, foster care placement, family or personal illness, or military leave. The statute also requires that the employer continue the employees' health insurance coverage and job protection. The FMLA is intended to provide families with the time and resources to deal with family emergencies, while also requiring employers to provide the time off.

The FMLA is where the federal government forces employers to allow employees to handle family problems that are medical or family-related.

Changes in Families

The Family and Medical Leave Act (FMLA) of 1993 allows employees not to have to make a choice between working and caring for their children, or elderly and extended family. It is social engineering that assumes that the government is better able to determine what is good for a family rather than the family itself.

It places the burden on the employer to hold open a job and continue to provide administrative support for employee benefits even though the employer may receive no direct benefit from doing so. The FMLA was signed into law on August 5, 1993 by President Bill Clinton.

FMLA Guarantees

An employee who takes unpaid leave in line with the FMLA rules is job-protected. That means the employee can return to the same job they had before they took FMLA leave. If the same job no longer exists the employer is required to provide a job that substantially equal in pay, benefits, and responsibility regardless of the necessity of the job. The FMLA mandates unpaid, job-protected leave for up to 12 weeks a year.

FMLA Qualifying

To qualify for FMLA leave and protection, an employee will have been employed by a business with 50 or more employees that operates within a 75-mile radius of the employee's job location. The employee must have worked for the employer for at least 12 months and worked at least 1,250 hours within the past 12 months. For more on employee and employer rights and responsibilities, see the Department of Labor's FMLA Informational Page (www.dol.gov/whd/fmla) or Fact Sheet #28 (www.dol.gov/whd/regs/compliance/whdfs28.pdf), which offer more details.

FMLA Purposes

The FMLA, as administered and recorded by the Department of Labor, has the following purposes as stated by law:

- To balance the demands of the workplace with the needs of families, to promote the stability and economic security of families, and to promote national interests in preserving family integrity.
- To entitle employees to take reasonable leave for medical reasons, for the birth or adoption of a child, and for the care of a child, spouse, or parent who has a serious health condition.
- To accomplish the purposes described in paragraphs (1) and (2) in a manner that accommodates the legitimate interests of employers.
- To accomplish the purposes described in paragraphs (1) and (2) in a manner that, consistent with the Equal Protection Clause of the Fourteenth

Amendment, minimizes the potential for employment discrimination on the basis of sex by ensuring generally that leave is available for eligible medical reasons (including maternity-related disability) and for compelling family reasons, on a gender-neutral basis.

- To promote the goal of equal employment opportunity for women and men, pursuant to such clause.

Important Note on 45S

 Internal Revenue Code Section 45S provides a tax credit for employers who provide paid family and medical leave to their employees even if the employer is not subject to FMLA requirements.

Eligible employers may claim the credit, which is equal to a percentage of wages they pay to qualifying employees while they're on family and medical leave. The credit generally is effective for wages paid in taxable years of the employer beginning after December 31, 2017. Originally this credit was only for 2018–2019. It was extended by the Taxpayer Certainty and Disaster Tax Relief Act of 2019 for tax year 2020. I expect it may well be extended for future years. For more information, see Notice 2018-71 (www.irs.gov/pub/irs-drop/n-18-71.pdf).

What Kind of Credit Is It?

This is a general business credit that employers may claim, based on wages paid to qualifying employees while they are on family and medical leave, subject to certain conditions. If you operate your business as a pass-through entity the credit flows through the K1 to your personal returns.

Policy to Allow Credit

Employers must have a written policy in place that meets certain requirements. The policy must allow for at least two weeks of paid FMLA qualifying leave per year. The paid leave must be paid at not less than 50% of the employee's normal wage.

Qualifying Employees

A qualifying employee is any employee under the FLSA who has been employed by the employer for one year or more and who, for the preceding year, had compensation of not more than a certain amount. For an employer claiming a credit for wages paid to an employee the employee must not have earned more than $72,000 in the previous year.

Qualifying Leave

Leave must be for one or more of the following reasons:

- Birth of an employee's child and to care for the child.
- Placement of a child with the employee for adoption or foster care.
- To care for the employee's spouse, child, or parent who has a serious health condition.
- A serious health condition that makes the employee unable to perform the functions of his or her position.
- Any qualifying crisis due to an employee's spouse, child, or parent being on covered active duty (or having been notified of an impending call or order to covered active duty) in the Armed Forces.
- To care for a service member who is the employee's spouse, child, parent, or next of kin.

If an employer provides paid vacation leave, personal leave, or medical or sick leave, other than leave specifically for one or more of the purposes stated above, that paid leave is not considered family and medical leave. In addition, any leave paid by a state or local government or required by state or local law will not be taken into account in determining the amount of employer-provided paid family and medical leave.

 I feel that if an employee takes a "mental health day" because they are unable to work, that this is a qualifying event. The Labor Department has not ruled that out as of the date this was written.

Calculating the Credit

The credit is a percentage of the amount of wages paid to a qualifying employee while on family and medical leave for up to 12 weeks per taxable year. The minimum percentage is 12.5% and is increased by 0.25% for each percentage point by which the amount paid to a qualifying employee exceeds 50% of the employee's wages, with a maximum of 25%. So if an employer sets up a policy that meets the requirements and fully pays the employee for the leave taken, the employer has a tax credit for 25% of the wages paid out.

Effective Dates

The credit is generally effective for wages paid in taxable years of the employer beginning after December 31, 2017, and it is not available for wages paid in taxable years beginning after December 31, 2020, as of publication.

When Must the Policy Be in Place?

Except for the first taxable year of an employer beginning after December 31, 2017, an employer can claim the credit only for leave taken after the written leave policy is in place. The written policy is in place on the later of the policy's adoption date or the policy's effective date.

FMLA Leave Policy

In their written policy (See chapter 17 for a sample policy) an eligible employer must allow at least two weeks of paid family and medical leave (prorated for part-time employees) for all qualifying employees at a rate of at least 50% of the wages normally paid to them. This must cover all employees who may not be covered under a mandated FMLA policy because of the employer's size.

Employers must make the leave available to all qualifying employees, which means all employees who've been employed for at least one year and had compensation from the employer for the preceding year that didn't exceed a dollar amount of $72,000 for the previous year. The law allows an employer to prorate the two-week leave period for part-time employees which means those employed for fewer than 30 hours per week on a regular basis.

Employer Is Not Required to Provide FMLA

If the employer's policy meets the requirements laid out above the employer is eligible to claim the credit even if the employer is not subject to the required FMLA mandate.

AFFORDABLE CARE ACT

The Affordable Care Act created a federally mandated insurance requirement on employers with more than 50 full-time equivalent employees. The Patient Protection and Affordable Care Act (PPACA), often shortened to the Affordable Care Act (ACA), was nicknamed Obamacare and was the US healthcare system's most significant regulatory overhaul and expansion of medical insurance coverage since the creation of Medicare and Medicaid in 1965.

This is a very complex issue both for large businesses and for individuals. It is not something, however, that the small businessperson needs to concern themselves with in regard to their business payroll until they approach the 50-person threshold. It is therefore outside the scope of this book.

If you get to the point that your business will be affected by the ACA, I would suggest that you work closely with your major medical insurance provider and your HR department. There are burdensome and expensive requirements that are placed on business.

However, there are some effects on all businesses regardless of size. Please see the following from the IRS directly about businesses with under 50 employees.

How ACA Affects Employers with Fewer Than 50 Employees

IRS Health Care Tax Tip 2015-31, May 13, 2015

 Most employers have fewer than 50 full-time employees or full-time equivalent employees and are therefore not subject to the Affordable Care Act's employer-shared responsibility provision (www.irs.gov/affordable-care-act/employers/employer-shared-responsibility-provisions).

If an employer has fewer than 50 full-time employees, including full-time equivalent employees, on average during the prior year, the employer is not an applicable large employer (ALE) for the current calendar year. Therefore, the employer is not subject to the employer shared responsibility provisions or the employer information reporting provisions for the current year. Employers with 50 or fewer employees can purchase health insurance coverage for its employees through the Small Business Health Options Program – better known as the SHOP Marketplace (www.healthcare.gov/small-businesses).

Calculating the number of employees is especially important for employers that have close to 50 employees or whose workforce fluctuates throughout the year. To determine its workforce size for a year, an employer adds its total number of full-time employees for each month of the prior calendar year to the total number of full-time equivalent employees for each calendar month of the prior calendar year, and divides that total number by 12.

Employers that have fewer than 25 full-time equivalent employees with average annual wages of less than $50,000 may be eligible for the small business health care tax credit if they cover at least 50 percent of their full-time employees' premium costs and generally, after 2013, if they purchase coverage through the SHOP.

All employers, regardless of size, that provide self-insured health coverage must file an annual information return (www.irs.gov/affordable-care-act /employers/information-reporting-by-providers-of-minimum-essential-coverage) reporting certain information for individuals they cover.

NEW HIRE REPORTING

The Personal Responsibility and Work Opportunity Reconciliation Act (PRWORA) of 1996, known as welfare reform, requires all employers to report certain information on their newly hired employees to a designated state agency.

New hire reporting is a process by which you, as an employer, report information on newly hired employees to a designated state agency shortly after the date of hire. As an employer, you play a key role in this important program by reporting all your newly hired employees to your state.

New Hire Information

States match new hire reports against their child support records to locate parents, establish a child support order, or enforce an existing order. In addition to matching within a state, states transmit the new hire reports to the National Directory of New Hires (NDNH).

State agencies operating employment security (unemployment insurance) and workers' compensation programs have access to their state new hire information to detect and prevent erroneous benefit payments.

In addition, each state can conduct matches between its own new hire database and other state programs to prevent unlawful or erroneous receipt of public assistance, including welfare, food stamps, and Medicaid payments.

National Directory of New Hires

It is estimated that more than 30% of child support cases involve parents who do not live in the same state as their children. By matching this new hire data with child support case participant information at the national level, the Office of Child Support Enforcement assists states in locating parents who are living in other states. Upon receipt of new hire information from other states, state child support agencies can take the necessary steps to establish paternity, establish a child support order, or enforce an existing order.

New Hire As Part of Welfare Reform Legislation

A major focus of PRWORA is the parents' responsibility to support their children. It contains strict work requirements for custodial parents receiving public assistance and increases the effectiveness of the child support program by including new hire reporting programs in each state. The federal government attributes tens of millions of dollars in collections to the use of new hire data.

Reporting Process for Employers

The majority of the information an employer submits is already collected when a new employee completes a Form W-4. Although the reporting process is an additional requirement, the majority of employers participating in state-established programs report "no" or a "minor" cost impact on their operations. To ease the process, states are working closely with their employers, offering them a variety of reporting methods.

Other Benefits to Employers

A potential benefit to employers is the reduction and prevention of fraudulent unemployment and workers' compensation payments. Timely receipt of new hire data allows each state to cross-reference this data against its active workers' compensation and unemployment insurance claimant files to either stop or recover erroneous payments. States have saved millions of dollars of erroneous unemployment insurance payments because of these tools.

Definitions

Employer Federal law states that an "employer" for new hire reporting purposes is the same as for federal income tax purposes (as defined by Section 3401(d) of the Internal Revenue Code of 1986) and includes any governmental entity or labor organization. At a minimum, in any case where an employer is required to have an employee complete a Form W-4, the employer must meet the new hire reporting requirements.

Date of Hire The "date of hire" is the day an individual first performs services for wages.

Newly Hired Employee The law defines a "newly hired employee" as:

1. an employee who has not previously been employed by the employer.
2. a person who was previously employed by the employer but has been separated from such prior employment for at least 60 consecutive days.

Rehired Employee If the employee returning to work is required to complete a new Form W-4, or has been separated from your employment for at least 60 consecutive days, you should report the individual as a new hire to the State Directory of New Hires (SDNH). If, however, the returning employee has not been formally terminated or removed from payroll records, or returns to employment within 60 consecutive days of separation, there is no need to report that individual as a new hire.

New Hire Report for Independent Contractors

⚠️ Some states do require the reporting of independent contractors through the "New Hire" reporting system. However, federal law does not require it. The State New Hire Reporting Contacts and Program Information matrix, available at www.acf.hhs.gov/programs/css/resource/state-new-hire-reporting-contacts-and-program-information, lists the state requirements including independent contractor requirements.

Temp Agency and New Hire Reporting

If you are a temp agency and paying wages to the individual, you must submit a new hire report. The individual needs to be reported only once except when there is a break in service from your agency of 60 days or more or that would require a new Form W-4. If your agency simply refers individuals for employment and does not pay salaries, new hire reports are not necessary. However, the employer who actually hires and pays the individual, whether on a part-time or full-time basis, will be required to report the new hire information.

Timing of Report

Federal law mandates that new hires be reported within 20 days of the date of hire. However, states are given the option of establishing reporting time frames that may be shorter than 20 days. You must adhere to the reporting time frame of the state to which you report. Be sure to check with your state new hire contact to learn your state's requirements (www.acf.hhs.gov/css/resource/new-hire-reporting-answers-to-employer-questions).

Form for Reports

Each new hire report must contain seven data elements:

1. Employee name
2. Address
3. Social Security number (SSN)
4. Date of hire (the date an employee first performs services for pay)
5. Employer name
6. Address
7. Federal employer identification number (FEIN)

Although most states require only these seven basic data elements, some states require or request additional data. Check with your state for reporting requirements.

Employee Quits before Report Is Due

Because the employer/employee relationship existed, and wages were earned, a new hire report must be submitted. Even though the employment period was short, the reported information may be the key to locating a noncustodial parent.

Address for Report

New hire reports should be sent to the SDNH in the state where the employee works. Federal law identifies three methods for submitting new hire information: first class mail, magnetic tapes, or electronically. For the convenience of employers, states offer additional options such as fax, email, phone, and online transmissions. Your state new hire contact can provide you with instructions on where and how to send new hire information.

Federal employers report new hire data directly to the National Directory of New Hires.

Reporting Time Frame for New Hire Reports

If you are an employer sending new hire reports by magnetic tape or electronically, you must make two monthly transmissions not less than 12 days and not more than 16 days apart. You should contact the state where you submit your new hire reports for all technical information regarding electronic reporting.

Information Security

Security and privacy of new hire data are important issues for all those involved in this nationwide program. Federal law requires all states to establish safeguards for confidential information handled by the state agency.

All state data is transmitted over secure and dedicated lines to the NDNH. Federal law also requires that the Secretary of Health and Human Services (HHS) establish and implement safeguards to protect the integrity and security of information in the NDNH, and restrict access to and use of the information to authorized persons and for authorized purposes.

Penalties

States have the option of imposing civil monetary penalties for noncompliance. Federal law mandates that if a state chooses to impose a penalty on employers for failure to report, the fine may not exceed $25 per newly hired employee. If there is a conspiracy between the employer and employee not to report, that penalty may not exceed $500 per newly hired employee. States may also impose nonmonetary civil penalties under state law for noncompliance.

Multistate Employer Issues

If you are a multistate employer, you have two reporting options. You may report newly hired employees to the states in which they are working, or alternatively, you may select one state where you have employees working to which to report all your new hires. If you choose to report to one state, your new hire reports must be submitted by magnetic tape or electronically. Also, you must notify the Secretary of HHS, in writing, of the state you have chosen. Fax or mail your notification to:

US Department of Health and Human Services
Office of Child Support Enforcement
Multistate Employer Registration
Box 509
Randallstown, MD 21133
(410) 277-9325 (fax)

You also can electronically submit a multistate employer notification form. The NDNH will maintain a list of multistate employers and their designated reporting locations.

Additional Information

The state where you operate a business can provide you with complete information and instructions, as necessary, regarding all aspects of its new hire program and your responsibilities as an employer. If you have additional questions or concerns, please refer to the State New Hire Reporting Contacts and Program Information (www.acf.hhs.gov/programs/css/resource/state-new-hire-reporting-contacts-and-program-information).

 LABOR POSTERS

The DOL requires that all employers post certain mandatory labor law posters in a prominent area within the workplace. Most businesses will also need to post their state's mandatory labor law posters in addition to these federal posters.

Please note that while the DOL publishes a large number of notices and posters, not all employers are required to display every poster. For example, some small businesses may not be covered by the Family and Medical Leave Act and thus would not be subject to the Act's posting requirements.

 For Labor Poster Resources please go to www.ThePayrollBook.com/resources/Labor-Posters.

To be sure that an employer is posting all the DOL posters that are required, the labor department has a website and algorithm that they can walk you through to make sure you have all the required posters: https://webapps.dol .gov/elaws/posters.htm.

Following are the most common of Federal Labor posters.

(Required) JOB SAFETY AND HEALTH PROTECTION from OSHA

www.osha.gov/Publications/poster.html

If you are in interstate commerce, you need to post.

There may be a penalty for not posting, so be sure to check to see if you are in Interstate Commerce.

(Required) EQUAL EMPLOYMENT OPPORTUNITY IS THE LAW from OFCCP

www.dol.gov/ofccp/regs/compliance/posters/ofccpost.htm

If you have contracts with the federal government or issue savings bonds.

They may affect your contracts if you don't update when they notify you.

(Not required) Fair Labor Standards Act (FLSA)

www.dol.gov/whd/regs/compliance/posters/flsa.htm

No citations or penalties for failure to post. This doesn't mean it's a bad idea to post, especially since you can get it for free. But you don't have to worry about a fine if you don't.

(Not required) Employee Right for Workers with Disabilities/Special Minimum Wage Poster

www.dol.gov/whd/regs/compliance/posters/disab.htm

No requirement to post therefore, no citations or penalties for failure to post.

(Not required) Employee Right for Workers with Disabilities/Special Minimum Wage Poster

www.dol.gov/whd/regs/compliance/posters/disab.htm

This is relevant for every employer having workers employed under special minimum wage certificates authorized by section 14(c) of the Fair Labor Standards Act.

However, there are no citations or penalties for failure to post.

(Required) YOUR RIGHTS UNDER THE FAMILY AND MEDICAL LEAVE ACT

www.dol.gov/whd/regs/compliance/posters/fmla.htm

Public agencies (including state, local, and federal employers), public and private elementary and secondary schools, as well as private sector employers who employ 50 or more employees in 20 or more work weeks and who are engaged in commerce or in any industry or activity affecting commerce, including joint employers and successors of covered employers.

Willful refusal to post may result in a civil money penalty by the Wage and Hour Division not to exceed $100 for each separate offense.

(Not required) UNIFORMED SERVICES EMPLOYMENT AND REEMPLOY-MENT RIGHTS ACT

www.dol.gov/vets/programs/userra/USERRA_Private.pdf

The full text of the notice must be provided by each employer to persons entitled to rights and benefits under USERRA.

No citations or penalties for failure to notify.

(Not required) NOTICE TO ALL EMPLOYEES WORKING ON FEDERAL OR FEDERALLY FINANCED CONSTRUCTION PROJECTS (Davis-Bacon Act)

www.dol.gov/whd/regs/compliance/posters/davis.htm

Any contractor/subcontractor engaged in contracts in excess of $2,000 for the actual construction, alteration/repair of a public building, or public work or building or work financed in whole or in part from federal funds, federal guarantee, or federal pledge which guarantee, or federal pledge which is subject to the labor standards provisions of any of the acts listed in 29 CFR 5.1.

The contractor or subcontractor is required to insert in any subcontract the poster requirements contained in 29 CFR 5.5(a)(l). The poster must be posted at the site of work, in a prominent and accessible place where it can easily be seen by workers.

Again, no citations or penalties for failure to post.

(Not required) NOTICE TO EMPLOYEES WORKING ON GOVERNMENT CON-TRACTS (Service Contracts Act)

www.dol.gov/whd/regs/compliance/posters/sca.htm

Every contractor or subcontractor engaged in a contract with the United States or the District of Columbia in excess of $2,500.

No citations or penalties for failure to post.

(Required) NOTICE: EMPLOYEE POLYGRAPH PROTECTION ACT

www.dol.gov/whd/regs/compliance/posters/eppa.htm

Any employer engaged in or affecting commerce or in the production of goods for commerce. Does not apply to federal, state and local governments, or to circumstances covered by the national defense and security exemption.

The Secretary of Labor can bring court actions and assess civil penalties for failing to post. You can get a copy of this if it applies.

(Required) NOTICE MIGRANT AND SEASONAL AGRICULTURAL WORKER PROTECTION ACT In English and Spanish www.dol.gov/whd/regs/compliance/posters/mspaensp.htm

Agricultural employers, agricultural associations and farm labor contractors.

A civil money penalty may be assessed, so download, print, and display if appropriate.

(Required) NOTIFICATION OF EMPLOYEE RIGHTS UNDER FEDERAL LABOR LAWS

www.dol.gov/olms/regs/compliance/EO13496.htm

Federal contractors and subcontractors must post the employee notice conspicuously in and around their plants and offices so that it is prominent and readily seen by employees. In particular, contractors and subcontractors *must post* the notice where other notices to employees about their jobs are posted.

Additionally, federal contractors and subcontractors who post notices to employees electronically must also post the required notice electronically via a link to the OLMS website. When posting electronically, the link to the notice must be placed where the contractor customarily places other electronic notices to employees about their jobs. The link can be no less prominent than other employee notices. Electronic posting cannot be used as a substitute for physical posting.

Where a significant portion of a federal contractor's or subcontractor's workforce is not proficient in English, they must provide the employee notice in languages spoken by employees. OLMS will provide translations of the employee notice that can be used to comply with the physical and electronic posting requirements.

The sanctions, penalties, and remedies for noncompliance with the notice requirements include the suspension or cancellation of the contract and the debarring of federal contractors from future federal contracts.

Please note that all of these are available free from the US Department of Labor. Many have not changed from year to year. Many don't even have penalties if you don't post them.

In 40 years of business, I have never had a federal or state inspector ever ask to see any posters anywhere I've worked. Furthermore, I've never had any of my thousands of clients tell me they have been asked. However, that doesn't mean it won't happen to you. If they're free and available, why not cover yourself?

If an employer doesn't want to go to the trouble of keeping up with labor posters, they can, use a commercial service. The service will provide you with complete federal and state labor posters and update them as new laws are passed or regulations changes. These services typically charge a few dollars a month to keep you fully up to date and many times offer a protecting guarantee that, in the event you are fined for not having the right posters up, they will pay the fine.

You can check with your state labor or wage and hour department to see if they have any state posters that you are required to post. They may well have a state minimum wage poster where the state minimum wage is different from the federal minimum wage. The link for each state labor or wage and hour department can be found at the *State Information Link*: www.dol.gov/whd/minwage/mw-consolidated.htm.

DAVIS-BACON AND WALSH-HEALY

If your business takes federal construction contracts, you should be aware of Davis-Bacon and Walsh-Healy federal laws and all that they entail. For those of you thinking of taking on federal construction contracts here is a summary of Davis-Bacon and Walsh-Healy to start you on your nightmare journey into politically motivated payroll requirements.

The Davis-Bacon Act

The Davis-Bacon Act and its companion acts require all contractors and subcontractors performing work on federal or District of Columbia construction contracts or federally assisted contracts in excess of $2,000 to pay their laborers and mechanics not less than the prevailing wage rates and fringe benefits for corresponding classes of laborers and mechanics employed on similar projects in the area. The prevailing wage rates and fringe benefits are determined by the Secretary of Labor for inclusion in covered contracts.

In addition to the Davis-Bacon Act itself, Congress added Davis-Bacon prevailing wage provisions to approximately 60 laws under which federal agencies assist construction projects through grants, loans, loan guarantees, and insurance (e.g., the Federal-Aid Highway Acts, the Housing and Community

Development Act of 1974, and the Federal Water Pollution Control Act). Generally, the application of prevailing wage requirements to projects receiving federal assistance under any particular related Act depends on the provisions of that law.

The US Department of Labor (DOL) has oversight responsibilities to assure coordination of administration and consistency of enforcement of the labor standards provisions of the Davis-Bacon Act. Under this authority, DOL has issued regulations establishing standards and procedures for the administration and enforcement of the Davis-Bacon labor standards provisions. Federal contracting agencies have day-to-day responsibility for administration and enforcement of the Davis-Bacon labor standards provisions in covered contracts for which they are responsible or to which they provide federal assistance under laws they administer.

Walsh-Healey Act Law

The Walsh-Healey Act or Walsh-Healey Public Contracts Act is a United States federal law passed in 1936. It requires contractors engaged in the manufacturing or furnishing of materials, supplies, articles, or equipment to the US government or the District of Columbia to pay employees who produce, assemble, handle, or ship goods under contracts exceeding $10,000, the federal minimum wage for all hours worked. It establishes overtime as hours worked in excess of 8 hours per day or 40 hours per week, sets the minimum wage equal to the prevailing wage in an area, and sets standards for child and convict labor, as well as job sanitation and safety standards.

 ## THE EQUAL PAY ACT (EPA)

The Equal Pay Act Requires Equal Pay for Equal Work

A federal law, the Equal Pay Act (EPA), requires employers to pay men and women equally for doing the same work – equal pay for equal work. The Equal Pay Act was passed in 1963 as an amendment to the Fair Labor Standards Act and can be found at 29 USC. § 206: //www.eeoc.gov/laws/statutes/epa.cfm.

Although the Equal Pay Act protects both women and men from sexual discrimination in pay rates, it was passed to help rectify the wage disparity experienced by women workers, and in practice, this law has almost always been applied to situations where women are paid less than men for doing similar jobs.

Who Is Covered

Virtually all workers are covered by the Equal Pay Act, which regulates the conduct of state, local, and federal governments and most private employers.

Making a Claim

To successfully raise a claim under the Equal Pay Act, you must show that you and an employee of the opposite sex are:

- Working in the same place.
- Doing equal work.
- Receiving unequal pay.

However, if the employer can show that the wage disparity has a legitimate basis – for example, that the higher earner has more seniority or more experience – the claim will be defeated.

Determining Equal Work

Jobs do not have to be identical for courts to consider them equal. If two employees are actually doing the same work, it doesn't matter if their titles or job descriptions differ. What counts is the duties the employees actually perform. In general, courts have ruled that two jobs are equal for the purposes of the Equal Pay Act when both require equal levels of skill, effort, and responsibility and are performed under similar conditions.

There is a lot of room for interpretation here, of course, but the general rule is that small differences in the skill, effort, or responsibility required do not make two jobs unequal. The biggest problems arise where two jobs are basically the same, but one includes a few extra duties. It is perfectly legal for an employer to pay more for the extra duties, but some courts have looked skeptically at workplaces in which the higher-paying jobs with extra duties are consistently reserved for male workers.

What "Equal Pay" Means

The EPA requires that employers pay workers at the same rate, but it doesn't require that employees receive the same total amount of compensation. If one worker earns more than another because of higher productivity – for example, because the higher-paid employee has made more sales – that does not violate the EPA.

The EPA requires more than equal wages. If employees do equal work, they are also entitled to equal fringe benefits, such as equal health and life insurance coverage, retirement plans or pensions, pre-tax medical or dependent care savings accounts, and use of company equipment. The EPA also applies to forms of compensation other than wages, including vacation time, profit sharing, and bonuses.

Title VII of the Civil Rights Act

The EPA was passed one year before Title VII of the Civil Rights Act. Both laws prohibit wage discrimination based on gender, but Title VII goes beyond ensuring equal pay to barring discrimination in all aspects of employment (www .eeoc.gov/laws/statutes/titlevii.cfm), including hiring, firing, promotion, and more. In addition, Title VII broadly prohibits other forms of discrimination, including that based on race, color, religion, and national origin.

PART TWO

Running a Payroll

n Part One, we dealt with many of the aspects of setting up payroll:

- We clarified who is an employee and offered other classifications for staff.
- We dealt with earnings, overtime, tips, and other types of pay.
- We discussed setting up deductions and taxes.
- We touched on various federal laws concerning taxes, payroll, child support, and new hires, among others.

If you have read all the previous chapters, you have the knowledge to set up your payroll.

In Part Two we'll go through what it takes to actually run a payroll, get your staff paid, and calculate and pay the government what they want you to pay.

CHAPTER NINE

Collecting Time

H ow do you collect the time that you need so that you can calculate the pay for each person, and why do you need to? The tradition in this country and the way most employment is paid is normally by the hour. So, you have to collect the hours that your staff works. We will talk about nonhourly pay a little later in his chapter. The best way to collect hours for hourly employees is a time clock.

 ## TIME CLOCKS

It is estimated that a company that *does not* use time clocks overpays the hours worked by about 10%, and that is a lot. There are a number of types of time clocks. Let's look at a few.

Manual Punch Time Clocks

This is the classic factory time clock that we see punched in the old movies. Picture a line of workers taking a paper time card and inserting it into a gray box with a clock face on the front. If you think these are no longer used, you would be wrong. These kinds of clocks are still sold and there are lots of companies that still make punch cards for time clocks. Google it and you will be surprised.

The card is taken by the employee whose name is on the top of the card from a rack and dropped into the time clock when they start work, to punch in.

The time clock stamps the time on the paper card in a sequential fashion from the first punch of the week (or other period) till the last punch of the week. The employee replaces the card in a similar rack on the other side of the time clock, to allow the line of workers to flow smoothly as they pass through and punch their time cards in the most efficient fashion. At the end of the shift, or possibly to account for a break time, the employee goes through the line in reverse to punch out and put the card back in the original rack in the appropriate slot. The slots in the rack are often labeled to make it easy for each employee to find their individual card, particularly if there are a large number of employees.

Many times, the procedure is overseen by a foreman or other company employee. This is to make sure that everyone punches in/out and nobody punches an additional card for another employee who is not present. This is called buddy punching.

Sometimes the clock will be available for only a couple of minutes before a shift to a couple of minutes after a shift, to keep employees from punching early or late. There are cases in which the time clock may be locked before and after the punching timeframe to prevent anyone from tampering with or removing a timecard.

Any problems with the punches are corrected in writing by a supervisor, right on the timecard itself, and initialed by the supervisor. This describes the time clock I used at a Colgate-Palmolive soap factory back in the early 1970s before I entered college.

The cards are collected at the end of the week and turned over to the payroll department. All of the time is then calculated by hand by subtracting the in-punch from the out-punch. Then, all the times for the workweek are added and totaled, normally right on the card. This facilitates the audit process if there is a question. The employee punches their own time on their own time card. If the punches are then subtracted and added correctly there is no dispute regarding the hours that the employee worked.

After the hours are calculated by hand, the hours are moved on to calculating pay.

You have to track the hours that your employees work and pay them for all of the work hours. The FLSA sets forth the requirements for a 40-hour workweek. However the congressional Portal-to-Portal Act first passed in 1947 modifies the FLSA in several regards.

Certain activities are not considered when working for compensation:

- Traveling to or from work.
- Engaging in incidental activities before or after work.

The US Supreme Court has ruled that the Act requires paying employees for activities that are "integral and indispensable" to an employee's principle on-the-job actions. An employee cleaning up before or after work is not normally considered work time for pay. However, if work includes working with dangerous material washing up may be "integral and indispensable" for safety purposes and therefore, the employer must pay the employee for that time, because it involves worker safety and is compensable.

Punching in or out of work, waiting in line for a paycheck, searches of workers for safety or antitheft screening are not considered working time that the employee must be paid for. But if you *require* the employee to attend a training class on any subject, the employer must pay for that time.

In 1993 Food Lion Inc. paid out over 16 million dollars to settle claims where the chain violated Federal Wage and Hour laws concerning what were worked hours, overtime hours, and violations of child labor laws.

The US Department of Labor investigated the chain and found "widespread and extensive" violations. This included teenagers operating dangerous machinery and being scheduled to work hours greater than were allowed under the law.

In addition there were instances where employees were forced to work off the clock, without pay, after their normal shift was over.

At the time this was the largest settlement ever for an instance where a company violated FLSA statutes.

Electronic Time Clocks

Electronic time clocks are newer and more efficient. There are a number of different types of electronic time clocks. Some use a plastic card such as a credit card with a magnetic stripe that identifies when an employee swipes a card to punch in and out. There are others where the employee punches in his assigned number to punch in and out. There are others that are handled by software on a computer network, where the employee enters a password to punch in and out.

The upside of these is that most are connected to a computer and the punches are automatically subtracted out and then added to get a total for the pay period. That information is used to calculate pay. Many times, they are actually connected to the payroll system so the hours are not re-entered into the payroll system; they are there automatically or get uploaded to the payroll system. All this saves time and errors of manual processing.

These systems do not prevent buddy punching, however. A worker can give his card or password to a friend to punch them in or out. A staff member can leave early and give his card or password to a friend to punch them out, even though they may have gone to a ballgame or the beach.

Biometric Time Clocks

Biometric is the latest method in clocking time . In 2007, Pay by Touch introduced biometric technology for the first time. These clocks use the staff members own body in one way or another to institute the time punch. They vary and can use hand geometry, voice, facial recognition, iris patterns, or other unique characteristics of the staff member that cannot be duplicated or shared. This eliminates buddy punching completely.

I discussed the concept of biometric time clocks with one of our clients, who employs about 200 workers. This is a medical services company with a large number of educated and professional staff. The office manager felt it was unnecessary to switch to a biometric clock. The company had a manual clock they used for years in a back corridor out of sight of any supervisory personnel. I finally talked her into installing a temporary surveillance camera of the time clock. At the end of a week she fired three employees for buddy punching and ordered a biometric time clock. The moral is, if the clock is not being watched, someone will probably scam it.

For time clock resources, please go to www.ThePayrollBook.com/resources.

TIMESHEETS

Timesheets are nothing but a manual clock without any of the timekeeping properties of a time clock. You are solely relying on the staff to be both conscientious and honest. They should fill in the timesheet when they come and go. Trying to fill it in at the end of the week is an exercise in futility. Can you remember the exact time you left and came back from lunch on Monday when you fill out your time sheet on Friday? I couldn't.

Five minutes here and there, no big deal, right? Five minutes a day for 250 working days is over 20 hours a year. That is several hundred dollars at a minimum that the employer is giving away, unknowingly. It also encourages less honorable employees to fudge their time even more, because they get away with it. It encourages other employees to do the same thing because they see their fellow workers doing it and prospering from it. Timesheets have all the weaknesses of time clocks and more, and few of the advantages.

SALARIED EMPLOYEES' TIME

You are paying a salaried employee a certain amount every pay period, right? Wrong. You learned in Chapter 3 that you can withhold payment from salaried employees under certain conditions for time not worked on a full-day basis. You also learned in Chapter 8 about the Section 45S tax credit for wages paid to employees who take time off that qualifies under FMLA circumstances if you have the correct policies in your Employee Handbook/Policy Manual (see Chapter 17).

Corrections

You need to track salaried employees hours/days worked by type and circumstances. Their paid time off needs to be recorded to make sure they don't take days off with pay that you as the employer have not authorized. You need to track the Section 45S qualified time so as to claim your tax credit at the end of the year.

No matter what system you use, there will always be corrections, for example, for people who forgot to sign in, sign out, or other issues. Your supervisors need to be vigilant about the timekeeping under their watch and make sure their corrections are real and not just fanciful suggestions from employees who would cheat their employer if they could. The people entering the time should not be the people approving the time. The people approving the time should not be the people entering time into the payroll system. The approval process is, of course, where unscrupulous supervisors can enter ghost punches for their ghost employees (see Chapter 10).

In addition, no matter how you collect time, you need to make sure that the equipment and/or software is protected so that it cannot be tampered with without notifying management that such tampering has happened.

CHAPTER TEN

Calculating Payroll

N ow that you have all the time entered to pay your staff, you can calculate earnings. You will have to calculate gross pay, taxable pay, after-tax pay, and net pay.

CALCULATE EARNINGS HOURLY

Let's start with your hourly paid staff. You know your workweek and your pay period (see Chapter 7). How many of the recorded hours are in the workweek? If a non-exempt employee has more than 40 hours of worked hours in the workweek, and the company is subject to FLSA, then those hours in excess of 40 are overtime. That company may well have, unless it pays weekly, more than one workweek in its pay period. The overtime hours will need to be calculated by workweek, not by pay period.

Example 1: You have a pay period from Saturday, June 1, to Friday, June 14. This has two workweeks in the pay period because you have set your workweek from 0:00 a.m. on Saturday through 11:59 p.m. on Friday. You will have to look at the hours worked in each workweek. If employees worked no more than 40 hours in each week, then there is no overtime. But if a staff member worked 50 hours from June 1 through June 7 and 30 hours from June 8 to June 14, they are due 10 hours of overtime pay, even though they worked an average of 40 each of the two weeks in the pay period. Overtime is calculated on a *per workweek basis*, not a per pay period basis.

Example 2: Your pay period is semimonthly. Again, it started at 0:00 a.m. Saturday morning on the first of June and ended at 11:59 p.m. on the fifteenth of June. You now have two full workweeks and part of a third workweek in the pay period. You have to look at the hours in the first week to check for overtime and the second week for overtime. There will be no overtime (under FLSA) in the third workweek which only had one day, June 15, in this workweek. But when you do the pay period of June 16 through June 30 you will have to look at the hours, if any, worked on the 15th to see if the first workweek in the June 5 through June 21 workweek had more than 40 hours, to see if you have to pay overtime. It can be confusing, which is why we recommend biweekly pay periods and not semimonthly pay periods.

Here is a calendar for 168-hour workweeks – and the periods (between the parenthesis) used for calculating overtime.

```
(  1  2  3  4  5  6  7 )
(  8  9 10 11 12 13 14 )
( 15 16 17 18 19 20 21 )
( 22 23 24 25 26 27 28 )
( 29 30  1  2  3  4  5 )
```

This is the calendar for calculating payroll for the semimonthly pay period. Note the disconnect.

```
( 1   2  3  4  5  6  7
  8   9 10 11 12 13 14
 15) (16 17 18 19 20 21
 22  23 24 25 26 27 28
 29 30)  1  2  3  4  5
```

Now you have regular and overtime hours for a staff member. You will multiply the total (regular and overtime) hours worked for the pay period by the staff member's rate of pay. Understand that the employee can have worked several jobs during the pay period and each pay week. These jobs can have different rates of pay.

In a restaurant, for example, the same person may work as waitstaff, bus help, and even cook at different times. That is fine, and they can have different pay rates for the different jobs. Next you'll multiply the hours worked (if necessary in each job) by the rate of pay for that job. In most cases it will simply be the total hours worked by the single normal rate of pay. This is known as regular earnings.

Next you will calculate overtime earnings. For a person who works at a single rate of pay, take 50% of the regular rate and multiply it by the overtime hours worked. This is referred to as the overtime premium.

Total hours worked: 45

45 total hours × $10.00 rate of pay = $450.00 regular earnings

5 hours of overtime × $5.00 overtime premium
= $25.00 overtime premium pay

Total earnings for workweek $450.00 + $25.00 = $475.00

OVERTIME IF A STAFF MEMBER WORKS DIFFERENT POSITIONS AT DIFFERENT RATES

If your staff works at multiple rates of pay during the workweek it is more difficult. You will have to calculate weighted overtime. Weighted overtime, also known as blended overtime, is the average of an employee's different pay rates. Employers might pay an employee different pay rates for each job they work.

Let say, for example, you have an employee, Joe, who works as a welder for $18.00 an hour who also does office cleaning at $10.00 an hour and front desk work at $12.00 an hour.

To find the weighted overtime, multiply the average pay rate by .5 to find their overtime premium.

Getting to the weighted overtime premium takes several steps.

1. Multiply hours worked for each position by the hourly rate for that position.
2. Add together the total wages from all positions to get the regular earnings.
3. Divide the regular earnings by the number of hours worked to get the average pay rate.
4. Multiply the average pay rate .5 to get the overtime premium.
5. Multiply the overtime premium by the overtime hours to get the overtime premium pay.
6. Add the total regular earnings and total overtime premium pay to get total pay.

We will follow Joe's payroll throughout this section all the way to the net pay.

Your employee, Joe, worked as follows:

Welder	20 hours	× $18.00	= $360.00
Cleaner	12 hours	× $10.00	= $120.00
Front Desk	16 hours	× $12.00	= $192.00
	48 total hours		$672.00 regular earnings

$672.00 regular earnings/48 hours = $14.00 average pay rate

$14.00 × 0.5 = $7.00 overtime premium

8 overtime hours × $7.00 overtime premium

= $56.00 overtime premium pay

$672.00 regular pay + $56.00 overtime premium pay $728.00 total pay

ADDITIONS TO EARNINGS

Now that you have total pay (regular earnings plus overtime premium pay), are there any additions to the pay for your hourly people? There are a lot of other earnings that may come into play, such as holiday pay or jury duty pay (see Chapter 3). These other earnings are usually calculated at an employee's regular rate of pay. Your employee handbook/policy manual should tell you and your employees about any additional pay and how it is calculated.

If the employee works at multiple rates, it may be a base rate that is established for the employee or may be an average rate, such as the one we calculated earlier for a weighted or blended overtime calculation.

Certain fringe benefits are taxable. If you provide taxable fringe benefits they are added to the employee's total wages and then taxed like any other earnings. Examples of taxable fringe benefits include:

- Reimbursement for business-related miles in their vehicle that are greater than the IRS standard mileage rate.
- The Tax Cuts and Jobs Act made moving expenses paid by the employer for the years 2018 through 2025 taxable.
- Bicycle commuting that was tax exempt was made taxable by the Tax Cuts and Jobs Act for the years 2018 through 2025.
- Clothing given to employees that is suitable for street wear is a taxable fringe benefit.
- Education reimbursements payments for educational assistance that is not job related or that exceeds the IRS exclusion are taxable.
- Cash awards are taxable unless given to charity. Noncash awards are taxable unless nominal in value or given to charity.

- Expense reimbursements not under a nonaccountable plan are taxable. The employee needs to provide adequate records or any expense reimbursement will be taxable to the employee.
- One common taxable fringe benefit is a company car that is available for personal use. See Chapter 3 and IRS Publication 15-B (www.irs.gov/pub/irs-pdf/p15b.pdf).

In our example Joe was reimbursed for mileage by his employer at a rate above what the IRS allows.

		Mileage reimbursement	$ 22.00
		Above the IRS allowance	
Plus	Total payroll		$728.00
Equals	Total gross payroll		$750.00

 ## REDUCTIONS TO EARNINGS

Now that you have total gross pay (regular pay, overtime premium pay and additional earning), are there any items to reduce pay? There are obviously several. We will discuss them in the order that they need to be applied to the total gross pay.

Pre-Tax Deductions

Pre-tax deductions such as POP insurance premiums, 401k deductions, Section 125 deductions, and others are discussed at length in Chapter 4. These deductions are the first thing used to reduce total gross pay. This is because the law allows for these deductions to come out of income before taxes are figured.

Example: Joe has a Section 125 deduction of $95.00 a week for qualifying health insurance.

	Total gross pay	$750.00
Minus	Pre-tax deduction	($95.00)
Equal	Taxable pay (or pre-tax pay)	$655.00

Tax Withholding

The next reduction to taxable pay is taxes withheld from the employee. This consists of multiple items and will vary by state, locality, amount of pay, and number of deductions claimed. Every employee should have filled out a W-4 form when hired. This form determines the withholding status of each employee and allows them to adjust their withholding based on circumstances outside of the job they are filling out the Form W-4 for.

The federal taxes that come out of the employee taxable pay are Social Security taxes and Medicare which are fixed percentages, and federal income tax (FIT), which will vary. IRS Publication 15 (also known as Circular E) and Publication 15-T have all the rules and tables you will need if you are figuring the payroll yourself, and not using payroll software or a third-party payroll service provider.

You will find references sometimes to FICA, which stands for Federal Insurance Contributions Act. This is the law that authorizes the deduction for Social Security taxes and is many times used instead of Social Security as the title for the Social Security tax withholding. You may also find Social Security withholding tax referred to as OASDI which stands for "Old-age, Survivors and Disability Insurance Program" and is the official name for Social Security.

Social Security is currently taxed at the rate of 6.2% (0.062 × taxable pay) of an employee's taxable pay, up to a dollar limit. The 2020 maximum taxable wages subject to Social Security tax withholding is $137,700 or a deduction of $8,239.80. What this means is that once an employee's taxable wages for the year equal $137,700, no more Social Security taxes are withheld from their pay.

Medicare tax on each employee is withheld at the rate or 1.45% (.0145 x taxable pay) without a limit on the amount withheld or the taxable income without limit. If the employee has taxable income of $100,000 the employer will withhold $1,450. There is an additional surcharge on highly compensated employees see Chapter 5.

 You need to be aware that Social Security taxes and Medicare taxes (not including the 0.9% surcharge) are matched by the employer. So when you deposit the Social Security and Medicare taxes you have withheld from the employee, you will add an equal sum that you pay as the employer. See Chapter 12.

The next tax to deduct form the employee's taxable pay is Federal Income Tax withholding. If you're doing this manually you will need a copy of Publication 15 and Publication 15-T. In fact, it is a good idea to keep both publications on hand. They will answer a number of payroll and payroll tax questions. They also have a full set of FIT withholding tables both for the pre-2020 Form W-4 and for the new Form W-4 for use after January 1, 2020.

Publication 15-T contains tables for single and married individuals for pay periods of daily, weekly, biweekly, semimonthly, and monthly in part three. Down the left hand side of the tables is the income; across the top is the amount of exemptions claimed. Select the correct table for single or married, as indicated on their Form W-4, and the correct pay period. Go down the left-hand side to the correct taxable pay amount and across to the number of exemptions claimed on the pre-2020 Form W-4. In the indicated box will be the amount of FIT to withhold, deposit, and report. In Joe's case the amount of federal income tax withheld is $26.00

The tables in part two are for those filing the new Form W-4 for January 1, 2020, and forward. There is a worksheet to figure the amount to withhold using the new tables for 2020 forward and the three status of "Married Filing Jointly," "Head of Household," or "Single or Married Filing Separately."

There are several additional ways to calculate withholding but you will seldom if ever need them. They are laid out in the Publication 15 and the new Tables are in Publication 15-T available at IRS.gov.

State and local income tax withholding comes next. Alaska, Florida, Nevada, South Dakota, Texas, Washington, and Wyoming do not have state income taxes; in addition, New Hampshire and Tennessee do not tax wages. None of the nine states withhold state income tax from wages. The rest of the country does. The rates in the states very widely. The details are available on each state's website.

Joe lives in New York. According to their table, for "weekly" and "married" with two exemptions, Joe's state income tax withholding should be $24.73, which would be $1,285.96 on an annual basis. Joe also lives in New York City. According to the New York City tax withholding table for "weekly" and "married" with two exemptions you will have to withhold $16.70 of city income tax, which would be on an annual basis of $868.40

Example: Joe is married and claims two additional exemptions

Joe's taxable pay (from the preceding example)	$677.00
Social Security tax withholding at 6.2%	($ 40.61)
Medicare taxes at 1.45%	($ 9.50)
Income tax withholding	($ 26.00)
State income tax withholding	($ 23.86)
NYC income tax withholding	($ 16.70)
Joe's pay after taxes	$538.33

Some states will impose taxes on residents who are permanent residents even if they work in a different state, and the reverse. You need to be very aware of the provisions of income tax withholding for your locale and surrounding areas that you might have employees living in.

 A list of states with reciprocal agreements with other states concerning income taxation can be found at www.ThePayrollBook .com/resources/reciprocal-agreements.

Most US cities and counties do not impose a local income tax, but they are imposed by 4,943 jurisdictions in 17 states, encompassing over 23 million Americans. Varying from minute amounts in several states to an average of 1.55% in Maryland, these taxes provide a long-standing and significant source of revenue to many cities in Rust Belt states in the northeastern states.

A list of local tax jurisdictions is given at taxfoundation.org/local-income-taxes-city-and-county-level-income-and-wage-taxes-continue-wane. If your business is in one, or you have employees who live in one, you need to be aware of the provisions. There are about 5,000 cities and/or counties that impose such taxes on about 7% of the population of the United States.

After-Tax Deductions

Deductions that come out of after-tax pay are the next items in order to reduce the amount that you pay an employee. In Chapter 4, we went through many of the common deductions. There are both voluntary and nonvoluntary deductions. Make sure that if you have voluntary deductions from an employee's pay that you have a signed agreement in the file allowing you to deduct the money. If you don't, and they object to the state labor department, you may well be forced to refund the amounts to them *even after* they have quit being an employee.

We are going to assume that Joe has two after-tax deductions. The first deduction is child support for $75.00 a week for a dependent child who is living with his ex-spouse and the second is a United Way contribution of $10.00

Joe's pay after taxes	$538.33
Child support deduction	($75.00)
United Way	($10.00)
Joe's net pay	$453.33

The net pay is what you pay the employee. You have now completed the calculation of Joe's pay. Make sure that you review pay-stub requirements in the next chapter.

Here is Joe's complete payroll at a glance.

Welder	20 hours	× $18.00 = $360.00
Cleaner	12 hours	× $10.00 = $120.00
Front desk	16 hours	× $12.00 = $192.00
	48 total hours	$672.00 regular earnings
Plus	Overtime premium	$ 56.00
	Mileage reimbursement	$ 22.00
	Above the IRS allowance	
Minus	Pre-Tax deduction (Section 125)	($ 95.00)
	Taxes	($122.17)
	Child support deduction	($ 75.00)
	United Way	($ 10.00)
Joe's net pay		$ 453.33

CHAPTER ELEVEN

Paying Your Employee

 METHOD OF PAYMENT

There are basically four methods of paying your employees, and we will discuss the pros and cons of each.

Cash

Cash is a legal way to pay employees in all states.

When you pay cash there are some distinct problems. You have to obtain and keep it safe on the premises to be able to pay it out. If you have an amount of cash on hand at a known time and known place, this is an invitation to get robbed. Also, cash mislaid is cash lost. Remember the scene in *It's a Wonderful Life* when the uncle put the cash into a folded newspaper, forgot it, and it was found by the greedy banker, who kept it? It was gone! The records for cash payments are the individual signatures and must be kept safe for a number of years. If you make a mistake and overcount out cash to someone, you won't be able to prove it and get the overpayment back. Your employees are then subject to carrying a large amount of cash that can be lost or stolen.

Advantages include no banking or check charges, no reconciliation of each payment except in relation to the cash held for payroll and paid out, and reduced banking costs.

Check

Some states require that if you use checks they have to be drawn on a financial institution in the state where the employees work. Some require that it be located conveniently for the employees. The employees must be able to cash their checks for full face value without a charge from the financial institution on which they are drawn.

Advantages include greater safety of the funds and reduced risk of theft or loss. Technically only the employee can cash the check and if it is lost or stolen it can be replaced at little or no cost to the employee. There is a traceable and verifiable payment of wages.

Disadvantages include restrictions that various states make. Check fraud is also one of the largest categories of crime in the United States and every time you write a check you are giving all the information a fraudster needs to try and defraud you via check fraud. The checks can be lost or stolen and you will have to replace and track the account to make sure that both checks are not cashed.

If you overpay a departing employee you will have a hard time getting an overpayment back. If a check does not get cashed it has to be escheated to the state (we will cover that later). You have banking costs for the checks and accounting costs for reconciling each check. Many employees will want time off to go to the financial institution and cash their check. You may feel obligated to prepare checks early for employees who are going on vacation and won't be there for payday. Storage costs for maintaining all the cashed checks for a number of years.

Payroll Direct Deposit

Payroll direct deposit is the electronic transfer of a payment from a company or organization into the checking or savings account of an employee, retiree, taxpayer, or shareholder. The payment can be divided among several different accounts and, in many cases, between different financial institutions. The most popular application of our direct deposit service is for payroll, but it can also be used for many other types of payments, including:

- Annuities
- Bonuses and commissions
- Dividend and interest payments
- Pensions
- Travel expense settlements
- Tax refunds
- Social Security or other government payment

Benefits

Direct deposit is the electronic transfer of a payment from a company or organization into an individual's checking or savings account. The benefits of direct deposit to both consumers and companies are numerous. This is why most large companies (100+ employees) offer direct deposit, and it has become a staple in today's employee benefit packages.

Direct deposit is safe, confidential, convenient, and fast. Employees who use direct deposit can access their pay in their accounts at their financial institution's opening of business on payday. With direct deposit there is no waiting for checks to clear and the bank should not put a hold on availability.

Problems with direct deposit are very rare. The chance of having a problem with a check is 20 times greater than with direct deposit. If a problem does occur, it is generally easy to resolve. Consumers usually only need to contact the company or organization that made the deposit, or their financial institution.

Surveys show that 97% of those who use direct deposit are very satisfied with it.

Companies can save anywhere from $0.50 to several dollars per payment by using direct deposit instead of checks in preparation, distribution, physical costs, and banking fees, let alone the reconciliation and accounting fees. For accounting reconciliation purposes, payment of employees by direct deposit is one entry on the cash side of the ledger, not one entry for every check.

Operation

By completing a standard enrollment form, a person authorizes a company or organization to make a direct deposit payment into one or more of his or her accounts. You will need a signed authorization form with the employee's banking information before you can start making direct deposits for the employee's payroll.

 A standard direct deposit enrollment form is available at www .ThePayrollBook.com/resource/directdepositform.

The company or organization making the direct deposit may perform a test run by sending the consumer's checking or savings account information, but no dollar amount, to the consumer's financial institution via the Automated Clearing House (ACH) Network. The employee's financial institution notifies the company or organization if the entry can't be posted or if any changes need to be made to the account information. This is called a prenote.

After processing the payroll and making any necessary changes, the company or organization or their payroll service bureau creates the ACH file that contains all the direct deposit information. They then deliver it, usually by electronic transmission or CD-ROM, to their financial institution, which becomes the Originating Depository Financial Institution (ODFI) for the ACH transactions. The ODFI strips out any transactions that are to remain in that institution.

The ODFI sends the remaining file to the ACH system operator, which is the Federal Reserve System. It is processed there and the pieces going to the various Receiving Depository Financial Institutions (RDFI) for each employee's account are created along with all other transactions going to that institution.

The RDFI picks up the file electronically and loads it into their internal system which makes the direct deposit available for the employee.

The ODFI and RDFI have a schedule when they send and receive files to/from the system operator. The time slot is called a *window*, a term taken from old bank terminology. The largest institutions have the most, as well as the latest in the day, windows to send/receive files. If the employer or service bureau miss the ODFI's last window, the file waits until the next day to go to the system operator. It takes the system operator as much as four hours (or more) to have the data assembled into the outbound file. The file waits for the RDFI's next window to be picked up.

Some RDFI's only have one window late in the day. Credit unions use a correspondent bank, not the system operator, to get their files, because they are not a bank. Credit unions usually pick up from their RDFI correspondent bank once a day in the afternoon.

If the direct deposit for the employee is not yet at the RDFI it won't be picked up that day and available for the employee.

So, lots of fingers and deadlines in the pot. If the ODFI is a large institution and sends early in the day, and the RDFI is a large institution with a late pickup window, the direct deposit may well only take one day to move through the system. Therefore if the ACH file gets to ODFI early Monday it may be available for the employee at the RDFI at opening of business Tuesday. Any delay or time slippage or having a credit bureau in the mix or dealing with smaller ODFIs/RDFIs will cause the direct deposit to not be available until the second business day. However the RDFI should not make the direct deposit amounts available to the employee until the effective date of the file, which is normally payday regardless of when the RDFI received the direct deposit information from the system operator.

What is true for direct deposit movement of funds also holds true for debit/pay cards.

State Rules

States have different rules on:

- Whether a company can insist on direct deposit.
- Fees incurred by employee.
- Who chooses the financial institution for the direct deposit.
- Other factors.

These rules are in constant change because of pressure by financial institutions and large employers as well as labor organizations. Should you have any questions about your state check with your state labor department or your payroll professional.

Pay Card

Payroll debit cards make all the sense in the world for small businesses, despite their recent bad publicity.

First, they are an adjunct to a direct deposit system. They can be used in concert with your direct deposit system for your unbanked employees, for partial payments to family members in college, family members out of state or out of country, etc.

The same information the employer uses for direct deposit (ABA and account number) are used for debit cards. You just send the file to your bank or you payroll service provider and they do the rest.

That's it, and everybody is paid on payday! All the advantages of direct deposit are available for your unbanked employees.

A properly designed payroll debit card program does not cost the employee anything as long as they follow a few simple rules. They can get all their money at a bank or as cash back at point of sale without a fee. But, if they want to use it as an ATM card there are fees. Under almost any circumstances it is cheaper than the cost of cashing a check if they don't have a bank account. Your employees can even, for a small fee, get additional cards. In addition, it brings them into the Internet age, allowing them a way to make online purchases. Pay cards also should not cost the employer anything. You don't make any money off a good system, but why would you want to make your employees pay you to get paid?

Your payroll processing company should be able to provide you with immediate issue cards. You keep a stack in the desk drawer. When you hire someone you give them a card, they complete an enrollment form, and sign it. The employer faxes it in to the payroll company, who puts it in the payroll system and notifies the issuer.

In the next pay period, the employee's pay is on the card. This doesn't get much simpler. After several deposits, the issuer may send out to the employee a personalized card. The ABA and routing number stay the same so the employer does nothing.

It provides the employee with greater security. The card should be a PIN-based card, and as long as the employee does not write the PIN on the card it is worthless if lost or stolen. A lost card can be replaced with a new card, for a small fee, with the existing balance already on it. The employee pays the small fee for the replacement card.

It provides the employer with greater security. No checks to be used for a check fraud scheme. No checks to be lost or stolen. No having to deliver a paycheck. It provides all the advantages of direct deposit to the employee and employer with no additional costs. The card should have a Visa or MasterCard logo on it to make it useable almost anywhere.

Fifty years ago there was still the occasional person who insisted on cash wages. In the next few years, checks will disappear and everyone will be paid electronically. This is the future!

Pay Stubs

The Fair Labor Standards Act (FLSA) does require that employers keep accurate records of hours worked and wages paid to employees. However, the FLSA does not require an employer to provide employees pay stubs.

The states of Alabama, Arkansas, Florida, Georgia, Louisiana, Mississippi, Ohio, South Dakota, and Tennessee have no requirements regarding pay stubs. The employer may provide them but is not required to.

The following 26 states require employers to provide their employees with a pay stub, though it is not specified that the pay stub be in writing or on paper. Many states have reasonably interpreted that employers can comply by providing either a written, printed, or electronic pay stub, as long as the employee has the ability to view their pay stubs. Some state agencies require the capability to print the electronic pay stubs.

Alaska	Missouri	Pennsylvania
Arizona	Montana	Rhode Island
Idaho	Nebraska	South Carolina
Illinois	Nevada	Utah
Indiana	New Hampshire	Virginia
Kansas	New Jersey	West Virginia
Kentucky	New York	Wisconsin
Maryland	North Dakota	Wyoming
Michigan	Oklahoma	

The following 11 states require employers to provide a pay stub that is printed or written. However, most states allow employers to provide electronic pay stubs that can be printed (with access to a printer ensured by the employer). Some states require employees to give consent to receive pay stubs electronically.

California	Maine	Texas
Colorado	Massachusetts	Vermont
Connecticut	New Mexico	Washington
Iowa	North Carolina	

Opt-Out States

Delaware, Minnesota, and Oregon provide employees the right to opt-out of receiving electronic pay stubs and receive paper pay stubs from their employer instead.

Opt-In States

Hawaii is the sole state that requires employers to obtain employee consent before implementing an electronic paperless pay system. Employers must provide a written or printed pay stub with details of the employee's pay information unless the employee agrees to receive their pay stub electronically.

What's in a Pay Stub?

A pay stub is a pay statement that itemizes the details of each pay period's wages. It typically contains the:

- Beginning and end dates of the pay period.
- Total gross earnings (pay before deductions).
- Pre-tax deductions.

- Federal taxes withheld.
- State taxes withheld.
- Local taxes withheld.
- Wage garnishments (such as child support).
- Voluntary deductions including pension/retirement contributions.
- Net pay (pay after all deductions).

It also may include:

- Contributions, such as to a retirement or pension plan.
- Year-to-date payroll earnings.
- Total number of hours worked for hourly workers and different types of hours worked, including regular, overtime, break time, double-time, etc.
- Pay rate.
- PTO/vacation hours (total available, accrued this period, used this period).
- Other information as the employer desires.

WAGES FOR DECEASED EMPLOYEES

The loss of an employee due to death is a difficult time for a business. Not only is it hard to lose a friend and colleague, but the business is faced with the need to hire and train a replacement, a loss of productivity, and potentially complicated legal issues.

One of these issues involves how to properly handle any wages that are due to a deceased employee.

There are several factors that determine whether or not the payment of that employee's wages are taxable, how the payments and taxes withheld should be reported, and to whom the wages should be paid.

These factors include the following:

- Whether the payment is for an uncashed paycheck or for unpaid accrued wages, vacation pay, taxable fringe benefits, or other types of accrued compensation.
- Whether the payments are made in the same year the employee died or in a following year.
- Whether or not there are state laws limiting the amount that can be paid, to whom the wages can be paid, and whether or not state income taxes should be withheld.

Handling a Deceased Employee's Paycheck

Uncashed Paychecks

If a paycheck has already been issued to an employee, but the employee dies before cashing it, a check has to be reissued for the same net amount of the original check, payable to the employee's beneficiary or personal representative.

The employer should also have the employee's personal representative sign a statement that the money being paid is for a deceased employee's uncashed paycheck. Since the final paycheck was already issued once, the necessary taxes have already been withheld, so the wages and taxes will be reported on the employee's Form W-2 at the end of the year.

One issue that must be addressed at this point is the definition of personal representative. Under federal law, an employee's personal representative is any person designated by an employee's will or determined by probate. If there is no will or if the employee's will or estate has not yet been probated, the check should be issued to the employee's estate.

Employers will want to check state law at this point, because it may designate that only certain individuals (such as a spouse, children, or parents) may be the employee's personal representative, and may limit how much may be paid directly to a personal representative.

Accrued Wages Paid the Same Year as the Employee's Death

Before a deceased employee's accrued wages can be paid, the employer should have the employee's personal representative or beneficiary complete a Form W-9 in order to obtain the person's Social Security number (SSN). Typically, if there is no personal representative, then the wages cannot be paid until the probate court has established the estate and the IRS has issued a tax identification number (TIN) for the employee's estate.

Wages paid in the year the employee died are subject to federal employment taxes (Social Security, Medicare, and FUTA). Therefore, the employer must withhold the Social Security and Medicare taxes from the employee's unpaid wages and deposit these taxes and the employer's share. [IRS Publication 15, pp. 23, 36.] At the end of the year the wages will be included on Form 940, subject to the FUTA tax. The employer will report the accrued wages and the federal employment taxes withheld in Boxes 3-6 on the employee's Form W-2. The gross amount of the unpaid wages should not be included in Box 1. [IRS Revenue Ruling 86-109.] The gross amount paid should be reported in Box 3 (other income) of Form 1099-MISC in the name and TIN of the

beneficiary, personal representative, or the employee's estate (see www.irs
.gov/pub/irs-pdf/i1099msc.pdf).

Wages Paid in a Year after the Employee's Death

The payment of accrued wages may not be paid until a later year because of
delays in probating the employee's estate. When this happens, IRS Revenue Ruling 86-109 states that "these payments are not considered wages for purposes
of the collection of income tax at source," and the payments are not subject to
federal employment taxes. These amounts will not be reported on a Form W-2.

Therefore, the employer will report the gross amount paid in Box 3 (other
income) of Form 1099-MISC in the name and TIN of the beneficiary, personal
representative, or the employee's estate.

CHAPTER TWELVE

Taxes Depositing and Filing

N ow that you have paid the employees, the rush to get the payroll out is over. But your job still continues. You have the following tasks.

Get all of your identification numbers! You will need these to deposit and file taxes.

- Federal employer identification number (EIN) via IRS Form SS4
- State revenue number for reporting state withholding, if required.
- State unemployment number (required).
- Local reporting number, if required.

Deposit the taxes that are withheld. Timing can vary from one day to the 15th of the following month.

- Federal
- State
- Local

Report the taxes that are withheld. These times vary widely.

- Federal (Form 941)
- State
- Local

At the end of the calendar quarter:

- Deposit federal unemployment taxes, if required.
- Calculate and deposit state unemployment taxes.

At the end of the year:

- Report federal unemployment taxes (Form 940), if required.
- Create and file W-2s and W-3 reporting wages and taxes to SSA.
- Create and file 1099s and 1096.

All of these are covered in Chapter 5. I list them here, so if you have come to Part Two to run a payroll, you don't forget that the job is not done.

PART THREE

Additional Essential Components

CHAPTER THIRTEEN

Record keeping

Every business must retain certain records on their current and past employees, but which ones and for how long?

On the federal level, there are two agencies that regulate record keeping. First is the IRS, which is responsible for enforcing the Internal Revenue Code. The second is the US Department of Labor (DOL). The Wage and Hour Division of the DOL is responsible for enforcement of the Federal Fair Labor Standards Act (FLSA), the Family and Medical Leave Act (FMLA), the Immigration Reform and Control Act (IRCA), and the laws governing wages paid by federal government contractors.

Both of these agencies have separate rules regarding the type of records that must be kept and the length of time you must keep the records. To further complicate your requirements, there are numerous state, local, and other regulatory agencies that may require additional record keeping. State agencies enforce state unemployment insurance tax acts, state wage and hour laws, child support and creditor garnishment laws, and unclaimed or abandoned wage requirements.

Keeping these records accurate and up to date is extremely important to the health of your business. Without the proper records, you will be unable to meet regulatory requirements should you be audited by any of various federal state and local agencies. Failing to meet these requirements can mean large penalties and the potential for large settlement awards should you be unable to provide the required information when requested.

INTERNAL REVENUE SERVICE

The following records must be *kept for four years* after the tax due date or the actual date paid:

- Name of employee.
- Address of employee.
- Occupation of employee.
- Social Security number of each employee.
- Total compensation and date paid including tips and noncash payments.
- Compensation subject to withholding for federal income, Social Security and Medicare tax.
- Pay period for each compensation period.
- Explanation of difference in total compensation and taxable compensation.
- Employee's Form W-4.
- Dates of employment (beginning and ending).
- Employee tip reports.
- Wage continuation made to an absent employee by employer or third party.
- Details of fringe benefits provided to employee.
- Copy of employee's request to use the cumulative method of wage withholding.
- Adjustments or settlement of taxes.
- Amounts and dates of tax deposits.
- Total compensation paid to employee during calendar year.
- Compensation subject to FUTA.
- State unemployment contributions made.
- All information shown on Form 940.
- Copies of returns filed (Forms 941, 943, W-3, Copy A of Form W-2 and returned Form W-2s).

DEPARTMENT OF LABOR

The following records must be *kept for three years* after date of last entry.

- Employee's name as it appears on Social Security card.
- Complete home address and date of birth if under age 19.
- Sex and occupation.
- The beginning of the employee's workweek.

- Regular rate of pay for overtime weeks.
- Hours worked each workday and workweek.
- Straight-time earnings including the straight-time portion of overtime earnings.
- Overtime premium earnings.
- Total wages paid for each pay period including additions and deductions.
- Date of payment and pay period covered.
- Records showing total sales volume and goods purchased.
- The following records must be kept for two years after the last date of entry.
- Employment and earnings records, employee hours of work, basis for determining wages and wages paid.
- Order, shipping, and billing records showing customers' orders and delivery records.
- Wage rate tables and piece rate schedules.
- Work time schedules that establish hours and days of employment.

In addition to the general requirements of both the IRS and the DOL mandated by several federal acts, there are others.

FAMILY AND MEDICAL LEAVE ACT (IF YOU HAVE 50 EMPLOYEES OR MORE)

- Basic payroll and employee data.
- Dates FMLA leave is taken.
- Hours worked by employee in the past 12 months.
- Hours of FMLA leave for exempt employee.
- Copies of employee notice to employer.
- Copies of general and specific notes given to employee.
- Copies of policy regarding taking of paid and unpaid leave by employee.
- Documents verifying premium payments of employee benefits.
- Records of FMLA leave disputes between employee and employer.

TITLE VII OF THE CIVIL RIGHTS ACT OF 1964 AND THE AMERICANS WITH DISABILITY ACT OF 1990

There are no general record requirements under the law, but to meet the requirements, all records relating to hiring, promotion, demotion, transfer, layoff or termination, rates of pay, and selection for training or apprenticeship should be kept for one year from date of action.

THE AGE DISCRIMINATION IN EMPLOYMENT ACT OF 1967

This Act requires that you keep the following records for *three years*.

- Name
- Address
- Date of birth
- Occupation
- Pay rate
- Compensation earned

You also keep the following for *one year* from the date of action.

- Job applications
- Résumé
- Response to advertised job openings
- Records related to the failure to hire an individual

You also must keep all records related to:

- Layoff or discharge of an employee.
- Job orders submitted to a placement agency.
- Employee, administrated by employee, physical exams used to make personnel decisions.
- Job advertisements.

THE IMMIGRATION REFORM AND CONTROL ACT

This requires that you must retain copies of the I-9 Form for *three years* after the date of hire.

PAYROLL AND DIRECT DEPOSIT RECORDS IN GENERAL

We recommend, all the prior notwithstanding, that you keep all payroll records for at least seven years. I mean *all records*, no matter how trivial, for all employees, current and past. If you want to keep them longer, that is not a bad idea, either. I have seen the IRS ask for 10 years of payroll records from a client of ours. We had them, to the surprise of the IRS. It made it easier for the client to win their case with the IRS.

EMPLOYEE HANDBOOK/POLICY MANUAL

You should keep a record of your employee handbook/policy manual as issued to your employees with all updates noted and retained by date issue. This will allow you to recreate the employee handbook/policy manual as of any particular day in the past.

You also need to keep copies of where your employees have acknowledged that they have received the employee handbook/policy manual, received any updates, and acknowledge they have read and understand them.

See the section "Employee Handbook/Policy Manual" in Chapter 17, on why you need one and what should be included in it.

MEDICAL INSURANCE

You will want to keep every enrollment for health insurance if you offer it. You will also want everyone who is eligible and does not take the health insurance to sign a form showing that they do not want coverage under a group health policy. If you can't prove they were offered insurance, if available, and they turned it down, you may find yourself liable for the insurance benefits for an employee or one of their family members, and not have the insurance company to pick up the tab. Companies have been successfully sued for insurance benefits, and lost, because they could not prove that an employee turned down the offer.

Years ago, there was a company in the Midwest, a grocery store chain later acquired by a major international food products company. It offered a very nice group health plan to its employees and their families for a reasonable employee contribution. One employee had not signed up for the plan and then his wife who was also not covered had a child with a major birth defect. The employee claimed he had never been offered the major medical coverage. The company could not prove that he had been offered it and turned down. The court ruled that the company was liable for the amount that the insurance would have paid. It ran well over a million dollars. So, if you offer medical insurance to all employees, make sure that you keep signed documents for those who signed up and those who refused it.

CHAPTER FOURTEEN

Workers' Compensation Insurance

Workers' compensation insurance is not strictly a payroll function. But if you have employees on payroll in any state except Texas, you may be required by law to carry it. So let's examine it because if you have payroll you will almost always have workers' compensation insurance.

 WHAT IS WORKERS' COMPENSATION INSURANCE?

The first workers' compensation law was enacted in the United States in 1911 by the state of Wisconsin. By 1948, every state had some form of "workmans' comp." Basically this is a government-mandated social insurance pact between employers and employees. Employers are forced to cover medical care and provide wage replacement for employees hurt on the job; in return, workers' compensation benefits become the only remedy available for workers. Even though courts have upheld this concept for almost one hundred years, occasionally in cases of bad faith courts have overridden this exclusive remedy.

Workers' compensation (referred to often as workers' comp) is a form of accident insurance paid by employers. No payroll deductions are taken out of employees' earnings for this insurance. If an employee is injured on the job or acquires a work-related illness, workers' comp will pay the employee's medical expenses. If the employee is unable to work it will also provide wage-loss compensation until the employee is able to return to work.

Benefits are usually paid by a private insurance company or state-run workers' comp fund. It also provides benefits to dependents if a person dies as a result of a job-related injury.

Not all employees are covered by state workers' comp insurance. Some federal employees are covered by other compensation laws administered by the US Department of Labor (DOL) or other special cases or occupations. Energy Employees Occupational Illness Compensation Program, the Federal Employees' Compensation Program, the Longshore and Harbor Workers' Compensation Program, and the Black Lung Benefits Program serve the specific employee groups. Some states and municipalities have an in-house program to cover workers' comp claims.

State Rules Cover What?

Every state sets its own exact rules. These rules cover a number of items, including:

- When an employer must get and keep coverage in place.
- A minimum number of employees, if more than one.
- What industries may not require coverage (for example, agricultural workers).
- What workers are covered (normally independent contractors are excluded).
- What illnesses are covered by workers' compensation.
- Compensation for injuries that are permanent.

What Injuries Are Covered?

Workers' compensation coverage is designed to cover accidents that happen on the job. It may include certain illnesses if the state defines them as work-related. For instance, in California, employees who suffer from work-related stress may be able to receive workers' compensation benefits under certain circumstances.

The work-related injury does not have to stem from a single instance. Repetitive stress injuries and conditions caused by long-term exposure to environmental hazards may be covered if the state specifies them.

Employees may not need to be at the work site to be covered. If the employee is involved in a work-related task at the employer's direction and receive an injury they may well be covered. Normally injuries while commuting are not covered.

Some states allow employees to be tested for substances such as alcohol or drugs which would have rendered the employee unfit to be working. If these substance are self-administered, the employer may be held not liable and the employee will be unable to collect benefits from a workers' comp policy. Workers' comp normally does not usually cover self-inflicted injuries or intentional acts. It may not also cover injuries deliberately caused by other employees or other parties.

Exclusive Remedy

Workers' compensation is often considered the "exclusive remedy" for job-related injuries because it generally gives employers immunity from lawsuits in exchange for coverage of medical costs, missed work, and other injury-related expenses. The employee is not required to prove fault in order to collect. However, immunity from lawsuits in exchange for workers' comp benefits is not absolute in all jurisdictions or situations. In rare situations the employee will be able to sue the employer for additional sums in excess of workers' comp benefits.

Employer Responsibilities

In addition to carrying and paying for workers' comp insurance, employers may be require to perform some or all of the following:

- Post notices of coverage.
- Provide emergency medical treatment.
- Provide continuing treatment if the employee does not choose a doctor.
- Report injuries to the appropriate state workers' comp office and their carrier.
- Comply with requests for information from the state workers' comp agency.
- Provide for employment when the employee is able to return to work.
- Not retaliate against an employee who files a workers' comp claim!

Employee Responsibilities

- Report any injury immediately.
- If you need medical attention seek it immediately.
- Cooperate with all parties; seek legal advice if you have questions.

MONOPOLISTIC STATES VERSUS NONMONOPOLISTIC WORKERS' COMP STATES

North Dakota, Ohio, Washington, and Wyoming do not allow private insurance companies to sell workers' comp policies in their states. These states are referred to as *monopolistic states* because employers must purchase workers compensation coverage from a government-operated insurance fund in that state. Unlike a competitive fund, a monopolistic state fund is the sole source of workers' compensation insurance in the state. It has no competitors because private insurance is not permitted.

Other states allow private companies to sell workers comp policies based on market forces. The state still sets requirements and coverage terms but not price. The employer is required to carry coverage by law. All states have assigned risk pool for companies where the company's calculated risk is too high for an insurance company to want to underwrite. This pool will use one of several mechanisms to provide coverage to those companies that cannot otherwise obtain the workers' comp coverage required by the state.

COST OF WORKERS' COMP COVERAGE

It is a little complicated to calculate workers' comp premium. The premium is based on several factors including:

- Class codes
- Number of employees
- Payroll
- Claims history

Class Code

The classification code (class code) is determined by each state or by National Council on Compensation Insurance (NCCI) and adopted by a state. Each code represents the type of work performed by the employees of the business. Each type of job has its own code. Every code has a rate attached. This rate is multiplied by the hours worked (see "Premium Calculation" further on). This code is designed to approximate the risk of a particular job. The more dangerous the job, the higher the attached rate (per hour), and therefore the higher the premium for hours worked in that job.

As you would expect there are times where codes do not match the actual job and something similar has to be used until the state sets up a new class code. This can cause problems, see the "Dirty Little Secret of Workers' Comp" further on.

Payroll

For workers' compensation purposes, payroll means money or payment other than money. Your premium calculations for the payroll number including the following:

- Wages or salaries including retroactive wages or salaries.
- Cash received by employees for commissions and draws against commissions.
- Bonuses.
- Extra pay for overtime work–not including the overtime premium.
- Pay for holidays, vacations, or periods of sickness.
- Payment to employees on any basis other than time worked, such as piecework, profit sharing, or incentive plans.
- Payment or allowance for hand tools or power tools used by hand provided by employees either directly or through a third party and used in their work or operations for the insured.
- The rental value of an apartment or a house provided for an employee.
- The value of lodging, other than an apartment or a house, received by employees.
- The value of meals received by employees.
- Davis-Bacon wages paid to employees or trusts.
- Excess expense reimbursements to employees.

Payroll does not include the following for workers' comp purposes.

- Tips and other gratuities received by employees.
- Payment by an employer to group insurance or group pensions plans for employees.
- The value of special reward for individual invention or discovery.
- Dismissal or severance payments except for time worked or for accrued vacation.
- Payments for active military duty.
- Employee discounts on goods purchased from the employee's employer.

- Expense reimbursements to employees on an accountable plan.
- Supper money for late work.
- Work uniform allowance.
- Third-party sick pay.
- Employer contributions to salary reduction, employee savings plans, retirement, or cafeteria plans
- Perks provided:
  - An automobile.
  - An airplane flight.
  - An incentive vacation (e.g., contest winner).
  - A discount on property or services.
  - Club memberships.
  - Tickets to entertainment events.

Claims History /Experience Modification (Mod)

Your experience mod is a comparison of your workers' comp claims with other companies of similar size operating similar businesses. It helps give you the ability to control your workers' comp costs by maintain a low claims rate to achieve a low experience mod. It is also why there is pressure by employers to not have employees report workers' comp claims, as it will raise their overall premium.

The actual process of calculating the experience mod is complex, but the purpose of the formula is pretty straightforward. Here's how it works: your company's actual losses are compared to its expected losses by industry type. Factors taken into consideration are: company size, unexpected large losses, and the difference between loss frequency and loss severity.

The experience mod for your company is calculated by the National Council on Compensation Insurance (NCCI) or in some states, by an independent agency. Experience rating is a required step that applies to all employers that meet a state's premium eligibility criteria for the plan.

The experience mod modifies your premium. If you have a mod greater than one because of your company's claim history your premium will be modified upward, increasing your cost. If your company has a lower-than-average claims history then your experience mod will be less than one and when applied to your premium it will lower the overall costs.

How to Maintain a Low Experience Mod

- Make sure your experience mod is accurate. Verify what is used to create the mod.

- The mod is more sensitive to many small claims rather than an occasional big one.
- Have a safety program that reduces accidents and therefore claims.
- Have a back-to-work program to reduce compensation payments.
- Educate first-level management about workers' comp, safety, and how to handle injuries. Where there are good relations between first level management and workers, history shows lower claims.
- Be careful whom you hire. Make sure the worker is right for the job. If they can't handle the job based on physical, physiological, training, experience, or any other reasons claims will be higher.

Premium Calculation

A premium calculation is a simple formula once you have the class code and modifier:

Class code rate × experience mod. × (payroll in dollars / 100) = premium

Premium is based on each $100.00 of wages paid. The class code determines the base premium rate for the wages

You have an employee with a class code of 8810 which is a Clerical Office Employee NOC (not otherwise classified). A rate for that clerk might be $0.35 per hundred dollars of earnings. So if you pay that clerk $25,000 per year your workers' comp premium would start at $87.50 per year. ($25,000.00 / 100 = 250. 250 × $0.35 = $87.50). If you have no modifier, then that is your premium for that clerk.

You have an employee who does commercial roofing with a code of 5551, which is Roofing – All Kinds (Commercial). A rate for that employee might be $5.40 per hundred dollars of earnings. So if you pay the employee $25,000.00 per year your workers' comp premium would start at $1350.00 per year. ($25,000.00 / 100 = 250. 250 × $5.40 = $1350.00). If you have no modifier, then that is your premium for that roofer. If you have a poor claims rate and an experience modifier of 1.25, the premium would rise to $1687.50 ($1350.00 × 1.25 = $1687.50).

Rates can vary from a few cents per hundred dollars of wages paid to over $12.00 per hundred dollars of wages paid before any experience modification.

Payment of Premium

Traditional Payment

Traditionally each company would estimate their workers' comp premium with their carriers and would be required to deposit as much as 20% of the annual expected premium at the start of the insurance contract that normally lasts for 12 months. The company would then be required to pay additional portions of the premium as the year went on. At the end of the year there would be an audit of the payroll and a calculation of the actual premium incurred. Additional payment or a refund would be paid depending on the audit outcome.

Pay as You Go

Because of the advent of computerized payroll it is now possible to calculate the workers' comp premium on a per payroll basis. Each employee is assigned their class code, or codes, in the case of multiple work functions. The premium is input into the payroll system for each appropriate class code. The payroll system or payroll provided can calculate the premium the carrier has earned to the penny. That amount can be transmitted to the carrier who automatically debits it from the insured's account.

There are substantial advantages to everyone in a pay-as-you-go system. The carrier does not have to calculate possible premiums for deposits, and they don't have to do an audit every year. They also don't have to issue refunds for overpayments or chase down clients for additional premium amounts.

For the employer there is no deposit, no audit, and they pay exactly what is due based on actual payroll and not a penny more.

 For workers' compensation resources, please go to www.ThePayroll Book.com/resources/Workers' Compensation.

Dirty Little Secret

 Workers' compensation insurance agents are paid commission based on the size of your company premium. The bigger the premium you pay, the bigger your agent's commission. Your agent may never cause your premium to go up unnecessarily, but has he done everything he can to reduce it and reduce his commission?

What is the "dirty little secret"? In 40 years of working with companies I have never gone into a company of any size and found that its employees are completely correctly classified for minimum premium. The classification process is many times as much of an art as it is a science. Different people can look at the same job and classify it differently sometimes with extremely different results affecting the premium. Many classification titles are very similar but with much different rates. There are many jobs that don't have a specific classification but have to be fit into something that makes sense. If the insurance company decides the classification, do you think it will be the best possible choice for the employer's lowest premium?

If an employer is not only knowledgeable but also aggressive about classifications, who is going to see to it that they are the lowest possible premium rates. The insurance company makes more money out of higher premium rate classifications. The risk to the insurance company does not rise if the employee is misclassified into a classification that commands a premium rate of, say, $10.13 per $100 of payroll as, say, a rate of $1.01 per $100 of payroll. The insurance company just makes 10 times as much revenue. If there is a claim, it will be paid at the same amount regardless of what the premium was.

The insurance agent that supposedly has the employer's interests at heart makes 10 times the commission if an employee is misrated as in the paragraph above. Is he going to take his time, energy, and effort to deliberately cut his commissions by suggesting rate changes over his company's objection?

As an employer you don't necessarily have an intimate knowledge of classification and ratings. You need to either get the knowledge or hire someone who has it. You may not be able to trust your agent to be objective about this. You are talking about taking money out of his pocket and out of the pocket of people that pay him. You don't pay him; the insurance company does. It pays him a commission on what he sells you, not necessarily on what you need. Your agent may be doing a bang-up job but wouldn't you like to be sure?

CHAPTER FIFTEEN

Payroll Security and Internal Controls

A n embezzlement of $50 million makes the news. What we don't see or hear about are all the small embezzlements and losses in small companies around the country on a daily basis.

Security is about managing both internal and external threats. In reality, the threats to the integrity of your payroll system are far more likely to be internal than external. We all see the articles about a million identities stolen. It makes great news. Let's go through payroll from beginning to end, and touch on some of the security problems in the following areas:

- Manuals and procedures
- Hiring
- Time collection
- Payroll calculation
- Identity theft
- Check and other fraud
- Tax filing and deposit errors and problems
- Internal controls

 ## MANUALS AND PROCEDURES

Probably the most important thing you can do in providing security is to write everything down. By having a procedure manual, everything you want to do

207

to insure the security of your system is in one place and can be followed to the letter. In addition, new people will have all the experience of the people that came before them. No institutional knowledge will get lost when someone quits or retires. Without this, everything is helter-skelter, and things that are important will be missed.

A good procedure manual is, however, not static. It changes and is updated on an ongoing basis. There are always going to be changes. Sometimes things come out wrong. You will figure out why and put a procedure in place so that it does not happen again. A procedure manual is a living document. But, it does not change willy-nilly. You must have a policy describing how your procedure manual is to be updated: when, how, what for, and by whom.

The point of the procedure manual is that anyone of requisite intelligence for the job could come in off the street and do the job correctly just by following the procedure manual. It might take them 20 times longer than it takes the person who does it now, but it would get done, correctly. You don't think that is possible? McDonald's has a manual for their restaurants that details everything from when the lights come on to the temperature of the grill to how long french fries are held, to how often the bathrooms are checked for cleanliness. There is a full and complete checklist for every day.

Your goal is to get your manual to that level. It is not something that many – if any – of you have. Some of you will never take the trouble to try and do it. But, it is important. It should be a goal for your company, regardless of its size.

The procedure manual is updated when there are incidents that show the system is not perfect. A payroll check is wrong. A report no longer shows what it should. An employee does not get paid or does not get paid correctly.

These problems and changes should all be documented in an incident report, and reviewed by management. The review is to see if the incident:

- Should create a revision to the procedure manual.
- Was an error that lies outside the procedure manual.

An error such as a keying error that was not caught by the error-catching routine is a personnel matter that involves retraining to the procedure manual rather than a manual change.

The manual will also change when:

- The local, state, or federal laws change.
- Tax rates change.
- Tax forms are revised.
- Other events occur.

Changes in the law may well cause updates and adjustments to the procedure manual as well. If the state mandates required time, off policies this may well lead to changes.

WHO ARE YOU HIRING?

Background Checks

There are security risks to your company in the hiring process. Are you actually hiring the person, with the actual set of skills, that you think you are hiring? Résumé inflation is rampant.

There have been documented instances where 20% of the resumes received would not stand up to a cursory background check. Resumes have been seen with degrees that were not obtained, criminal convictions not listed, jobs that were never held, and duties described that were never performed by the résumé writer.

 In 2012, the CEO of Yahoo, Scott Thompson, was terminated after four months on the job when it was discovered that he did not have the computer science degree he claimed on his résumé. How could the company not have know that? If you hire somebody with supposed qualifications that they don't have, and their actions on the job create a liability situation, you have a problem. If those qualifications were crucial to an action that created the liability and you can't prove the employee had the qualifications, you may not be able to prevail in an action against the company. There is substantial legal liability if there is a problem and a person's qualifications prove to be bogus.

 An example I am aware of was a truck driver. He was hired because he showed a commercial driver's license and said he had a clean record. He, in fact, had a suspended license and a conviction for driving a commercial vehicle under the influence of drugs. When he had another accident with a resulting injury while under the influence of drugs the company ended up in bankruptcy.

Is it legal for the person you are hiring to actually work in this country? We are all aware of the problem of undocumented workers in this country. It is illegal to hire them. The penalties for doing so are stiffer than in the past. More than one person has gone to jail for making a practice of hiring undocumented workers. You need to make sure that every new employee fills out a Form I-9 and provides documentation that appears to be proper. I recommend that copies of the documents be kept in the employee's file. If you have someone doing the hiring, make sure that someone else is checking the paperwork, a person who is not under the influence or control of the hiring person. This is all part of internal control, which we will discuss further on.

If you are hiring hourly laborers you may not think it is important. Until you find that you have hired an employee who has several lawsuits against previous employers for workers' compensation claims, sexual harassment claims, discrimination, or other such items.

Do you want to hire a serial litigant?

Hiring for in-the-office work can be worse. Does the job you are hiring for entail handling money?

One of our clients hired a very nice young lady from an employment agency into the accounts payable department. The staffing agency had supposedly run a background check on her. When my client ran their own background check they found a felony conviction for embezzlement. Needless to say, they terminated the employee and the staffing company.

We ourselves had a nice young student in on a part-time basis to do some office clerical work. We wanted to hire her into our payroll processing center until our background check with the local authorities found that her boyfriend was known for passing bad checks.

Ghost Employees

Let's also discuss *ghost employees*. These are employees whom you are paying who don't exist. You need to have adequate controls to make sure that everybody who is on the payroll is really working for you. It is not uncommon for some supervisors with too much authority to "hire" a person and report "hours" for that person only to be taking the check and cashing it themselves for the employee that does not exist, i.e., a ghost employee.

Equipment Protection

Equipment safety includes actually securing the physical equipment from being able to be tampered with by insiders or outsiders. If you use a computerized system, it includes keeping it safe from spy software. A simple key logger can give away not only your payroll password but every password and informational module you have on that computer. If your time clock is not locked and protected, it can be accessed and compromised.

Remember the movie *Ferris Bueller's Day Off*, where Ferris went into the school's computer and changed records? In reality, that is more likely to be attempted these days than when the movie was made.

How do passwords get disclosed? I have seen them written and taped to the bottom of a keyboard or on a pullout shelf at a desk; I have even seen them on sticky notes on the monitor. That is all it takes to compromise your whole system.

Passwords must be controlled and changed on a regular basis. I know it is a pain to track and maintain a number of passwords, but you must have your staff change them on a regular basis. Most systems these days will allow you to set the complexity and change frequency. You need to set these and enforce them.

If you are really concerned and don't mind the price, you can upgrade to a system from several vendors where you have a token that generates a random number based on time and an algorithm; this code is verified with a server that maintains the same algorithm and time and compares the two. This is a two-part authentication and is very effective. All my banks use it for my accounts that have online access. Even the IRS is moving to two-part authorizations for tax professionals.

Calculating Payroll

Now you have accurate time collection and secure systems. It is time to do payroll. The systems range from doing it by hand, a piece of paper, a calculator, and a Circular E open next to you, is all that you actually need. I don't recommend it. I am not going to talk about doing payroll by hand. It is not worth the effort, problems, mistakes, and the time it takes. This is not the 1960s, don't do it.

You can buy inexpensive PC-based systems. They normally work okay. It depends on how complex your payroll is, how large it is, your payroll tax situation, your payroll staff, and other associated factors.

Let's talk about the risks of in-house automated systems. These can range from a simple off-the-shelf PC shrink -wrapped package to the very complex custom system for your company. Our assumption is that the system does the arithmetic calculations correctly: 40 hours at $10.00 an hour is $400.00 gross pay.

However, is that system up to speed on all the changes that are imposed at the various levels of government? Does it have updating service to keep you up to speed on the changes during the year? Does it have adequate security levels to maintain your internal control policies? Can it handle your retirement program? Can it handle multiple levels of matching in the 401(k) based on seniority? Can it handle overtime and Chinese overtime? Will it keep you fully compliant with FLSA, the IRS, and your state agencies? Make sure your system does what you need it to do; don't try to stretch a $100 system to handle a payroll that needs a $1,000 system.

In the end, no system, regardless of how expensive, can take the place of a trained and experienced payroll tax expert when it comes to compliance problems. No software can answer the letter from the IRS. (See Chapter 6, "Tax Penalties.") Over half of the employment tax penalties the IRS issues are abated by people who know what they are doing and who take on the IRS directly. That basically means that the IRS issues billions – yes, billions – of dollars of penalties every year that they shouldn't . . . which boggles the mind.

As with software, the same is true with hardware choice. Make sure you have adequate equipment for your needs. If you have expensive software, you may well need expensive hardware to make it run the way it was designed to run. Don't skimp.

Calculation is the simple part. You collected 40 hours. How do you guarantee that 40 hours is entered in the system and not 44? How do you make sure the employee is being paid $10.00 per hour and not $11.00 per hour? This is where electronic time clocks can be a real help. Once the supervisor has signed off on the hours for his department, they are transferred directly to the payroll system. No hand-keying means fewer mistakes.

 Obviously, the person inputting and verifying hours should not be the same person as the one that puts in rates of pay and rate changes. The segregation of these duties is part of the internal controls that keeps one individual from bypassing controls to game the system.

The employee puts in their hours, the supervisor checks and approves them, HR puts in any approved rate changes, and accounting runs the payroll, calculating and creating the checks and reports. Then, if necessary, HR hands out the checks. No one person has access to all of the system. No person should have access to the system in excess of what is needed to do their job.

Again, anytime there is a problem, an incident report needs to be created and sent up the chain of command. Is the incident a simple training problem? Is it a software or hardware problem? Does the procedure manual need to be changed to address a flaw that has previously gone undetected? That needs to be analyzed and management needs to implement the appropriate fix.

Review

 Periodically, management needs to look at the whole system and follow some of the transactions from beginning to end. Or, have the payroll function examined closely as a part of the financial audit every few years. A number of years ago I was brought in to a small single-location bank with the idea of providing payroll services for the bank. As the consultant who had brought me in and I got deeply into the payroll process, we found that the policy in the payroll department was to pay overtime for more than eight hours of work in a day, regardless of how many hours were worked in a week. When I explained that this was not the way to calculate overtime in the state of Texas or under FLSA, I was given the boot by the payroll supervisor. She, her staff, and their friends liked the way overtime was calculated. The hourly employees of the bank were the beneficiaries of overtime pay on one or more long days every week, even though their total workweek might not exceed 40 hours. The cost to the bank was in excess of a half-million dollars a year. No one in management was aware of the policy, which had existed in the payroll department for an unknown number of years, costing the bank unknown millions of dollars of wasted payroll.

Internet Transfers and Internet Security

Do you transfer any data over the Internet? If so, you need to look carefully at your firewalls and encryption. The firewall needs to keep people out of your system. Not only are crooks after your money these days, they are also after your employees' information. Identity theft is still on the rise.

Your payroll computer has all the information an identity thief needs to know about your employee: name, address, SSN, probably age, and possibly bank account information. In your HR files are mentions of next of kin, maybe insurance policies, and who knows what else. As important as it is to keep paper information under lock and key with access restricted to only those with "need to know" to accomplish their job, it is as important to keep all computer records secure as well.

Your IT person or consultant should be able to assist you in this matter. There are firewalls, secured servers, and other devices to restrict access. A strong password is one very important part of the computer/Internet security problem. With the growth of cloud-based computing and storage, you are taking on additional risks of your data being hacked while in someone else's control. You may well want to keep payroll data on a spare computer that has limited or even zero interface with the rest of the company network. You need to control your backup from multiple viewpoints.

One of our clients was backing up with a local ISP who one day simply went out of business. The door was closed, the owner was gone, and the office was empty. My client never did find out what happened to his backup files.

You need to have a series of backups. You might want to plan for one backup every day for a week, then every week for a quarter, and then every quarter for at least five years to be able to recreate government filings, if necessary.

Years ago, we kept boxes of green bar paper reports and filled filing rooms with them. That is not necessary with current technology, but now if you don't keep adequate backup files, then you have nothing to access if there is a problem.

You need to be able to quickly reload a file deleted by accident. You need to be able to recreate the whole system if a disaster happens to your facility. This requires offsite storage. This again makes you vulnerable to loss. You will always have to take some risk in offsite storage, but it can be minimized by good planning, good equipment, and dependable vendors.

Let's talk a moment about upgrading software. If you are just upgrading the version of your existing software, it should not be a big deal. But by making a full copy of your system before you upgrade, if there is a problem, you restore and go on. If you don't make a full backup, you are at the mercy of your software vendor to make things right. If they had fully tested the upgrade there would not have been a problem. So, if there is a problem they probably don't know what went wrong or necessarily how to fix it, because you need to run payroll right now. If you are installing an entirely new standalone system, you need to take the time and trouble to complete due diligence on the new software. Perhaps you can see it in operation in another location and ask questions.

Then, you need to run in parallel after installation of the new software. I know it may be a major pain in time and effort. You have just managed to learn a new system and you still have to use the old one and double up all of your processes. That is the only way to make sure that, if there is a problem, you can still pay everyone. One processing may be enough to make you feel comfortable or it may not; you will need to run in parallel until you are comfortable.

If you decide to outsource from in-house to a service bureau, still be prepared to run again in-house if you have to. If you go with a competent, experienced vendor it should not be a problem, but sometimes things can happen. If you are switching from one vendor to another, don't burn your bridges behind you; if the new vendor can't accomplish the task the old vendor will probably welcome you back with open arms.

Payments/Fraud/Errors

Now the payroll is processed and you're ready for the output. Many companies still write checks. The check stock has to be protected and accounted for. If you use prenumbered checks, then you need to account for each check, whether it is used or destroyed. If the payroll system numbers the checks, then you have to be even more careful with the blank stock because in this day and age it is simple to create fraudulent checks. Plain stock is available on the Internet to anyone that wants it.

You should be using a high-quality check stock with lots of built-in protection features. It should not be able to be copied on a copy machine. It should have toner lock so it can't be erased and a different dollar amount typed on. There are a number of other safety features your check stock provider and your banker should be able to help you with. Regardless of what you do, people will try to forge your payroll checks. It is not a matter of *if*, it is a matter of *when*. Anybody with a PC and a laser printer can create forged checks. They can copy a signature and imprint it on a fraudulent check. No matter how safe your checks are, the information can be put on other check stock and thieves can try to pass them. Check fraud is one of the largest white-collar crime industries in the country today.

Positive Pay

So how do you stop check fraud? The first way is to have positive pay. This is where you give your bank the information on the checks you issue. We send a file every day to each of our banks detailing the checks that were issued that day for our clients. When a check is either presented to be cashed, or is deposited and presented to one of our banks, the bank runs the information against the positive pay file. They can check the date, the amount, and the payee and if it has ever cleared before. If it does not match the file as a good item the bank notifies us and we have the ability to release the check anyway—if we missed sending the file or missed a manual check, etc. If we don't respond to the bank the default action for the bank is to return the item if it is not on the positive pay file or has been presented before.

 Another type of check fraud that has cropped up is double-cashing a check. This happened to us recently. One of our client's employees went to a check-cashing place and they took an image of the check and gave her back the check and a debit card that would be good in three days. The three days would allow the bank to be sure the check was good before activating the debit card in their system for use. After getting the card the employee decided she could not wait three days and deposited the check in her Wells Fargo account. The Wells Fargo deposit reached our bank first and cleared through positive pay. When the copy from the check-cashing company arrived, our bank returned it since it had already cleared. The check-cashing company called our client and threatened them, saying that the check-cashing company was a "holder in due course" and wanted to be paid on the check. They were, in fact and law, a "holder in due course," and were due their money. The employee had committed fraud but that did not let my client off the hook. My client talked to the employee and she made everything good with the check-cashing company. If she hadn't, my client would have been responsible for the check amount and would have had to take measures, civil or criminal, to recover their money.

We have all seen the commercials where you can deposit your check via a picture with your smartphone. What if you do that and then cash the physical check at the issuing bank? By the time the image (or images) arrive at the issuing bank and are sent back, the now ex-employee has removed the money from his account where he deposited it by smart phone. The bank that cashed the image for the employee is going to hold you responsible as they are a "holder in due course." This all is now possible because of Check 21 and the like allowing the movement of checks as images instead of paper. This was accelerated after 9/11, when all airplanes were grounded and physical checks could not move overnight. We suspect this problem is going to get worse, not better.

For Direct Deposit

The second, and the best way, to prevent check fraud is to not have checks. We encourage direct deposit wherever possible and for those who are unbanked we recommend debit cards.

How many of you use direct deposit? Obviously direct deposit goes from your bank through the local automated clearinghouse system to your employee's bank. It is very secure and has lots of advantages. There is no physical image of a check to be copied or duplicated.

Your bank has to guarantee good funds on outbound direct deposit, so you will not have any float on the direct deposits. They will all be charged to your account no later, and maybe earlier than payday.

 We had one case in a divorce in which the ex-wife kept the bank account and took her husband's name off it. He did not notify the company that he had opened a different account and the receiving bank deposited his paycheck to the account number that belonged to his ex-wife. In this case, she was amenable to giving him the money, but it could have been ugly.

For Debit Cards

Debit cards work just like direct deposit except the employee's bank account is effectively on the card. A well-designed program does not have to cost the employee or the employer any money as long as they all understand the limits.

I know there has been some bad publicity on payroll debit cards recently, but that has to do with either poorly designed or poorly understood systems, or because of employers who want to make additional money off the card system.

You should know that if you make a mistake on an employee's direct deposit and overpay them, you have the right to take the excess amount back out of their account. Your employees often don't know that by granting you the power to deposit into their account they are also granting you the power to take money out of their account.

The employee, of course, can notify the bank that the draft by their employer was not authorized and that the bank must put the money back in the employee's bank account. This requires that the employee be aware of NACHA (National Automated Clearing House Association) rules.

Another fraud we have seen is that an employee will say they did not get their direct deposit for one reason or another, such as closing the bank account. The company feels the need to get the employee paid and in some states the state regulators may be heavily on the employee's side. The problem is that it takes several days for a direct deposit to a closed account to work its way back, if it ever does. Many banks will take a direct deposit to a closed account and reopen the account and keep the deposit on their books. If you have a Friday payroll it may well be the next Thursday before your bank knows that a direct deposit has been returned and deposited back to your account. Then the bank has to tell you or you have to check the account every day. If you issue a check on Monday or Tuesday based on what the employee says, you may be in for a surprise if the direct deposit is not returned to you. We suggest to our clients that they don't issue a check for a failed direct deposit until the direct deposit is back in their bank account.

Washed Checks!

Another fraud is check washing. The employer issues a new check and at some time in the future the first check gets cashed as well. Don't reissue the same check – issue a new one instead. Positive pay, as previously discussed, will solve that particular fraud. But you need to make sure that you update the positive pay file with the information that the first check is no longer valid. It is always best to ask for the remains of the check for the file; of course if it is simply lost, you can't get the remains.

Employee Self-Service

Newer payroll systems designed to run on a network many times have what is called employee self-service. This complements a number of things that happen in the payroll and HR area. It is accessed by the employee using a secured server and a password. The server in fact may not be a company server but either way you must be very conscious of security. All of an employee's check stubs may well be on the self-service server. This allows your payroll to be paperless. This is good for saving time, money, and effort. It also helps promote a "green" environment with all that goes with that. By having the employee check pay stubs online you don't have to issue vouchers that use paper and contain information that can be used for identity theft. The employee always has access and need not trouble HR if they need copies of pay stubs for a mortgage application or another reason. Employee self-service may also be a platform for rolling out benefit enrollments. The employees may be able to update a Form W-4 and submit it to HR to approve before going into the payroll system. It may well be a place to keep and update emergency contact information and much more. But security, again, is a prime concern because of the dangers of identity theft.

Tax Deposits and Filings

Okay, you have now processed and paid payroll successfully! It is time for the tax man. Are you still making your deposits via the phone instead of the computer? Do you have a foolproof system to make sure that all your deposits are made in a timely manner? We used to make deposits at the bank with coupons. Oh, how times have changed! Your Circular E will keep you up to speed on most changes in filings, but not all. The last few years the IRS have changed, on the fly, some forms such as the Form 941X have to be manually adjusted for certain years. The IRS never got around to making a correct form for 2011 and 2012 employee FICA corrections at 4.2% instead of 6.2%.

Are your tax deposits correct? Did the system kick out the correct amounts? Does the system tell you when they have to be made? The penalties from the IRS for incorrect and/or late deposits are ridiculously high.

 INTERNAL CONTROLS

Internal control is critical to the security of your payroll system. I am going to list a few items here to think about, but talk to your controller or outside CPA – they are trained in internal control and can help you design a system. Even if you don't employ all the people you need for complete segregation of duties, there are ways to increase controls. Embezzlement is a growing crime and more common in small businesses than most people would guess.

Segregation of Duties

Segregation prevents one person from doing something both incorrectly (by accident or on purpose) and without oversight. No one should be able to take an action without someone else reviewing that action. In a small business, that may end up being the owner, but it is still necessary.

The person verifying the hours for people should not be the one handing out paychecks. Paychecks should be delivered in person, if possible. If not possible, then it should be done occasionally on an unannounced basis. Hiring personnel should not be entering rates into the payroll system. No employee should be processing their own payroll.

Record Storage

Records should be available only to the person who needs to see them and/or enter the data into the payroll system. The rest of the time, records need to be in secured storage. All undistributed paychecks need to be under lock and key. Management needs to be notified of all undistributed checks or vouchers.

Best Practices

- Authorized signatures for checks, reports, input, changes, and so on need to be reviewed and updated on a regular basis.
- The permission and ability to change timekeeping records needs to be reviewed on a regular basis and changed as needed.
- Passwords need to change on a regular basis, preferably as often as monthly.
- Access needs to be reviewed on a regular basis to make sure that everybody with access to the payroll systems only has access to the level of their need and responsibility.
- Review attendance, pay, overtime and other payments regularly and compare with your company policy manual to make sure all policies are being followed.
- Review monthly payroll cost reports, compare actual to budgeted, and investigate variances in detail.
- All incident/discrepancy reports need to be reviewed and signed off on by management.
- Audit procedures and internal controls, on a regular basis to make sure everything is being done.

DISASTER RECOVERY

A Checklist for Disaster Recovery

A disaster can happen almost anytime, anywhere, and in many ways. A disaster may be natural, such as tornados, floods, hurricanes, dams breaking, thunderstorms, torrential rain; or can be an unnatural disaster, such as arson, electrical outage, water pipes breaking, terrorism, or even mistakes made by employees or management.

Here is a checklist with some steps that may be useful in planning for what to do in a disaster. The most important thing in disaster recovery is to have thought about it and hopefully tested a plan before disaster strikes.

Payroll Is a Critical Function

Your employee wants to be paid whether there is a disaster or not. Many of them are living paycheck to paycheck already, before any disaster occurs. You need to be able to run your payroll regardless of the disaster from where you are or from someplace else. You need to run payroll as close to on time as possible.

Update Your Plan

Regularly meet with all appropriate parties and review your disaster recovery plan. Update it as circumstances and technology change. Test your plan from time to time and make changes as appropriate for identified problems.

Procedures

Who is going to do what, and if they are not available, then who is next? What will be done first, second, third, and so on? Have a plan to achieve what you need and in a disaster work the plan.

Know What You Will Need

What systems and backups will you need? What hardware is needed? If what you have is gone, how and where is hardware and software you can use? Who is going to do it, and if they are not available, who will you contact?

Backup Locations

Where is your data backed up? There are three electrical grids in the United States – is your backup on at least two of them? If one goes down, and your backup is present, you could be dead in the water. If the East Coast is hit by another Hurricane Sandy, will your backup be affected? Do you test your backup regularly?

Hardcopy Documents

In this day and age every hardcopy document should be available in an electronic format. You should not be held hostage to paper. If you have not put a system in place to copy everything to electronic format and back it up, you need to start on that project now.

Conclusion

I know this sounds like a lot and some of it may be overkill for small businesses, but you need to think about all of these points and what you or the person who replaces you in an emergency will do. Have it in writing and available on-site and in another known site for the people who need to know. Disaster planning is part of the job, as distasteful as it may be. You will be very happy to have a disaster recovery plan in place if something occurs that would otherwise put you out of business.

 FORM 944

Hopefully you won't get saddled with a Form 944 requirement when you start in business. It is for very, very small businesses with probably one very part-time person. This form is designed so the smallest employers (those whose annual liability for Social Security, Medicare, and withheld federal income taxes is $1,000.00 or less) will file and report those taxes only once a year instead of every quarter. However, your deposit requirements are still those of a Form 941 filer.

Once you exceed $2,500.00 of federal employment tax liability (FIT and Social Security and Medicare) taxes, you will be a monthly depositor. If you're required to file Form 944 and your employment tax liability for the year is less than $2,500, you may pay the taxes for the year with your timely filed return instead of making deposits. If you're required to file Form 944 and your employment tax liability for the fourth quarter is less than $2,500, you may pay your fourth quarter liability with your timely filed return, as long as you've made deposits for the first, second, and third quarters according to the applicable deposit rules. Employers below the $2,500 threshold who aren't required to make deposits and instead remit employment taxes with their Forms 941 or Form 944 may choose to deposit the taxes or pay the amount shown as due on the Form 941 or Form 944, as provided by the form instructions.

CHAPTER SIXTEEN

US Citizens Abroad, Resident and Nonresident Aliens, and Illegal Aliens

Wages paid to US citizens and to resident aliens employed outside the United States are generally subject to Social Security and Medicare tax if the employer is an American employer.

The term *American employer* means a person who is:

- An individual who is a citizen or resident of the United States.
- A partnership, if two thirds or more of the partners are citizens or residents of the United States.
- A trust, if all of the trustees are citizens or residents of the United States.
- A corporation organized under the laws of the United States or of any state or the District of Columbia.

In some situations, a foreign country will impose its own Social Security tax on the wages of a US citizen or resident alien employed in that foreign country by an American employer. This could create a situation in which an employee's wages are subject to Social Security taxes imposed by two different countries. The United States has entered into agreements with some countries in order to avoid this double taxation.

For a list of other exempt services, refer to Publication 15, Circular E, and Employer's Tax Guide (www.irs.gov/forms-pubs/about-publication-15).

NONRESIDENT ALIEN SERVICES PERFORMED OUTSIDE THE UNITED STATES

Compensation paid to a nonresident alien for services performed outside the United States is not considered wages and is not subject to graduated withholding or 30% withholding.

PAYING NONRESIDENT ALIENS INSIDE THE UNITED STATES

Any employer who hires aliens (non-US citizens or residents) to perform services within the United States must follow these general procedures with respect to the reporting and withholding of federal income taxes:

- Identify all aliens (non-US citizens) on the company's payroll.
- Divide the aliens into two groups: "resident aliens" and "nonresident aliens" as defined by Internal Revenue Code section 7701(b), which defines residency status for aliens. Refer to Determining Alien Status (www.irs .gov/individuals/international-taxpayers/determining-alien-tax-status) for more information on the residency status of aliens.
- For income tax withholding purposes, treat resident aliens the same as US citizens.
- For income tax withholding purposes, treat nonresident aliens according to the following special withholding rules that apply to nonresident aliens, as described in Chapter 9 of Publication 15 (Circular E) (www .irs.gov/forms-pubs/about-publication-15) and Publication 515, Withholding Taxes on Nonresident Aliens (www.irs.gov/forms-pubs/about-publication-515).
  - A nonresident alien should follow the special instructions in Notice 1392, Supplemental Form W-4 Instructions for Nonresident Aliens (www.irs.gov/forms-pubs/about-notice-1392) to complete Form W-4.

A nonresident alien needs to consult Notice 1392, Supplemental Form W-4 Instructions for Nonresident Aliens before completing a new Form W-4.

- Some nonresident aliens are eligible for exemptions from federal income tax withholding on wages because of tax treaties (www.irs.gov/individuals /international-taxpayers/claiming-tax-treaty-benefits). To claim the exemption they must file Form 8233, Exemption From Withholding on Compensation for Independent (and Certain Dependent) Personal Services of a Nonresident Alien Individual (www.irs.gov/forms-pubs/form-8233-exemption-from-withholding-on-compensation-for-independent-and-certain-dependent-personal-services-of-a-nonresident-alien-individual) with the employer.
- Nonresident aliens who fail to file, or file an invalid Form W-4, as required by IRS regulations shall have federal income taxes withheld at the rates pertaining to single status with no adjustments.
- Employers must report wages exempt under a tax treaty paid to a nonresident alien on Form 1042, Annual Withholding Tax Return for US Source Income of Foreign Persons, and Form 1042-S, Foreign Person's US Source Income Subject to Withholding. Any additional wages paid to a nonresident alien over and above the exempt amount are reported on Form W-2 in the normal manner. Even in situations in which all of a nonresident alien's wages are exempt from federal income tax under an income tax treaty, and in which all his federal wages would be reported on Form 1042-S, the filing of a Form W-2 for such an alien is usually also required in order to report state and local wage amounts and state and local income taxes withheld on such alien's wages.
- Some income tax treaties allow alien students and scholars who have become resident aliens of the United States to exempt part or all of their US source wages from US taxation. Treaty-exempt wages paid to a resident alien in these situations should be reported on Form W-2, and not on Form 1042-S. In these situations, block 2 (Federal Income Tax Withheld) of Form W-2 may show zero or a reduced amount of federal income tax withheld because of the tax treaty exemption. Refer to Publication 519, US Tax Guide for Aliens, for instructions on how a resident alien claiming a tax treaty benefit should file his/her US federal individual income tax return.

EXCEPTIONS TO MANDATORY WITHHOLDING OF FIT ON NONRESIDENT ALIENS

Wages or nonemployee compensation are exempt from withholding of federal income tax (FIT) if all three of the following conditions are met (per IRC 861(a)(3) and 864(b)(1)):

- The nonresident alien performing services is present in the United States for a total not exceeding 90 days in a taxable year.
- The compensation for such services does not exceed $3,000.00.
- The nonresident alien performs the services as an employee of, or under contract with, a nonresident alien individual, a foreign corporation, or a foreign partnership not engaged in a trade or business in the United States or the foreign office of a US citizen or resident alien individual, a US corporation, or a US partnership (including from within a US possession).

Wages or nonemployee compensation are exempt from withholding of federal income tax if both of the following two conditions are met (per IRC 872(b)(3)):

1. The nonresident alien is present in the United States in F, J, M, or Q nonimmigrant status.
2. The compensation for services is paid by a nonresident alien individual, a foreign corporation, or a foreign partnership or the foreign office of a US citizen or resident alien individual, a US corporation, or a US partnership (including from within a US possession).

PAYING ILLEGAL ALIENS

The following provides a summary of an employer's responsibilities for withholding and reporting of employment taxes on wages paid to illegal aliens. For purposes of this book, an illegal alien is an individual, resident in the United States, who is not a citizen or a lawful permanent resident and who has not been given authorization to work by the US Citizenship and Immigration Services.

Employment Eligibility Verification

The Immigration Reform and Control Act made all US employers responsible to verify the employment eligibility and identity of all employees hired to work in the United States after November 6, 1986. To implement the law, employers are required to complete Employment Eligibility Verification forms (Form I-9) for all employees, including United States citizens. Anyone employing an illegal alien without verifying his or her work authorization status is guilty of a misdemeanor.

Employment Taxes

In general, if employers pay wages to illegal aliens, they must withhold income tax, Social Security, and Medicare taxes in the same manner as they would for their employees who are US citizens or lawful permanent residents. Wages paid are subject to graduated income tax withholding based on information reported to the employer on Form W-4, Employee's Withholding Allowance Certificate. Employers are also required to withhold Social Security and Medicare taxes from their employees' wages and pay a matching amount of these taxes. Wages paid to illegal aliens are subject to Social Security and Medicare taxes even though the illegal aliens are not eligible for Social Security benefits. The Federal Unemployment Tax Act (FUTA) provides for payments of unemployment compensation to workers who have lost their jobs. Employers are required to pay FUTA tax; it is not deducted from the employee's wages.

Each year employers are required to file a Form W-2, Wage and Tax Statement, for each employee from whom income, Social Security or Medicare taxes are withheld. Forms W-2 are filed with the Social Security Administration (SSA) and a copy is required to be furnished to each employee. Employers are required to report their employees' Social Security numbers on Forms W-2 to ensure that earnings are properly posted to the employees' Social Security accounts. When SSA receives Forms W-2, a match is performed against the name and Social Security number on the forms and SSA's records. If the information does not match, the earnings are held in a suspense file waiting for reconciliation.

IRS Individual Taxpayer Identification Numbers (ITINs)

An ITIN is a tax processing number for certain nonresident and resident aliens and their spouses and dependents. The ITIN is only available for individuals who cannot receive a Social Security number (SSN) and is utilized for tax purposes *only*. The Internal Revenue Service, not the Social Security Administration, assigns a tax identification number. It is issued to certain nonresident and resident aliens, their spouse, and dependents. Taxpayers need to file Form W-7,

Application for IRS Individual Taxpayer Identification Number, with the IRS to obtain an ITIN. For detailed information, see www.irs.gov/pub/irs-fill/fw7.pdf.

The ITIN is only available to individuals who cannot get a Social Security number (SSN). It is a nine-digit number, beginning with the number 9 and formatted like an SSN (XXX-XX-XXX) with the fourth and fifth digits ranging from 70 to 80. ITINs are used exclusively for tax purposes in order to identify and process the individual tax returns.

.The issuance of an ITIN does not:

- Entitle a recipient to Social Security benefits or the Earned Income Tax Credit (EITC).
- Create an inference regarding the individual's immigration status.
- Give the individual the right to work in the United States.

Caution: *An individual with an ITIN who later becomes eligible to work in the United States must obtain an SSN. The ITIN is not valid for employment purposes.*

For more information on ITINs, visit the IRS website's information on Individual Taxpayer Identification Numbers at www.irs.gov/individuals/article/0,, id=9628700.html or refer to IRS Publication 1915, IRS Individual Taxpayer Identification Numbers, which is available online at www.irs.gov, or call 800-829-3676.

Illegal Use of Social Security numbers (SSNs)

Since ITINs are for tax purposes only and are by no means a legal identification number for employment, individuals are utilizing erroneous or stolen SSNs when applying for employment.

Correct names and Social Security numbers (SSN) on W-2 wage documents are keys to successful processing of annual wage report submissions.

Verification of Social Security numbers

The Social Security Administration (SSA) offers employers and authorized reporting agents two methods for verifying employee SSNs. Both methods match employee names and SSNs.

Telephone Verification

To verify up to five names and numbers, call 800-772-6270. To verify up to 50 names and numbers, contact your local Social Security office.

Large Volume Verification

The Employee Verification Service (EVS) may be used to verify more than 50 employee names and SSNs. Preregistration is required for EVS or for requests made on magnetic media.

For more information, call the EVS information line at 410-965-7140 or visit SSA's website for employers at www.ssa.gov/employer/SSNV.htm.

CHAPTER SEVENTEEN

Other Issues

PROFESSIONAL EMPLOYER ORGANIZATION (PEO)

Advantages and Disadvantages

PEO stands for professional employer organization. The trade organization for PEOs is the National Association of Professional Employer Organizations (NAPEO), which was known as the National Staff Leasing Association up to 1994, after 10 years in business.

According to NAPEO, a PEO allows businesses to outsource a number of employee-associated functions, including human resource management, employee benefit management, employee payroll, and workers' compensation insurance in a cost-effective manner, thus allowing a business not to have to spend time on those functions and freeing it to concentrate on other areas. The NAPEO goes on to say they relieve their clients of the burden of administering critical employee-related functions, which reduces liabilities, increases competitiveness, and improves the bottom line of their clients.

What PEOs really do is provide a way for employers to buy insurance products, payroll processing, and possibly some basic HR services in a single package with a high administrative cost added on top. PEOs will say that they "assume certain employer rights, responsibilities, and risk." Many of the states they operate in disagree. Most states have rules that PEOs are co-employers, or joint employers, and that the actual employer retains all of the risk.

PEOs began in the 1960s as a way to escape federal ERISA requirements. If you had no employees, you were exempt from ERISA. Those rules have been long since repapered by the federal government. PEOs have been used to reduce workers' compensation costs to their clients. Several PEO principles have gone to jail for improperly reporting workers' compensation risks and thereby illegally reducing the premiums they were being charged. PEOs were front and center in the state unemployment dumping scandals to improperly reduce state unemployment taxes for a company. This all stopped when the antidumping law was signed by George Bush in 2004 and similar rules were adopted by most states.

What it comes down to is this: a PEO says it will use the large number of employees it has to negotiate better rates for medical insurance policies than small businesses can. But if you are the small business, you have to take the policy that the PEO has negotiated. Since high benefit policies are easier to negotiate, small businesses will (many times) find they are buying a Cadillac health insurance policy when they want to buy a Ford. The Cadillac policy is cheaper than what the small business could buy it for, but it is still way more expensive than the Ford policy they could have negotiated on their own.

The PEO will do the same thing with workers' compensation insurance. They will bundle up a whole bunch of risks and try to get a better rate from the insurance company. They may also maintain a staff whose sole purpose is to minimize payouts of workers' compensation claims to your employees. Those payouts affect the PEO's experience rating and drives up their costs. When your employees don't get compensation for their injuries, in the manner or the amount they think they should, are they going to blame the PEO or you, their employer?

PEOs have attracted, over the years, the worst risks because those risks received the greatest benefit from a better workers' compensation rate from the PEO. This, of course, was a self-defeating proposition for the PEO. Those bad risks drove up the premium cost to the PEO with no benefit to the PEO. In the current environment, many states and many workers' compensation carriers require individual underwriting of each client company of the PEO. Since the underwriting is just the small businessperson's company and the experience rating (only accidents involving his employees) and since rates are set by the state, the advantage of being in a PEO employment pool is gone. It's no more than an extra charge for the PEO administering your workers' compensation, which for many companies is worth little or nothing.

Many of the PEOs brag about their human resource departments and what they offer. For many small businesses that is little or nothing. They don't hire people for you. They don't fire people for you. When an employee has a complaint, the PEO is off in some other city or state. When an employee has a personal problem and needs a shoulder to cry on, it is still the small business owner's shoulder that gets cried on. Since most small business don't have heavy HR requirements, a heavily staffed HR department is a cost that the small business owner neither needs nor wants. Now that your employees are in a much larger pool, it makes them subject to more, not less, federal and state regulations.

 For a fraction of what the PEO charges, a business can retain an online HR service like ThinkHR.com, which can provide online and live person help and lots of electronic resources for HR problems or situations, including employee handbook/policy manuals.

One final thing a PEO does is process your payroll. They do pay the taxes and file the forms as the employer of record. If the PEO goes out of business, is the IRS going to write off any unpaid taxes? The small businessman will find that the IRS deems them the "responsible party" and they will be forced to pay the taxes that the PEO did not.

So how does the PEO bill you? Normally they calculate their costs, plus an administrative fee, plus a profit margin, and they add that as a percentage to your payroll costs. Each pay period you turn in your hours and salaries, and the PEO tells you what you have to wire to them so that they can process the payroll. The administrative fee can run from 4% of the real costs to much higher. The PEO will normally be very reluctant to discuss their actual costs so that you can really see what you are paying for.

Our experience with PEOs began when they were still called staff leasing. We've learned that PEOs try to make their bills absolutely impenetrable, and by "we" I mean CPAs and people who are experts at deciphering this financial stuff. They also may neglect to lower your costs as your employees max out for SUTA, FUTA, and even FICA. Many PEO do not reduce their fees even though they are not paying the additional taxes.

Our experience over the past 20 years is that it is never cheaper to use a PEO. If you negotiate your own medical and workers' compensation insurance, have a good online HR service when needed, and use a good payroll processing service bureau with CPAs on staff *you will save money.*

In our experience the savings are always at least $1,000 per employee per year and sometimes twice that or more.

A recent allowance by the IRS is the certified professional employer organization (CPEO). Employers may enter into a service contract with a CPEO in which the CPEO agrees to take over some or all of the employer's federal employment tax withholding, reporting, and payment responsibilities and obligations. The start and end of these contracts must be reported to the IRS on Form 8973, Certified Professional Employer Organization/Customer Reporting Agreement. Form 8973 also notifies the IRS of the tax returns the CPEO will file, reporting wages or compensation paid to employees performing services for the customer.

A CPEO files aggregate employment tax returns for all its customers using the CPEO's employer identification number (EIN). The CPEO must attach the appropriate Schedule R, Allocation Schedule for Aggregate Filers, to its employment tax return to allocate to each customer the aggregate information reported on the employment tax return. The CPEO deposits and pays for tax liabilities the CPEO has aggregated and reported using the CPEO's EIN, according to the CPEO's deposit requirements. CPEO customers cannot view federal tax deposits and payments made by the CPEO using the Electronic Federal Tax Payment System (EFTPS).

Generally, the CPEO is solely liable for paying the customer's employment taxes, filing returns, and making deposits and payments for the taxes reported with regard to remuneration it pays to worksite employees (as defined in IRC 7705(e)). However, a CPEO and its customer may both be liable with regard to remuneration the CPEO pays to non-worksite employees. For a detailed definition of *work site employee*, see section 1 of Revenue Procedure 2017-14.

One of our best customers, a business owned by doctors with 150 or so employees, got talked into looking at a PEO a few years ago. One of the doctor-owners' golfing buddies was in the PEO business. The business manager was a very sharp person and had minimized costs for years. The PEO quote was $300,000 per year higher for the same services that the business was getting. Needless to say, the doctor changed his mind and his golf partner.

Before signing on with a PEO, analyze what they are offering you and what it is really worth to you. With the SHOP exchanges and the rest of the Affordable Care Act, a one-stop shop is going to be very enticing. But if you have 20 employees you may be talking about a $20,000-plus hit to your bottom line and getting little or nothing out of it.

Talk to a payroll company, preferably with CPAs on staff. They should be able to bring in one or more independent insurance agents and one or more online HR services. We do that for our clients. We think you will be surprised. If you are already in a PEO we suggest the same thing. We think you will be amazed at the available savings. Why do you think the big payroll companies are pushing their PEO divisions so hard? It is because they are much more profitable than any other service they provide.

HUMAN RESOURCE MANAGEMENT OR HR

Human resource management (HRM or HR) is an approach to the management of people in an organization. The idea is to make the most effective use of the human capital that the company has available and to add or reduce that as required by circumstances. It should help maximize performance. HR is normally in charge of benefits management, recruiting, termination, training, employee reviews, and the like. It may also be in charge of union bargaining and enforcing government regulations.

ESCHEAT

Concept of Escheat

The power of a state to acquire title to property for which there is no owner.

One of the more common reasons that an **escheat** takes place is that an individual dies intestate, which means there is no valid will indicating who is to inherit his or her property, and without relatives who are legally entitled to inherit in the absence of a will. Each state legislature has the authority to enact an escheat statute, and all have.

Property Subject to Escheat

Originally, only real property was subject to escheat on the death of the owner. Now the definition of property subject to escheat has expanded to include things such as stocks and bonds, bank accounts, shares of stock or brokerage accounts, and more.

Property escheats to the states under state statute. But the state cannot solely and arbitrarily choose what it is going to declare abandoned and subject it to escheat. That capability could lead to real abuses. Such state statutes are subject to federal oversight under the Constitution and the Fifth Amendment of the Bill of Rights.

The state is required to have a procedure to publicize what property has been escheated and provide a way for people whose property has been escheated to regain their property. The state must also adopt a procedure for notifying the public and must provide persons having a claim to the property an opportunity prove that it was escheated incorrectly. This is the source of unclaimed property sites and lists that every state maintains and publishes. If your forgotten bank account is escheated to the state and you remember it, you can reclaim it from the state. If you don't, the state keeps it forever.

Escheat in Relationship to Payroll

It may seem highly unlikely, but the problem of what to do with unclaimed checks that are uncashed by employees is an ongoing payroll problem. The problem arises where an employee is discharged or resigns, and fails to pick up or claim any wages owed. Or the ex-employee does not cash a check for whatever reason, or a direct deposit returned and never reclaimed by the employee. According to state abandoned property laws, unclaimed wages become a form of "abandoned property" that the employer must pay over to the appropriate state treasury if they remain unclaimed for a certain number of months or years. The state laws governing abandoned property are known as escheat laws, because the property escheats to the state. Every state does this. Type your state name and the word "escheat" into your search engine and the state department that handles unclaimed property should be number one or two result.

Most states require employers to contact employees in an attempt to keep unclaimed wages from becoming abandoned property. They are also generally required to file annual reports with the state that include each employee's name, last known address, amount, and payment date of the unclaimed wages, and the date of last contact with the employee. With that report, the wages need to be sent to the State Treasury, which will "hold on" to the money indefinitely for the individual. Some states put a minimum level such as $50.00, below which the unclaimed wages do not have to be reported or sent to the state because it is not worth it to the State to process such small amounts.

As an employer your responsibility for paying those wages is over when you have submitted those funds and complete information to the State. It does not in any way change your tax obligations at any level.

 ## TECHNOLOGY/OUTSOURCING

Business processes are incorporating new technologies at every turn. Payroll is no different.

Payroll technology is changing the way companies do their own payroll and the way third-party processors complete payroll tasks for hire. Following are five areas where technology is making an impact.

The Cloud

Everything is going to the cloud. No matter what business process you're talking about, you're likely to use the word "cloud" during the conversation. Cloud technology is helping both companies and payroll processing companies improve their payroll procedures and simplify them. It improves accuracy, efficiency, and access to the systems and its results.

In addition, it cuts costs. You have no physical infrastructure to support a cloud based system. You don't have hardware or technical services to support such hardware.

Smartphones

Mobile is an offshoot of cloud-based systems. The smartphone allows anyone from anywhere access to payroll systems. The cloud or the in-house server becomes the central collection and disbursement point with no need for people or paperwork to flow to and from it. Workers can submit their time and receive their paystubs and Form W-2s remotely. They can also access employee self-services and request time off, change withholding, change personal information, and more.

Independent contractors working remotely are becoming more and more common every day. It is critical for these workers to have mobile payroll services.

Integrated Systems

Technology supports integration. Mobile systems allow HR functions to be accomplished at a distance. Payroll and HR can be merged so that a single entry of data runs into both systems. Time-clock systems where employee data is created by the HR entry of employee data that also feed the payroll system. Payroll and accounting integration and/or the ability of the payroll system to feed the information directly into the accounting system even from third party payroll processors.

Compliance

Compliance is a major component of payroll. Governments are imposing more, not less, requirements on companies to be the source of tax payments for government rather than government doing it directly. The ACA is a perfect example of government imposing a whole new level of regulations and reporting without compensating companies for the work.

It is almost impossible for an individual to keep up with the changing payroll regulation landscape. They have to rely on others to keep up with all the changes, particularly in a multistate environment, and let employers know what they need to know.

Data-Driven Strategy

Payroll and HR professionals are both automating and integrating their mundane tasks, which frees up time to look at the strategic considerations of their jobs and companies.

The automated systems that create the time to make strategic considerations also provide seemly unlimited data with which to drive those decisions.

FEDERAL LAWS BASED ON THE NUMBER OF EMPLOYEES

There are a number of laws passed by Congress that affect different sizes of employers based on the number of employees. We are listing the various statutes based on the lowest numbers of employees you must have to come under the jurisdiction of that particular law, and what the enforcing department is.

One or More Employee

Fair Labor Standards Act (FLSA), enforced via DOLEmployers must properly classify and pay employees a corresponding minimum wage, while following overtime and child labor standards. Defines exempt (not entitled to overtime) versus nonexempt (entitled to overtime and scheduled breaks) employee restrictions.

Immigration Reform and Control Act (IRCA), via DOL
>Employers may hire only those who can legally work in the United States and must maintain up-to-date I-9 forms for all employees.

Employment Retirement Income Security Act (ERISA), via DOL
>Employers' private pension and health plans must give participants information about plan features, funding, and responsibilities. One key ERISA amendment includes COBRA (see further on).

Federal Income Tax Withholding
>Employers must withhold and pay the federal government a set percentage of employee wages for the federal government.

Federal Insurance Contribution Act (FICA)
>Employers must withhold and pay the federal government a set percentage of employee wages for Social Security and Medicare.

Equal Pay Act (EPA)
>Employers must pay male and female employees the same wage for the same job. One key amendment includes the Lilly Ledbetter Fair Pay Act that updates the original 1963 Equal Pay Act (In our experience the savings are always at least $1,000 per employee per year and sometimes more than twice that).

Uniformed Services Employment and Reemployment Rights Act (USERRA)
>Employers must permit employees to be absent from work for military duty and retain reemployment rights for up to five years, as well as make reasonable efforts to accommodate veterans' disabilities.

National Labor Relations Act (NLRA), via NLRB
>Employers cannot prohibit employees from or discipline them for forming or joining unions. One key amendment, the Labor Management Relations Act, grants employers an equal position in union-employee-employer disputes and outlines dispute procedures.

Uniform Guidelines for Employment Selection Procedures
>Employers may not discriminate against employees or applicants on the basis of race, color, religion, sex, or national origin.

Employee Polygraph Protection Act (EPPA)
> Employers cannot use lie detector tests in pre-employment screening or during employment (with some exceptions).

Sarbanes-Oxley Act (SOX)
> Public companies must follow set mandates to enhance corporate responsibility, combat fraud, and provide financial disclosures.

Consumer Credit Protection Act (CCPA)
> Employers must follow employee wage garnishment requirements.

Fair and Accurate Credit Transactions Act (FACT)
> Employers must carefully dispose of consumer credit information to prevent unauthorized access.

Health Insurance Portability and Accountability Act (HIPAA)
> Employers cannot receive health care information about employees from health care providers.

Occupational Safety and Health Act (OSHA)
> Employers must follow federally-set standards providing safe employment conditions, hazard communication, and personal protective equipment.

Eleven-Plus Employees

Recordkeeping. The Occupational Safety and Health Act (OSHA)
> Employers of this size must maintain records in compliance with OSHA, mentioned above.

Fifteen-Plus Employees

Americans with Disabilities Act (ADA)
> Employers may not discriminate against people with disabilities in employment, transportation, public accommodation, communications, and governmental activities.

Genetic Information Nondiscrimination Act (GINA)
> Employers may not discriminate against employees or applicants based on genetic information (genetic risk factors, family medical history, disease susceptibility, etc.).

Title VII, Civil Rights Act of 1964
> Title VII prohibits sexual harassment and other forms of sex discrimination in workplaces. Key expansions and amendments include the Lilly Ledbetter Fair Pay Act and the Civil Rights Act of 1991.

Twenty-Plus Employees

Age Discrimination in Employment Act (ADEA)
Employers may not discriminate in hiring practices against workers age 40 and older.
Consolidated Omnibus Budget Reconciliation Act (COBRA)
Employers must offer covered employees and their families the option to continue health insurance for 18–36 months after ceasing employment (duration depends on circumstances). Employees may be required to pay full insurance premiums.

Fifty-Plus Employees

Affordable Care Act (ACA)
Employers of this size are classified as Applicable Large Employers (ALEs) under the ACA and must offer affordable health insurance options, as defined by the law, with strict recordkeeping requirements. Note that this mandate applies to 50-plus "full-time equivalent" workers.
Family and Medical Leave Act (FMLA),
Employers must offer up to 12 weeks of unpaid, job-protected leave to eligible employees following the birth, adoption, or foster placement of an employee's child or serious family illness.
Affirmative Action Program (AAP)
Employers must create programs to actively recruit and train minorities, women, disabled persons, and covered veterans, with accompanying recordkeeping requirements.

One Hundred-Plus Employees

Worker Adjustment Retraining Notification Act (WARN)
Employers must notify employees at least 60 calendar days in advance of workplace closings and mass layoffs.

1. EEO-1 Survey Filing (Title VII, Civil Rights Act of 1964)
In compliance with Title VII, employers must maintain diversity records for workplaces and individual employees. If the organization is a federal contractor, this threshold becomes 50-plus employees.

Employers with Federal Contracts, Any Size

Employers of all sizes with federal contracts have additional compliance requirements and modified thresholds mandated by laws not outlined above, including:

- Davis-Bacon Act
- Drug Free Workplace Act
- Contract Work Hours and Safety Standards Act (CWHSSA)
- McNamara-O'Hara Service Contract Act (SCA)
- Executive Order 11246
- Vietnam Era Veterans' Readjustment Act
- Vocational Rehabilitation Act
- Walsh-Healy Act
- Copeland Act

There may be additional state-specific laws that apply to businesses in your state, some of which may set forth different or conflicting obligations than those described here.

THE EMPLOYEE HANDBOOK/POLICY MANUAL

An employee handbook/policy manual is an important communication tool between you and your staff. In the employee handbook/policy manual, you detail everything that you want your staff to know about how to work within your business. It sets an expectation for your new hire of what you expect from them as well as what they can expect from your company.

Additionally, legal information is also included, such as an employee's right to work, Family Medical Leave Act (FMLA), nondiscrimination laws, and company policies: sick time paid holidays and earned vacation, uniform, working conditions, and more. It is a document that is provided to every staff member upon hire.

Why should you create an Employee Handbook/Policy Manual?

Consider this: *All it takes is just one employee to cause you and your business problems*. One.

Have These Scenarios Ever Happened to You?

 An employee is repeatedly late for work. You talk to him about it, give him warnings that he could lose his job if he is continually late. But he keeps being late. Do you have cause to fire him? Nope.

An employee is not doing her daily tasks to keep her work station clean and stocked, and it's noticeable. Supplies in her room are too low, trash is not being emptied, and food scraps are strewn over the work area; the list goes on. You ask them politely to please keep their work area stocked, organized, and clean. The next day, the same thing. And the next day. You ask again, and again. You are fed up and want to fire that worker. Can you fire them for cause? No, you can't.

Why not? The answer is simple: You don't have a written policy that states that an employee may be terminated if they are late a specific number of times over a specific period of time. You don't have a written task list, that your employee has acknowledged receipt of, which says she will do these tasks daily (or even at all) and maintain certain standards. The possible result if you fire them without those policies in place? Paying unemployment or even getting hit with a lawsuit.

Benefits of Creating an Employee Handbook/Policy Manual

While writing a employee handbook/policy manual may seem like an insurmountable task, it's really not. There are lots of resources on the Internet that can give you a great starting point, especially to handle the legal jargon.

There are many benefits to having your own manual.

- It introduces your new hire to your company, company values, and culture.

  Set a strong foundation by sharing your mission and vision for your company, allowing for a faster introduction to the level of standards you expect from them, as well as give them an easier sense of belonging.
- It elaborates for the employee what is going to be expected of them.

  Roles, responsibilities, policies, and procedures for requesting time off, how to handle sick days, timekeeping, and more.
- It provides detailed information on what the employee can expect from you and management.

  Leadership style, management best practices, and other legally required information is detailed in this section.
- It clearly communicates your specific company policies.

  Standards of conduct; compensation; daily, weekly, and monthly tasks that are required of your employee; uniform/appearance; arrival time; and tools policy are some areas you can address here.
- It provides an easy way to share the benefits and perks your company offers.

  Vacation pay, sick pay, general PTO days, health insurance, maternity leave, 401(k), gym membership, or any other benefits and perks are clearly listed, as well as any eligibility requirements for each benefit.

- It keeps you compliant with state and federal laws.

    Family Medical Leave Act (FMLA), Military Leave, Fair Labor Standards Act (FLSA), Occupational Safety and Health Act (OSH), are some of the laws you'll want to include here.
- It protects you against employee claims.

    In the next section we will review having your employee sign an acknowledgment document stating they received a copy of the employee handbook/policy manual and reviewed it. This is your safety net if you are hit with a lawsuit from a terminated disgruntled employee.

If anything at all, the last point should get your attention and solidify why you need to have your own employee handbook/policy manual.

What Goes into an Employee Handbook/Policy Manual?

There are some things you *really need* to include in your employee handbook/policy manual:

Equal Employment and Nondiscrimination Policies

"Per the U.S. Equal Employment Opportunity Commission (EEOC): The U.S. Equal Employment Opportunity Commission enforces federal laws prohibiting employment discrimination. These laws protect employees and job applicants against employment discrimination when it involves:

- Unfair treatment because of race, color, religion, sex (including pregnancy, gender identity, and sexual orientation), national origin, age (40 or older), disability or genetic information.
- Harassment by managers, coworkers, or others in the workplace, because of race, color, religion, sex (including pregnancy), national origin, age (40 or older), disability or genetic information.
- Denial of a reasonable workplace accommodation that the employee needs because of religious beliefs or disability.
- Retaliation because the employee complained about job discrimination, or assisted with a job discrimination investigation or lawsuit."[1]

However, not everyone is covered under the EEOC.

1. To be covered under the EEOC for general discrimination categories listed above, a business must have a minimum of 15 employees for at least 20 calendar weeks. Otherwise, they are not covered.

2. To be covered under the EEOC for age discrimination practices, the business must have a minimum of 20 employees for at least 20 calendar weeks. Otherwise, they are not covered.
3. To be covered under the EEOC for pay discrimination practices, the business must have a minimum of one employee. So, basically, as soon as you hire your first employee, you're bound by this law.

Learn more about what may or may not be covered in your business, go to www.eeoc.gov/employers/coverage_private.cfm and www.eeoc.gov /employers/smallbusiness/requirements.cfm.

Family Medical Leave Act Policies

"The FMLA entitles eligible employees of covered employers to take unpaid, job-protected leave for specified family and medical reasons with continuation of group health insurance coverage under the same terms and conditions as if the employee had not taken leave. Eligible employees are entitled to:

- Twelve workweeks of leave in a 12-month period for:
  - The birth of a child and to care for the newborn child within one year of birth.
  - The placement with the employee of a child for adoption or foster care and to care for the newly placed child within one year of placement.
  - To care for the employee's spouse, child, or parent who has a serious health condition.
  - A serious health condition that makes the employee unable to perform the essential functions of his or her job.
  - Any qualifying exigency arising out of the fact that the employee's spouse, son, daughter, or parent is a covered military member on "covered active duty."
- Twenty-six workweeks of leave during a single 12-month period to care for a covered servicemember with a serious injury or illness if the eligible employee is the servicemember's spouse, son, daughter, parent, or next of kin (military caregiver leave).

Some states have more liberal rules for family leave than the federal policies. *If your state has policies about family leave, they need to be incorporated in your employee handbook/policy manual.* In almost all cases, you will be required to follow the policies that give the most benefit to the employee.

Workers' Compensation Policies

Workers' compensation is a type of insurance that provides employees injured on the job with medical benefits and dollar benefits for lost wages and permanent disabilities. In return for providing this coverage for on the job injuries, the employer is relieved of tort liability for such injuries that are due to negligence.

Workers' compensation policies vary from state to state. Every state requires that you have workers' compensation coverage, except Texas.

What Else Should You Include in an Employee Handbook/Policy Manual?

This list has some of what you may want to include in your employee handbook/policy manual. It is no means exhaustive, as you may add whatever you consider important for your company and it provides additional topics to consider that may not have been covered. Regardless, make sure that the last item of acknowledgement is present and returned to you signed for inclusion in the employee's personnel file or the manual is a waste of time, as it will not be enforceable without proof that the employee has read and understood the Employee Handbook/Policy Manual.

Introduction
- Welcome Message
- Company History, Values
- Mission Statement
- Ethical Code
- Proprietary Information Policy

Employment Policies
- EEOC Policy
- Sexual Harassment Policy
- Nondiscrimination Policy
- At-will Employment Policy
- Attendance Policy
- Promotion Policy
- Termination Policy
- Rehiring Policy
- Personnel File Policy

Workplace Policies
- Dress Policy
- Drug/Alcohol/Smoke Free Workplace
- Workplace Violence
- Weapons at Work
- Safety and Security
- Workplace Visitors
- Gift Receipt Policy
- Travel Policy
- Mileage Reimbursement Policy

Performance
- Employee Conduct and Performance
- Immediate Employment Termination
- Progressive Discipline
- Conflict Resolution
- Complaint Procedure
- Employment Termination
- Return of Company Property

Compensation and Benefits
- Benefits
- 401(k) Plan or Other Retirement programs
- Bonuses
- Workers' Compensation
- Time Clocks
- Expense Reimbursement
- Employee Discounts

Time Off
- Paid Holidays
- Paid Time Off (PTO)
- Family and Medical Leave (FMLA)
- Military Leave (USERRA)

Equipment and Electronics
- Telephone Use
- Company Tools, Equipment, and Supplies

- Email, Computer, Voicemail, Internet, and Telephone Usage
- Surveillance and Search Searches

Acknowledgment
- Employee Handbook/Policy Manual Employee Receipt and Acknowledgement

---

 There are many resources available to help you create an Employee Handbook/Policy Manual, ranging from templates to what to include. Here are a few to get you started.

www.ThinkHR.com

www.employee-checklists.com/res/pdf/EmployeeHandbook.pdf

http://spasalon.com/services/employee-handbook/

www.legalnature.com/lp/eh-295/Employee-Handbook?utm_source=Google&utm_medium=ppc&utm_term=what%20should%20an%20employee%20handbook%20include&utm_campaign=Employee+Handbook+%7C+Ex&fid=15365803&da=1&nl=1

https://formswift.com/employee-handbook

www.business-in-a-box.com/doc/employee-handbook-D712

www.shrm.org/resourcesandtools/tools-and-samples/pages/employee-handbooks.aspx

---

Providing Your Employee Handbook/Policy Manual to Staff

If you have written your own employee handbook/policy manual rather than using an outsource service you may want to have an employment attorney review it before releasing. They can check for policies that are self-contradictory, language that does not succinctly convey your meaning, and for policies or language that contradict the actual law.

Then when you have had it reviewed and are ready to provide it to all of your employees, follow these guidelines:

- **Communicate It:** All current employees need to have a current copy of the employee handbook/policy manual. You should have the signed acknowledgment page in their personnel file. Put a digital version on your internal webpage for your employees to be able to check at anytime.

- **Use It:** The employee handbook/policy manual needs to be your HR bible. Follow it! It has the procedures for dealing with employee issues. Using it hit or miss will lead to it becoming unenforceable and create legal problems if you then try to enforce it later. If you find a circumstance that is not covered, update and republish (with required acknowledgements) as soon as feasible.

The Importance of an Acknowledgment Document

You invest a lot of time into writing your employee manual, have it reviewed by your attorney, and make any necessary changes. It's ready to distribute. Wait.

It's vital to have an "Employee Handbook/Policy Manual Employee Receipt and Acknowledgment" document that is provided to the new hire with the manual. This way even if the employee's copy of the manual is lost, there is proof it was provided to them and they said they had read it and understood it. They cannot say they were unaware of the policies in place when they were hired. You should also get a new acknowledgement every time you promulgate revisions to the handbook/policy manual.

The moment the employee acknowledges the employee handbook/policy manual in writing they are required to follow it. This protects you in the future if you have to apply policies that the employee or their attorney don't like. They have agreed to them, in writing! If they don't want to sign and acknowledge the policy manual you have a legal safety net to terminate them without legitimate backlash.

Make sure you keep a copy in your locked personnel files.

An acknowledgment document can be very simple or more complex. Either way, be sure to include these basic components:

1. Instructions to read the employee manual, agreement that they understand everything in the handbook/policy manual and agreed to abide by the policies, sign and date the document.
2. Due date in which they must return to you the signed document. This can be within days from the hire date for new employees and a specific date when issuing a revised handbook.
3. A warning that this acknowledgment is going to be kept permanently.

Conclusion

*T*he *Payroll Book* has been a labor of love (really!) for us here at GetPayroll. We enjoy helping employers, customers and noncustomers alike, to navigate the treacherous waters of the world of payroll and payroll taxing authorities.

We have tried to make a comprehensive payroll guide for small businesses and start-ups, and I am sure that some detail has slipped away in the process, and for that I apologize in advance.

This is a reference book, and not a sit-down-and read cover-to-cover type of book, although if that's what you prefer, that's also fine. As you encounter new problems as a small business owner during your journey in payroll processing, come back to this book. Look up your questions, and you'll most likely find the answers. Keep this payroll bible close by, as it is inevitable that issues will crop up.

Things change in this world on a constant basis, and I am sure that by the time this is published something will have changed. We keep information updated on our website at www.ThePayrollBook.com. Feel free to sign up for our free newsletter while you are there, and we will automatically keep you updated on changes as they happen. Also pay attention to IRS.gov and your state websites.

We welcome suggestions and comments on this book as we hope to be updating and enhancing it on an ongoing basis.

If you have a payroll question for a small business or start-up that we have not addressed in the book, please feel free to send it via email to cjr@getpayroll.com or give me (Charles) a call at 972-353-0000 and I will see if I can answer it.

Best wishes to you and your business, and may you prosper.

Charles Read
June 2020

Appendix:
Payroll Tax Calendar

f you have any questions about federal employment tax due dates, visit this IRS page for more details:

www.irs.gov/businesses/small-businesses-self-employed/employment-tax -due-dates

All or most states also have an online calendar for due dates. Google your state's name and "Employment Tax Calendar" to find what you need.

Glossary

This glossary includes not only items used throughout this book, but additional payroll-related items, in case you need to know them.

Abate To reduce or eliminate a penalty imposed by a taxing authority.

ABC Test A set of criteria used by many states to determine the relationship of a worker to the organization for which services are performed. A worker meeting these criteria is considered an independent contractor under the state unemployment insurance law.

ACA The Patient Protection and Affordable Care Act (PPACA), often shortened to the Affordable Care Act (ACA) or nicknamed Obamacare, is a US federal statute enacted by the 111th United States Congress and signed into law by President Barack Obama on March 23, 2010.

Accelerated Deposit Rule Also known as the one-day rule, it requires employers that accumulate a tax liability of $100,000 or more during a deposit period to deposit the withheld taxes on the next banking day after the day the liability was incurred.

Acceptance Agent A financial institution, college or university, federal agency, or professional tax return preparer that operates under an agreement with the IRS to aid aliens in processing their requests for Individual Taxpayer Identification Numbers.

Account The representation of assets, expenses, liabilities, and revenues in the general ledger, to which debit and credit entries are posted to record changes in the value of the account.

Accountable Plan An employer's business expense reimbursement plan that satisfies all IRS requirements regarding substantiation, business connection, and return of excess amounts in a reasonable period of time.

Accounting Period The period covered by an income statement (e.g., month, year).

Accrual The recognition of assets, expenses, liabilities, or revenues before receipt.

ACH Automated Clearing House.

Actual Deferral Percentage (ADP) The percentage of wages deferred by employees participating in a salary reduction plan (e.g., §401(k) plan). The IRS uses the ADP to determine whether the plan meets the agency's nondiscrimination requirements.

ADA Americans with Disabilities Act of 1990.

AD&D Accidental death and dismemberment insurance.

ADEA Age Discrimination in Employment Act of 1967.

Adjusting Entry An entry made to update a general ledger account before financial statements are prepared.

Administrative Denotes regulations, interpretations, announcements, and so forth issued by government agencies empowered to enforce laws, such as the Internal Revenue Service, the Department of Labor, the Social Security Administration, and the Equal Employment Opportunity Commission.

Adoption Assistance Financial benefit provided by an employer to an employee to help with the child adoption process. Within certain limitations, it is excluded from federal income tax withholding, though not Social Security and Medicare taxes.

Affordable Care Act See ACA.

After-Tax Deduction A deduction from an employee's pay that does not reduce the employee's taxable wages. It is taken out only after all applicable taxes and other deductions have been withheld (e.g. union dues, garnishments, charitable contributions).

Age Discrimination in Employment Act of 1967 (ADEA) Federal law that prohibits employment discrimination on the basis of an individual's age (40 or older).

Alien A citizen of a country other than the United States or one of its territories or possessions.

Allocated Tips Amounts your employer assigned to you in addition to the tips you reported.

Americans with Disabilities Act of 1990 (ADA) Federal law that broadly prohibits discrimination against individuals with disabilities who can perform the essential functions of a job with or without reasonable accommodation.

Annual Wage Reporting (AWR) The Social Security Administration's system of recording wages reported annually by employers on Forms W-2.

APA American Payroll Association.

Application Service Provider (ASP)   An outsourcing arrangement in which the outsourcing company hosts each application at its location and the client gains access to the application through an Internet connection.

ASP   See Application Service Provider.

Assets   Resources acquired by a business.

Assignment   See Wage Assignment.

Attachment   See Wage Attachment.

Audit   A review of a business's records and procedures to determine their accuracy and completeness.

Authorization Agreement   In general, a written agreement authorizing an employer to withhold and distribute a portion of an employee's wages to a third party designated by the employee (i.e., direct deposit, union dues, savings bonds, voluntary bankruptcy payments, certain insurance premiums (i.e., AFLAC).

Automated Clearing House (ACH)   A Federal Reserve Bank or private financial institution acting on behalf of an association operating a facility that serves as a clearinghouse for direct deposit transactions. Entries are received and transmitted by the ACH under the rules of the association.

AWR   Annual wage reporting.

Back Pay Award   A cash award made to an employee that generally results from legal action to remedy a violation of federal or state wage-hour or employment discrimination laws.

Backup Withholding   Income tax withholding required from nonemployee compensation when the payee fails to furnish the payer with a taxpayer identification number or the payer is notified by the IRS that the payee's TIN is incorrect.

Balance   The value of an account, as determined by calculating the difference between the debits and credits in the account.

Balance Sheet   A financial statement that presents a business's financial position in terms of its assets, liabilities, and equity as of a certain date.

Base Period   When dealing with unemployment compensation, it generally consists of the first four quarters of the last five completed quarters immediately preceding the claimant's benefit year.

Base Period Wages   Wages earned during the base period. The amount is generally one of several criteria used in determining a claimant's eligibility for unemployment compensation.

Batch Processing   Processing data as a group, either to increase controls or processing efficiency.

BCIS   Bureau of Citizenship and Immigration Services.

Behavioral Control   The right of a business to direct and control the details and means by which a worker performs the work to be done.

Benefit Ratio   In the context of unemployment compensation, a type of experience rating system that bases an employer's unemployment tax rate on the ratio of the employer's benefit charges to its taxable payroll for a specific period of time.

Benefit Wage Ratio   In the context of unemployment compensation, a type of experience rating system that bases an employer's unemployment tax rate on the ratio of the employer's benefit wages to its taxable payroll for a specific period of time.

Benefit Wages   In the context of unemployment compensation, an amount charged to an employer's account when a former employee receives unemployment benefits. The amount is determined by the base period wages paid by that employer to the claimant.

Benefit Year   In the context of unemployment compensation, the 52-week period beginning on the first day a claim for benefits is filed.

BLS   Bureau of Labor Statistics.

Bona Fide   Actions taken in good faith, without pretense or fraud.

BSO   Business Services Online.

Bureau of Citizenship and Immigration Services (BCIS)   A federal government agency, part of the Homeland Security Department, to which the employment eligibility functions of the Immigration and Naturalization Service have been transferred.

Business Services Online (BSO)   Suite of electronic employer wage-reporting options available through the Social Security Administration's website.

Business Standard Mileage Rate   A cents-per-mile figure issued annually by the IRS. Reimbursements for employee transportation expenses incurred while using their vehicles for business are not included in income up to the business standard mileage rate.

Cafeteria Plan   A plan that offers flexible benefits under IRC section 125. Employees choose their benefits from a menu of cash and benefits, some of which can be paid for with pretax deductions from wages.

Cash or Deferred Arrangement (CODA)   An arrangement under a retirement plan that allows employees to either receive cash or have the employer contribute an equivalent amount to the plan.

Catch-up Contributions   Elective deferrals by an employee to a defined contribution retirement plan or IRA above any statutory or plan-mandated limit.

CCPA   Consumer Credit Protection Act.

Central Information File (CIF)   A file maintained by an Automated Clearing House (ACH) that contains depository financial institution names, routing numbers, addresses of contact persons, settlement and delivery information, and output medium requested.

Child Support Withholding   The process of withholding amounts from an employee's compensation to satisfy a child support order from a court or a state child welfare administrative agency. The employer is responsible for withholding the amounts and paying them over to the party named in the withholding order.

Circular E   IRS Publication 15, Employer's Tax Guide. This publication contains the basic rules, guidelines, and instructions for withholding, depositing, reporting, and paying federal employment taxes.

COBRA   Consolidated Omnibus Budget Reconciliation Act of 1985.

CODA   Cash or deferred arrangement.

COLA   Cost-of-living adjustment.

Common Law Employee   A worker who is an employee under the common law test.

Common Law Test   A test that measures the control and direction that an employer has the authority to exercise over a worker. Where the employer has the right to direct the worker as to how, where, and when the work will be completed, in addition to controlling the result of the work, the worker is a common law employee.

Common Paymaster   One of two or more related corporations that pay employees who work concurrently for the related corporations. Under this arrangement, the related corporations are treated as a single employer for employment tax purposes.

Compensation   All cash and noncash remuneration given to an employee for services performed for the employer.

Compensatory Time   Paid time off granted to an employee for working extra hours. The Federal Wage Hour Law places severe restrictions on the use of compensatory time to avoid paying overtime, although special exemptions are allowed for public sector employees.

Concurrent Employment   Working for more than one related corporation under a common paymaster arrangement.

Consolidated Omnibus Budget Reconciliation Act of 1985 (COBRA)   Federal law that requires employers with group health care coverage to offer continued coverage to separated employees and other qualifying beneficiaries.

Constructive Payment   An IRS rule that considers wages to have been paid to an employee when the employee has access to the wages without substantial limitations or restrictions.

Consumer Credit Protection Act (CCPA)   Federal law that restricts the amount of an employee's earnings that can be garnished to pay creditor debts, including child support.

Consumer Price Index (CPI)   A measure of the change in prices of certain basic goods and services (e.g., food, transportation, and housing) developed and published by the Bureau of Labor Statistics (BLS).

Control Group   A group of key or highly compensated employees in a company whose proportion of benefits is limited under the qualification requirements of certain benefit plans (e.g., §125 or §401(k) plans). Also, employers may not use the commuting valuation method for such employees when determining the value of their personal use of a company-provided vehicle.

Cost-of-Living Adjustment (COLA)   An adjustment of wages or benefit payments to account for changes in the cost of living, generally based on changes in the Consumer Price Index (CPI).

Cost-of-Living Index   See Consumer Price Index.

Covered Employees   For each law affecting payroll and human resources, this term defines those workers who are subject to the law.

CPA   Certified Public Accountant.

CPI   Consumer Price Index.

CPP   Certified Payroll Professional.

Credit   An accounting entry that increases liabilities and revenues and decreases assets and expenses.

Credit Reduction   A reduction in the credit an employer receives against FUTA tax owed for state unemployment taxes paid, where the state has not repaid a federal loan under the joint federal/state unemployment compensation program.

Critical Path   Management strategy that maps out deadlines that must be met to finish a project within the time allowed.

CSEA   Child Support Enforcement Agency.

De Minimis   Anything that is too insignificant to merit legal scrutiny, such as a fringe benefit that is provided occasionally and is too small to justify accounting for or recording it. This does not apply to cash or cash equivalents except in very specific instances such as supper money.

Debit   An accounting entry that increases assets and expenses and decreases liabilities and revenues.

Deduction   An amount subtracted from an employee's gross pay to reach net pay, or an amount allowed to taxpayers as an offset against income.

Deemed Substantiation   Safe-harbor rules under which IRS requirements regarding the substantiation of amounts spent on employee business expenses are considered to have been met (e.g., per diem allowances).

Deferred Compensation   In general, the postponement of a wage payment to a future date. Usually describes a portion of wages set aside by an employer for an employee and put into a retirement plan on a pretax basis.

Defined Benefit Plan   A retirement plan that uses a formula (generally based on an employee's salary and length of service) to calculate an employee's retirement benefits and is not funded by employee contributions to the plan.

Defined Contribution Plan   A retirement plan with benefits determined by the amount in an employee's account at the time of retirement. The account may be funded by contributions from both the employer and the employee.

Dependent Care Assistance Program   An employer plan providing dependent care services or reimbursement for such services.

Dependent Group-Term Life Insurance   Term life insurance that gives an employee death benefits should the employee's spouse or other dependents die.

Direct Deposit   The electronic transfer of an employee's net pay directly into financial institution accounts designated by the employee, thus avoiding the need for a paycheck.

Disaster Recovery   A plan for keeping the payroll function operational after a shutdown of the system is caused by a natural or man-made disaster.

Discrimination   In the context of employee benefits, favorable treatment of highly compensated employees under an employer's plan.

Dismissal Pay   Amounts paid to employees who are terminated from employment, also known as payments in lieu of notice, termination pay, or severance pay.

Disposable Earnings   That part of an employee's earnings remaining after deductions required by law (e.g., taxes). It is used to determine the amount of an employee's pay that is subject to a garnishment, attachment, or child support withholding order.

Double-Entry Accounting   The recording of equal debits and credits for every financial transaction.

Early Retirement Age   The earliest age at which Social Security retirement benefits can be received, currently age 62. Individual company retirement plans may provide for benefits at an earlier retirement age.

Economic Growth and Tax Relief Reconciliation Act of 2001   Significant tax cut legislation enacted in 2001 that reduced income tax rates and increased pension plan elective deferrals.

EDI   Electronic data interchange.

Educational Assistance Program   An employer plan providing for payment or reimbursement of an employee's educational expenses.

EEOC   Equal Employment Opportunity Commission. This federal agency is responsible for administering and enforcing the Civil Rights Act of 1964, the Age Discrimination in Employment Act of 1967, the Americans with Disabilities Act of 1990, and the Equal Pay Act of 1963.

EFT   Electronic funds transfer.

EFTPS   Electronic Federal Tax Payment System.

EFTPS-Direct   An electronic tax payment method that allows employers to access the Electronic Federal Tax Payment System by computer or phone to report its employment tax deposit information.

EFTPS-Online   An EFTPS-Direct payment option that allows employers to deposit taxes, monitor the status of current deposits, and check their recent payment history over the Internet.

EFTPS-Through a Financial Institution   An electronic payment method where an employer instructs its financial institution to originate a federal tax deposit through the ACH system to the US Treasury.

EGTRRA   Economic Growth and Tax Relief Reconciliation Act of 2001.

EIC   Earned income credit.

EIN   Employer identification number.

Elective Deferral   The amount of pretax dollars that an employee chooses to have the employer contribute to a qualified deferred compensation plan (e.g., a §401(k) plan) in the employee's behalf, also known as pretax contributions or employer contributions.

Electronic Federal Tax Payment System (EFTPS)   System that allows employers to make federal tax deposits electronically through the ACH network.

Electronic Filing   The process of filing tax and information returns directly from one computer to another.

Electronic Funds Transfer (EFT)   The transfer of money electronically from an account in one financial institution to an account in another financial institution (see Direct Deposit).

Electronic Tax Application (ETA)   The term for the same-day settlement procedures for electronic tax deposits made through the Electronic Federal Tax Payment System.

Employee   An individual who performs services for another individual or an organization in return for compensation. See also Common Law Employee and Covered Employees.

Employee-at-Will   An employee can be terminated for any reason and without warning.

Employee Business Expenses   Amounts spent by an employee for travel, lodging, meals, and so forth, while on the employer's business. Reimbursements for such expenses may be excluded from income if they are properly accounted for.

Employee Retirement Income Security Act of 1974 (ERISA)   Federal law regulating the operation of private sector pension and benefit plans.

Employee Self-Service   An application that gives an employee access to personal and company data and allows the employee to review, print out, and/or update certain portions of that data. It can be accomplished by phone, at a centralized computer workstation, or on individual personal computers.

Employee Stock Purchase Plan (ESPP)   An employer plan under which all employees are given the opportunity to buy the employer's stock at a discount, subject to strict limitations.

Employee Verification Service (EVS)   A service offered by the Social Security Administration allowing employers to verify the accuracy of their employees Social Security numbers by sending in a paper listing, magnetic tape, or diskette of their data for review by the SSA.

Employee's Withholding Allowance Certificate   The federal Form W-4 or an equivalent state or local form on which the employee states the number of withholding allowances the employee claims. The form is used by the employer to determine the amount of federal, state, and local income taxes to withhold from the employee's compensation.

Employer   An individual or organization that hires individuals to perform services in return for compensation, and that has the authority to control and direct the work of those individuals as part of the employer employee relationship.

Employer Identification Number (EIN)   The employer's account number with the Internal Revenue Service, it consists of nine digits (XX-XXXXXXX).

Employer's Supplemental Tax Guide   IRS Publication 15-A. This publication provides more detailed information for employers than Circular E

(Publication 15), especially in the areas of employee status determinations and sick pay taxation and reporting.

Employer's Tax Guide to Fringe Benefits IRS Publication 15-B. This publication provides detailed information for employers on fringe benefits that are excluded from employees income, as well as the valuation, taxation, and reporting requirements for taxable fringe benefits.

Employment Tax E-file System The IRS's electronic filing system for Forms 941 and 940.

Employment Verification The process of determining whether a newly hired employee is authorized to work in the United States under the Immigration Reform and Control Act.

emTRAC Employer's tip reporting alternative commitment.

Enterprise Coverage A test for determining whether an employer's entire operation is covered by the Fair Labor Standards Act. It is based on the employee's involvement in interstate commerce and the employer's annual volume of revenue.

EPA See Equal Pay Act.

Equal Pay Act (EPA) A federal law requiring equal pay for men and women performing work requiring equal skill, effort, and responsibility under similar working conditions. It was made part of the FLSA in 1963.

ERISA Employee Retirement Income Security Act of 1974.

Escheat In the context of payroll, the turning over of unclaimed wages to the state after a period of time determined by state law.

ESPP Employee stock purchase plan.

ETA Electronic tax application.

EVS Employee Verification Service.

Excess Deferral The amount of an employee's deferred compensation that exceeds the IRS's annual contribution limit.

Exempt Employees While this term can refer to anyone not covered as an employee under a certain law, it generally means those employees who are exempt from the minimum wage, overtime pay, and certain recordkeeping requirements of the Federal Wage-Hour Law.

Exercise Price The price an employee pays for a stock when a stock option granted by an employer to an employee is exercised by the employee.

Expatriate For US payroll purposes, a US citizen or resident alien who lives and works outside the United States.

Experience Rating In the context of unemployment compensation, it is the employer's past record of unemployment claims activity. This past record is used as part of the determination of the employer's unemployment tax rate (i.e., the higher the turnover rate, the higher the tax rate).

Extended Benefits Unemployment benefits paid beyond the normal 20 or 26 weeks allowed by most states (authorized by federal legislation).

External Audit An audit of an organization's financial statements by a disinterested third party (e.g., an outside CPA or CPA firm).

Fair Labor Standards Act (FLSA) See Federal Wage-Hour Law.

Family and Medical Leave Act of 1993 (FMLA) Law guaranteeing 12 weeks unpaid leave to most employees to care for newborn or newly adopted children, or to deal with a serious illness or injury suffered by the employee or an ailing child, spouse, or parent of the employee.

FASB Financial Accounting Standards Board.

Federal Wage-Hour Law The Fair Labor Standards Act of 1938, as amended. It regulates such areas as minimum wage, overtime pay, and child labor for employers and employees covered by the law.

FICA Federal Insurance Contributions Act. It also describes the combined taxes levied for Social Security and Medicare.

Field Service Advice (FSA) Written advice to IRS field agents and examiners from the IRS Chief Counsel's office to guide them in handling particular factual situations.

Filing Information Returns Electronically (FIRE) The IRS's system for filing information returns (e.g., Form 1099-MISC) electronically.

Financial Accounting Standards Board (FASB) Group that sets the standards for sound financial management.

Financial Control The right of a business to direct and control the economic aspects of a worker's job.

Financial Statements Reports that summarize a business's financial position and operating results (comprised of a balance sheet, income statement, and statement of cash flow).

FIRE Filing information returns electronically.

FIT Federal Income Tax.

FITW Federal Income Tax Withholding. FIT withheld from an employee's wages when they are paid.

Flat Rate Withholding See Supplemental Wages.

Flexible Benefits The option to choose from a menu of benefits offered by an employer. See Cafeteria Plan.

Flexible Spending Arrangement (FSA) An arrangement that allows an employee to have pretax dollars deducted from wages and put into an account to pay for health insurance deductibles and copayments and dependent care assistance (separate accounts for medical and dependent care FSAs).

FLSA   Fair Labor Standards Act (see Federal Wage-Hour Law).

Fluctuating Workweek   An arrangement between an employer and a nonexempt employee to pay the employee a fixed weekly salary even though the employee's hours may vary from week to week.

FMLA   Family and Medical Leave Act of 1993.

FMV   Fair market value. Used to determine the value of noncash, employer-provided benefits for payroll tax purposes, or the value of facilities provided to employees in lieu of wages.

Foreign Country   A country or territory not under the jurisdiction of the United States government.

Foreign Earned Income Exclusion   An election by a United States citizen or resident alien working abroad to exclude up to a certain amount of foreign earned income from the taxpayer's gross income.

Foreign Housing Cost Exclusion   An exclusion from income for reasonable foreign housing expenses exceeding a base housing amount that is available to United States employees working abroad whose tax home is not in the United States.

§401(k) Plan   A cash or deferred arrangement that allows employees to authorize their employer to place pretax dollars in a retirement plan that invests the money. The contributions (including those matched by the employer) and any earnings on them are not subject to federal income tax (most state income taxes also) until they are withdrawn.

§403(b) Annuity   An annuity or mutual fund that provides retirement income for employees of public schools and certain tax exempt organizations.

§457 Plan   A deferred compensation plan that provides retirement income for employees of public sector employers (e.g., state and local governments) and certain tax exempt organizations.

Fringe Benefits   Compensation other than wages provided to an employee, such as health and life insurance, vacations, employer-provided vehicles, public transportation subsidies, etc., that may be taxable or nontaxable.

FSA   Flexible spending arrangement.

FTD   Federal tax deposit.

FUTA   Federal Unemployment Tax Act. It requires employers to pay a certain percentage of their employee's wages (up to a maximum wage limit) as a payroll tax to help fund unemployment compensation benefits for separated employees.

GAAP   Generally accepted accounting principles.

GAO   General Accounting Office.

Gap Analysis   Comparison of the functionalities of old and new payroll systems to determine if there are any gaps in the functionality of the new system that need to be addressed before going live.

Garnishee   In a payroll context, an employer that receives an order requiring withholding from an employee's wages to satisfy a debt. A garnishee can also be a debtor against whom a creditor has brought a process of garnishment.

Garnishment   A legal proceeding authorizing an involuntary transfer of an employee's wages to a creditor to satisfy a debt.

GASB   Governmental Accounting Standards Board.

GAW   Guaranteed annual wage.

General Ledger   A ledger containing all the transactions in the debit and credit accounts of a business.

Generally Accepted Accounting Principles (GAAP)   A set of rules and procedures set forth by the Financial Accounting Standards Board that outline accepted accounting practices broadly and in detail.

Golden Parachute   Payments made to business executives in excess of their usual compensation (e.g. stock options, bonuses) in the event the business is sold and the executives are terminated from employment.

Governmental Accounting Standards Board (GASB)   Group that sets the standards for sound governmental financial management.

Graphical User Interface (GUI)   Software that interacts between the user and the application in a user friendly manner to simplify user tasks and shorten the learning curve. GUIs use a mouse to maneuver around a window.

Green Card   INS Form I-551, Permanent Resident Card, which entitles the bearer to permanent resident status in the United States and provides proof of work authorization and identity under the Immigration Reform and Control Act (formerly known as the Alien Registration Receipt Card).

Gross-Up   An IRS-approved formula that employers can use to determine the taxable gross payment when the employer wishes to pay the employee's share of tax.

Group Legal Services Plan   An employer plan providing for the advance provision or prepayment of personal legal services for employees and their dependents.

Group Term Life Insurance (GTL)   Term life insurance that is provided to employees, with the cost being borne by the employer, the employee, or both.

GTL   Group term life insurance.

Guaranteed Annual Wage (GAW)   A plan guaranteeing employees their annual income (regardless of the work available) or that they will be kept on the payroll (although possibly at a lower wage).

GUI   Graphical user interface.

HCE   Highly compensated employee.

Health Insurance Portability and Accountability Act (HIPAA)   Law passed in 1996 restricting the right of group health plans to limit participation by newly hired employees and their dependents because of preexisting medical conditions.

Health Reimbursement Arrangement (HRA)   An employer-funded arrangement under which the employer reimburses an employee and the employee's spouse and dependents for medical care expenses up to a maximum dollar amount for the coverage period.

Health Savings Account (HSA)   Tax-exempt trusts or custodial accounts created exclusively to pay for the qualified medical expenses of the account holder (e.g., employee) and his or her spouse and dependents.

HI   Hospital insurance (the Medicare component of FICA).

High-Low Substantiation Method   A safe-harbor method (deemed substantiation) for reimbursing lodging, meal, and incidental expenses incurred by an employee who is traveling overnight on the employer's business.

Highly Compensated Employee (HCE)   In the context of certain fringe benefit plans, an employee who is an owner or officer of a business or whose salary exceeds a certain amount (indexed each year for inflation). Many benefits offered by employers do not qualify for favorable tax treatment if they discriminate in favor of highly compensated employees. And employers may also be restricted in their use of safe-harbor valuations of benefits provided to such employees.

HIPAA   Health Insurance Portability and Accountability Act.

Housing Allowance   Payment made to a US citizen or resident alien working abroad to make up the added cost of obtaining reasonable living quarters in a foreign country.

HRA   Health reimbursement arrangement.

HRIS   Human resource information system.

HRMS   Human resource management system.

HSA   Health savings account.

ICE   Immigration and Customs Enforcement Agency.

IIRIRA Illegal Immigration Reform and Immigrant Responsibility Act of 1996.

Illegal Immigration Reform and Immigrant Responsibility Act of 1996 Law enacted in 1996 that amends IRCA by reducing the number of documents that employers must accept to prove a new hire's identity and work authorization.

ILM Internal Legal Memorandum.

Immigration Reform and Control Act of 1986 (IRCA) Law enacted in 1986 that prohibits employers from hiring persons who are not authorized to work in the United States and from discriminating against those who are based on their national origin or citizenship.

Impute The addition of the value of cash/noncash compensation to an employee's taxable wages in order to properly withhold income and employment taxes from the wages.

Incentive Stock Option (ISO) A stock option plan that gives an employee the opportunity to buy the employer corporation's stock at a fixed price for a certain period of time, and that offers favorable tax treatment if certain conditions are met.

Income Statement A financial statement showing a company's results of operations for an accounting period or fiscal year.

Income Tax Treaties Treaties between the United States and foreign countries that may have provisions governing the tax treatment of United States employees working in those countries, as well as aliens from those countries working in the United States.

Indefinite Assignment See Long-Term Assignment.

Independent Contractor A nonemployee contracted by a business to perform services. Although the business specifies the result of the work to be performed, it has no right to control the details of when, how, or who will ultimately perform the work.

Individual Retirement Arrangement A trust created or organized for the exclusive benefit of an individual or his or her beneficiaries.

Individual Taxpayer Identification Number (ITIN) A tax reporting identification number issued to aliens in the United States who cannot get a Social Security number but are required to file a tax or information return with the IRS.

Information Return A return sent to the IRS (e.g., 1099 series) or the SSA (e.g., Form W-2, Copy A along with Form W-3 or 6559) that indicates information relevant to tax liability.

Information Statement   A statement sent to a payee (e.g., 1099 series) or an employee (e.g., Form W-2) that indicates payments made and taxes withheld by the party issuing the statement.

Interactive Voice Response (IVR)   In the employment context, a telephone system that allows employees to make changes by touchtone phone to their payroll and personal data.

Internal Audit   An audit of a business's policies, procedures, operations, and records carried out by employees of the business as opposed to outside parties.

Internal Control   Measures used by a company to safeguard company assets by preventing errors, waste, embezzlement, and fraud.

Internal Legal Memorandum (ILM)   An interpretation of a point of tax law designated for internal use by the IRS.

Internal Revenue Bulletin (IRB)   Issued regularly (weekly except during the summer) by the IRS, the IRB contains recently issued regulations, revenue procedures, and other agency announcements.

Internal Revenue Code (IRC)   Federal tax laws. Generally referred to as the Internal Revenue Code of 1986, which was the year of the latest major overhaul of the Code. The IRC also comprises Title 26 of the United States Code.

Internal Revenue Service   Federal agency charged with interpreting, implementing, and enforcing the tax laws of the United States

Internal Revenue Service Restructuring and Reform Act of 1998   Law enacted in 1998 to reform the governance structure of the IRS to make it more responsive to taxpayers and to promote electronic filing of information.

Interstate Commerce   The exchange of goods and/or services across state lines. It provides a basis for congressional and federal government agency regulation of wages and hours of work and other employment-related matters.

IRA   Individual retirement arrangement.

IRB   Internal Revenue Bulletin.

IRC   Internal Revenue Code.

IRCA   Immigration Reform and Control Act.

IRS   Internal Revenue Service.

ISO   Incentive stock option.

ITIN   Individual taxpayer identification number.

IVR   Interactive voice response.

Journal   A record of financial transactions that debit or credit an account.

KAC   Knowledge assessment calculator.

Key Employee   In the context of certain fringe benefit plans, an officer or owner (of all or a significant part) of a business whose annual pay exceeds a certain amount. Many benefits offered by employers do not qualify for favorable tax treatment if they discriminate in favor of key employees. In the context of the Family and Medical Leave Act, a high-salaried employee who may not be entitled to reinstatement after FMLA leave if doing so would cause the employer serious economic injury.

Kiosk   A centrally located, specialized workstation located for easy employee access, where employees can inquire about and modify their payroll and personal data, as well as view company-provided information.

Knowledge Assessment Calculator (KAC)   Online tool for employees and managers with payroll-related responsibilities to assess the employees' strengths and weaknesses and recommend training offerings from the American Payroll Association that address those shortcomings.

LAN   Local area network.

Leased Employees   Employees of a leasing agency who are hired and trained for the client firm through the agency. Withholding, depositing, and reporting responsibilities remain with the leasing agency.

Levy   An attachment to satisfy a tax debt or a court judgment.

Liabilities   Debts of a business that have yet to be paid.

Local Area Network (LAN)   A network in which all computers are physically attached to each other and data are transmitted at high speeds over short distances.

Local National   An employee who works in the country where his home base is located, even though the employee may actually be a citizen of another country.

Long-Term Assignment   A job assignment that is realistically expected to last more than 12 months.

Long-Term Care Insurance   An insurance contract providing for coverage of qualified long-term care services, including diagnostic, preventive, treating, mitigating and rehabilitative services, which is treated as an accident and health insurance contract for payroll tax purposes.

Lookback Period   The 12-month period running from July 1 of the second preceding calendar year through June 30 of the preceding calendar year. The employer's payroll tax liability during this period determines its depositor status for the current year. The period may be different for some employers.

Magnetic Media Reporting   Use of a computerized method of filing information with government agencies, such as magnetic tape, diskette, cartridge, or electronic filing from one computer to another.

Magnetic Media Reporting and Electronic Filing (MMREF) Specifications   Set of specifications for filing Forms W-2 and W-2C with the Social Security Administration on magnetic media or electronically.

Mainframe   Large, powerful computer that is generally used for companywide computing since it can handle multiple users and tasks at the same time.

Matching Principle   Matching revenue earned during an accounting period with the expenses incurred in generating the revenue.

Medical Savings Account (MSA)   An arrangement through which an employer or an employee (but not both) can put tax-preferred contributions into an account for the payment of health care deductibles under a high deductible health insurance plan.

Medical Support Withholding   The process of withholding amounts from an employee's compensation to satisfy a medical support order from a court or a state child welfare administrative agency. The employer is responsible for withholding the amounts and paying them over to the party named in the medical support withholding order.

Medicare   A federal hospital insurance program for individuals age 65 or older and some disabled persons. It is funded through the hospital insurance (HI) component of FICA tax.

Merit Rating   See Experience Rating.

Minicomputer   Smaller than a mainframe computer, but they can still handle multiple users and tasks on a more limited basis; often used to handle departmental computing needs in large organizations.

Minimum Wage   The lowest amount that an employer can pay its employees per hour under federal or state law.

MMREF   Magnetic media reporting and electronic filing specifications.

Monopolistic State   A state that administers workers' compensation premiums and benefits solely through a state fund, prohibiting employers from purchasing insurance from a private insurance carrier.

MQGE   Medicare Qualified Government Employee, who only has the Medicare component of FICA, but not Social Security, withheld from wages.

MSA   Medical savings account.

Multiple Worksite Report (MWR)   A report developed by the Bureau of Labor Statistics to help it collect statistical information on United States businesses with multiple worksites.

MWR   Multiple worksite report.

NACHA   NACHA, The Electronic Payments Association.

National Council States   For workers' compensation purposes, states that adhere to the uniform classification codes in the *Basic Manual for Workers' Compensation*, published by the National Council on Compensation Insurance.

National Medical Support Notice (NMSN)   Document provided by a state child support agency to an employer requiring that an employee's child be enrolled in medical insurance coverage provided by the employer and that an amount be withheld from the employee's wages to pay premiums for the coverage.

Negative Account Employer   An employer whose state unemployment tax payments are less than the benefits charged to its unemployment reserve account.

Negative Election   A salary deferral to fund pre-tax employee benefits that is begun without the employee making an affirmative election to begin the deferral.

Net Pay   That part of an employee's wages that remains after all deductions have been subtracted (e.g. taxes, health insurance premiums, union dues, etc.).

Network   System connecting computers and applications that consists of the physical connection (topology) and the software.

New Hire Reporting   The reporting of newly hired and rehired employees to state agencies to facilitate the collection of child support and/or to uncover abuse in the state's unemployment compensation, workers' compensation, or public assistance programs.

NLRB   National Labor Relations Board.

NMSN   National Medical Support Notice

No-Additional-Cost Services   A tax-free fringe benefit for employees consisting of free services offered by an employer at no substantial additional cost to the employer.

Nonaccountable Plan   An employer's business expense reimbursement plan that does not meet the requirements regarding business connection, substantiation, and returning excess amounts. Payments made under the plan are included in employee's income.

Noncash Fringe Benefits   Benefits provided to employees in some form other than cash (e.g., company car, health and life insurance, parking facility, etc.), which may be taxable or nontaxable.

Nondiscrimination Testing Tests that determine whether benefit plans provided by an employer discriminate in favor of highly compensated or key employees. If such discrimination is found, the employer will lose its favorable tax treatment for the benefit. Benefits provided under the plan may be taxable to employees receiving them.

Nonexempt Employees Employees who are covered by the minimum wage and overtime provisions of the Fair Labor Standards Act. They may be paid on an hourly or salary basis.

Nonqualified Plan In the context of employee benefits, an employer plan that does not meet IRS qualification requirements.

Nonqualified Stock Option (NSO) See Nonstatutory Stock Option.

Nonresident Alien An individual from a foreign country working in the United States who does not pass either the green card or substantial presence residency test, but is subject to federal income tax on US source income.

Nonstatutory Stock Option (NSO) A stock option plan that gives an employee the opportunity to buy the employer corporation's stock at a fixed price for a certain period of time, without the conditions that apply to an incentive stock option.

Normal Credit Amount of an employer's required contributions paid timely into a state unemployment insurance fund, to a maximum of 90% of the employer's basic federal unemployment tax rate, taken as a credit against the employer's federal unemployment tax.

Normal Retirement Age Currently 66 years and 2 months, the age at which retirees may receive unreduced Social Security benefits. Individual company retirement plans may use a different age.

NSO Nonqualified stock option; nonstatutory stock option.

OASDI Old Age, Survivors, and Disability Insurance, also known as Social Security.

Obamacare See ACA.

Obligee A person to whom a debt is owed.

Obligor A person who owes a debt.

OCSE Office of Child Support Enforcement.

ODFI Originating Depository Financial Institution.

OMB Office of Management and Budget.

On-Call Time Nonwork time during which employees are required to be available to handle job-related emergencies.

Online Processing Processing performed under direct control of the computer (can be batch or real-time).

Operating System   The computer program that controls the basic operations of a computer (e.g., MS-DOS, UNIX, Linux, OS2, Windows 95/98/XP).

Opportunity Wage   A reduced minimum wage that can be paid to teenagers during their first 90 days at work.

Originating Depository Financial Institution (ODFI)   A financial institution that is qualified to initiate deposit entries submitted by an employer as part of the direct deposit process.

OSHA   Occupational Safety and Health Administration.

Other Compensation   Compensation not subject to federal income tax withholding that an employer must report on an employee's W-2.

Outplacement Services   Services provided by employers to help employees find a new job after a layoff or reduction in force.

Overtime   Hours worked in excess of maximums set by federal or state law that must be compensated at a premium rate of pay (e.g., under the FLSA, all hours worked over 40 in a workweek must be paid at no less than one and one half times the employee's regular rate of pay).

Owner's Equity   The assets of a company minus its liabilities.

Participating Depository Financial Institution (PDFI)   A financial institution that can accept direct deposits and transmit or receive entries.

Paycards   Stored value debit cards that are funded by employers with employees' net pay. Employees can access their net pay by using the cards to make purchases or withdraw cash.

Payroll Period   The period of service for which an employer pays wages to its employees.

Payroll Register   A report listing and summarizing the compensation paid and deductions taken from each employee's wages for the payroll period.

Payroll Tax   Any tax levied by a government agency on employees' wages, tips, or other compensation.

PDFI   Participating Depository Financial Institution.

PEO   Professional employer organization.

Per Diem   A flat daily rate of reimbursement for business expenses (e.g., meals, lodging, and incidentals) incurred by employees while traveling overnight on business.

Percentage Method of Withholding   One allowable method for calculating federal income tax withholding from an employee's wages, most often used when the calculation is automated.

Patient Protection and Affordable Care Act (PPACA)   See ACA.

Positive Account Employer An employer whose state unemployment tax contributions are more than the benefits charged to its unemployment reserve account.

Preliminary and Postliminary Activities Time spent by employees to get ready for work or to get ready to leave work, which is generally not compensable time unless the activities are essential to the employee's principal work activity.

Premium Pay In a payroll context, it can have two meanings. It can be the extra pay above an employee's regular rate of pay that is paid for working overtime hours. Or it can be a special pay rate for work done on weekends, on holidays, during undesirable shifts, or for doing dangerous work.

Pretax Deduction A deduction taken from gross pay that reduces taxable wages.

Private Delivery Service (PDS) A private sector company that delivers packages. If their services are designated, by the IRS, materials delivered to them by a taxpayer for delivery to the IRS are considered postmarked on the date the delivery to the PDS is recorded on their database or marked on the package.

Private Letter Ruling (PLR) A ruling provided by the IRS when requested by a taxpayer who wants to know how the tax laws apply to a particular factual situation. The ruling applies only to the taxpayer requesting it, and cannot be relied on by other taxpayers.

Professional Employer Organization (PEO) An employee leasing firm that arranges with clients to lease their employees back to the client and handle all payroll and human resources functions for the client.

Public Sector Employer An employer that is a state or local governmental unit (e.g., county, town, village) or a political subdivision of such a unit (e.g., school district, sewer district).

Qualified Plan A benefit plan that meets IRS qualification requirements for tax-favored treatment (e.g. nondiscrimination).

Qualified Retirement Planning Services Certain retirement planning advice or information provided by an employer, the value of which is excluded from employee's income if it is provided in a nondiscriminatory manner.

Qualified Transportation Fringe Certain employer-provided transportation benefits that can be excluded from employees' income up to certain annually adjusted limits (i.e., transit passes, vanpools, parking).

Qualifying Event One of several events that results in the loss of group health insurance coverage for employees or their dependents and entitles them to continued coverage under the Consolidated Omnibus Budget Reconciliation Act of 1985 (COBRA).

RDFI   Receiving depository financial institution.

Reasonable Basis Test   A standard used to determine whether a worker can be treated as an independent contractor whether or not the common law test is met, based on prior court and administrative rulings, IRS audits, or longstanding practice in the industry.

Receiving Depository Financial Institution (RDFI)   A financial institution that qualifies to receive direct deposit entries from an Automated Clearing House.

Reciprocity   In payroll, a relationship between states under which privileges granted by one are returned by the other (e.g., reciprocal enforcement of child support orders, reciprocal agreements not to tax nonresidents working in a state).

Reconciliation   The process of ensuring that amounts withheld, deposited, paid, and reported by employers agree with each other and that if they do not, determining the reasons and making the necessary corrections.

Regular Rate of Pay   An hourly pay rate determined by dividing the total regular pay actually earned for the workweek by the total number of hours worked.

Regulations   The means by which government agencies administer and enforce laws (e.g., rules issued by the IRS to enforce the tax laws).

Rehabilitation Act of 1973   A federal law prohibiting discrimination against qualified disabled individuals by federal government contractors and grantees.

Reimbursement Financing   An unemployment insurance financing system that allows employers to pay back to the state unemployment trust fund any benefits paid to their former employees, rather than paying a tax based on their experience rating. This form of financing is most often used by nonprofit groups and public sector employers.

Reimbursement Fund   See Flexible Spending Arrangement.

Related Corporations   A group of corporations meeting certain common ownership and concurrent employment requirements that may be treated as one employer for Social Security, Medicare, and FUTA purposes.

Relational Data Base (RDB)   A file management system that organizes data into a series of tables, each containing a series of related data in columns and rows.

Reserve Ratio   In the context of unemployment compensation it is a type of experience rating system that bases an employer's unemployment tax rate on the ratio of taxes less benefits to taxable payroll.

Resident Alien In the context of payroll, an individual who passes either the green card or substantial presence test for determining resident status in the United States. Resident aliens are generally subject to federal income tax withholding and Social Security and Medicare taxes on the same basis as United States citizens.

Revenue Procedures (Rev. Proc.) Official statements from the IRS on how to carry out tax compliance.

Revenue Rulings (Rev. Rul.) Published decisions issued by the IRS that apply the tax laws to a particular set of facts. They can be used by taxpayers to determine their tax liability in similar factual situations.

Roth IRA An individual retirement arrangement to which nondeductible contributions may be made (subject to certain AGI phase-outs), and the distributions of which are generally nontaxable.

RRTA Railroad Retirement Tax Act.

Safe Harbor An IRS-approved alternative method for complying with IRS rules, regulations, and procedures (e.g., per diem allowances and high-low substantiation).

Salary Reduction Arrangement See Cash or Deferred Arrangement.

Savings Incentive Match Plans for Employees of Small Employers (SIMPLE Plans) Retirement plans for employees of small employers (no more than 100 employees) that have simpler administrative and nondiscrimination requirements than other retirement plans.

SCA Service center advice.

SDI State Disability Insurance.

SDU State Disbursement Unit.

SECA Self-Employment Contributions Act.

Segregation of Duties A basic principle of internal control that prevents individuals from having responsibility for all phases of a job process, thus guarding against misuse or misappropriation of company assets.

Self-Employment Contributions Act (SECA) This law requires self-employed individuals to pay both the employer and employee share of Social Security and Medicare taxes.

SEP Simplified employee pension.

Service Center Advice (SCA) An opinion on a point of tax law as applied to a specific set of facts provided to an IRS service center from the IRS Chief Counsel's office.

Severance Pay A payment offered by some employers to terminated employees (usually those who are terminated through no fault of their own) that is designed to tide them over until new employment is secured.

Shared Services The consolidation of related functions and integration of the processes involved with them throughout an entire organization.

Shift Differential Extra pay received by employees for working a less-than-desirable shift (e.g., evenings or late nights).

Short-Term Assignment A job assignment that is realistically expected to and in fact does last less than 12 months.

SIMPLE Plans Savings Incentive Match Plans for Employees of Small Employers.

Simplified Employee Pension (SEP) An individual retirement arrangement (IRA) with special participation requirements that is available to certain small employers.

SIT State income tax.

Social Security The Old Age, Survivors, and Disability Insurance (OASDI) component of FICA.

Social Security Administration (SSA) The federal government agency that administers Social Security.

Social Security Number (SSN) An individual's taxpayer identification number, it consists of nine digits (XXX-XX-XXXX).

Social Security Statement The earnings and benefit verification statement sent by the Social Security Administration annually to employees over age 24 in the United States who are not currently receiving Social Security benefits.

Special Accounting Rule A safe-harbor rule that allows employers to treat certain noncash fringe benefits provided to employees in November or December as received in the following year. If an employer uses the special accounting rule, the employee must also report the benefit for the same period.

Special Wage Payments Payments made to employees or former employees for services performed in an earlier year. These payments require special reporting by employers so that retirees' Social Security benefits are not reduced under the annual earnings test because of amounts earned in prior years.

Split-dollar Life Insurance An arrangement where an employer pays that part of an annual life insurance premium representing the increase in the cash surrender value of the policy during the year, while the employee pays the remainder of the premium.

Split Shifts A workday that is divided into two parts separated by a spread of hours longer than the conventional rest or meal period.

SSA See Social Security Administration.

SSN   See Social Security number.

State Disbursement Unit (SDU)   A centralized location for the collection and disbursement of withheld child support payments throughout a state.

Statute of Limitations   A period of time established by law during which parties can take legal action to enforce their rights.

Statutory Employees   Special groups of employees identified by law (e.g., full-time life insurance salespeople, certain homeworkers) whose wages are not subject to FITW, but are subject to FICA and FUTA.

Statutory Nonemployees   Special groups of workers who may qualify as common law employees but are treated under the law as independent contractors (e.g., qualified real estate agents and direct sellers) whose compensation is not subject to federal income tax withholding or employment taxes.

Statutory Stock Option   An incentive stock option or an option exercised under an employee stock purchase plan.

Straight Time   The standard number of work hours during a workweek for which an employee's regular rate of pay will be paid.

SUB   Supplemental Unemployment Benefits.

Substantiation   In the context of reimbursed employee business expenses, the requirement that employees keep records of the time, place, and business purpose of reimbursable expenses they incur, including receipts (also used to track business use of company-provided vehicles).

Substitute Forms   Tax forms that are printed by private printers rather than the Internal Revenue Service. They must meet certain specifications to be acceptable for filing.

SUI   State Unemployment Insurance.

Supper Money   The irregular and occasional payment of amounts to employees who work late to cover the cost of meals eaten during that extra working time.

Supplemental Unemployment Benefits (SUB)   Employer plans that provide supplements to state unemployment compensation benefits.

Supplemental Wages   Compensation received by employees other than their regular pay, such as bonuses, commissions, and severance pay. Income tax may be withheld from such payments at a flat rate under certain circumstances.

Table I   Refers to IRS Uniform Premium Table I, which is used to calculate the value of group-term life insurance over $50,000.

Take-Home Pay   In the context of a federal tax levy, the amount of an employee's wages that remains after all normal deductions in effect at the time of the levy have been subtracted.

TAMRA '88   Technical and Miscellaneous Revenue Act of 1988.

Tax Cuts and Jobs Act of 2017   The 2017 Congressional Act that revamped the Tax Code substantially.

Tax Equalization Plan   A plan offered by an employer to an employee working abroad that would provide the employee with the same take-home pay he or she would have in the United States.

Tax Protection Plan   A plan offered by an employer to an employee working abroad that would guarantee the employee a foreign tax obligation no larger than he or she would have in the United States.

Tax Reform Act of 1986 (TRA '86)   Sweeping tax reform legislation that lowered tax rates and sought to eliminate many of the loopholes in the tax laws.

Taxable Wage Base   The maximum amount of employee compensation subject to Social Security, FUTA, and state unemployment insurance taxes.

Taxpayer Identification Number (TIN)   A Social Security number or employer identification number, which serves as the taxpayer's account number with the IRS.

TCJC17   See Tax Cut and Jobs Act of 2017.

TEFRA   Tax Equity and Fiscal Responsibility Act of 1982.

Temporary Assignment   See Short-Term Assignment.

Temporary Help Agency Employees   Workers hired through temporary help agencies who are screened and trained by the agency to provide services for client firms. They are employees of the agency, rather than the client firm.

TFA   Treasury Financial Agent.

Third-Country National   In the context of United States payroll, someone who is a non–US citizen working in a country other than the United States.

Third-Party Sick Pay   Payments made by a third party, such as a state or private insurer, to employees because of non-job-related illness or injury.

Third-Party Designee   An individual authorized by an employer to correspond with the IRS regarding the completion and processing of an employment tax return (e.g., Form 940, 941, 945).

Time-and-a-Half   Payment of one and one-half times an employee's regular rate of pay for hours worked over 40 in a workweek, as required by the Federal Wage-Hour Law (for nonexempt employees only).

TIN   Taxpayer identification number.

Tip Credit   A reduction in the minimum wage allowed for tipped employees (e.g., 50% of the federal minimum wage).

Tip Rate Determination Agreement (TRDA)   An agreement by an employer with the IRS on a certain tip percentage and a requirement that 75%

of the tipped employees agree to report at least the tip percentage found in the agreement.

Tip Reporting Alternative Commitment (TRAC) An agreement between a hospitality employer and the IRS that bases FICA assessments on employee audits and requires the employer to educate its employees on tip reporting.

Title VII The employment discrimination portion of the Civil Rights Act of 1964, which prohibits job bias based on race, sex, color, religion, or national origin.

Totalization Agreements Agreements between the United States and foreign countries that prevent double Social Security and Medicare taxation of United States employees working abroad and aliens working in the United States

TRA .86 Tax Reform Act of 1986.

TRAC Tip Reporting Alternative Commitment.

TRDA Tip Rate Determination Agreement.

Trust Fund Taxes The amounts withheld by employers from employees pay for federal income, Social Security, and Medicare taxes. They are referred to as trust fund taxes because the money is held in a special trust fund for the United States government. Amounts withheld for state and local income taxes are held in trust for the state or local government.

§218 Agreement An agreement between a state or local government employer and the state Social Security agency under which the employees are subject to Social Security and Medicare coverage.

UC Unemployment compensation.

UI Unemployment insurance.

UIFSA Uniform Interstate Family Support Act.

Uniform Interstate Family Support Act (UIFSA) Model state child support enforcement law under which employers must put into effect a child support withholding order from another state's child support enforcement agency if the order appears regular on its face..

Uniformed Services Employment and Reemployment Rights Act of 1994 (USERRA) Federal law guaranteeing, among other things, the right of United States veterans to make additional elective deferrals under their employer's §401(k) plan for the time they spent in military service.

Universal Availability A requirement that employers provide an equal opportunity for employees to make elective deferral catch-up contributions.

USC United States Code, where federal laws are compiled.

USERRA   Uniformed Services Employment and Reemployment Rights Act of 1994.

Voluntary Contribution   Advance payments of unemployment tax that can reduce an employer's state unemployment tax rate.

Wage Assignment   A voluntary agreement by an employee to transfer portions of future wage payments (e.g., insurance premium deductions, credit union deductions).

Wage Attachment   An involuntary transfer of an employee's wage payment to satisfy a debt.

Wage-Bracket Withholding Method   A procedure for calculating the amount of federal income tax to be withheld from an employee's wages based on wage-bracket tables classified by the employee's marital status and payroll period.

Wage Continuation Sheet   A periodic report (e.g., quarterly) from employers to state unemployment agencies containing employee's names, total wages, and unemployment taxable wages.

Wage-Hour Law   See Federal Wage-Hour Law.

Wage Orders   State agency directives that set wage and hour standards, usually for specific industries.

WAN   See Wide Area Network.

WC   Workers' Compensation (Insurance).

Web-Enabled Application   An application that uses the Internet as another means of accessing an organization's data and the HRMS application logic itself.

White Collar Employees   In the context of the Federal Wage-Hour Law, these are executive, administrative, professional (including computer-related professionals), or outside sales employees who are exempt from the law's minimum wage, overtime pay, and certain recordkeeping requirements.

Wide Area Network (WAN)   A computer network in which information is transmitted over long distances.

Withholding   Subtracting amounts from an employee's wages for taxes, garnishments or levies, and other deductions (e.g., medical insurance premiums, union dues). These amounts are then paid over to the government agency or other party to whom they are owed.

Work-sharing Plan   An agreement to reduce some employees' hours to avoid laying off other employees. Those employees whose hours were reduced receive partial unemployment benefits.

Worker Classification The process of determining whether an individual performing services for a business is an employee or an independent contractor.

Worker Classification Settlement Program A process that allows IRS agents and businesses to resolve worker classification cases as early in the enforcement process as possible with a settlement of past liabilities and an agreement to treat the workers as employees in the future.

Workstation In the context of computers, a powerful personal computer that is generally faster than a standard PC.

Workweek The basis for determining an employee's regular rate of pay and overtime pay due under the Fair Labor Standards Act. It can be any consecutive seven-day (168-hour) period chosen by the employer

Index

401(k) plan, 87, 171, 243, 247

A

Acknowledgment document, importance, 249

Administrative employees, exemptions, 33–34

Adoption assistance plans (cafeteria plan selection), 88

Affirmative Action Program (AAP), 241

Affordable Care Act (ACA), 145–146, 241

Age Discrimination in Employment Act (1967), 194, 241

Agent-drivers (statutory employees), 19

Agricultural employers, tax reporting, 106

Agricultural labor, man-days (nonusage), 51

Allowances, 56

American employer, definition, 223

Americans with Disability Act (ADA), 193–194, 240

Annuity payments (Railroad Retirement Tax Act), 69, 70

Armed service-connected disability payments, 69

Attachment orders, usage, 69

Auto-gratuities, 45

Automated Clearing House (ACH) Network, 180

B

Background checks, 209–211

Backup withholding (BWH), 111–112

credit, 112

payments, 111–112

Bad checks, employer deduction (inability), 86–87

Bankruptcy orders, 81–82

Base salary, commission (addition), 42

Behavioral control, 16

Bereavement pay, 54–55

Biometric time clocks, 164

Birthday pay, 58

Bonuses, 55

Built-in transfer restrictions, 7

Business
self-operation, advantages, 9
spouse continuation, 10–11

Business entities, 3

C

Cafeteria plans (Section 125), 87–88

Cash shortages, employer deduction (inability), 86–87

Cash tips, 43

C Corporations (C-Corp), 4

tips, 43–46

uncashed paychecks, processing, 185

uniforms, usage requirement, 85

W-2/W-3 forms, 114–121

wages, employer reporting, 106

work absence, deductions (permission), 37

work state laws rule, usage, 75

Employer Identification Number (EIN), 111, 187, 234

Employers

administrative fee, 75

American employer, definition, 223

charity share reporting burden, 68

definition, 148

employees, relationship, 47, 49, 80

federal contracts, 241–242

federal holiday recognition, 54

FIT/FICA taxes, withholding (report), 47

garnishment order, out-of-state orders, 80

holiday recognition, 54

independent contractor usage, advantages, 13

insurance bonds, purchase, 87

intern employment, 23

report tip, 45

salary payroll deductions, timing, 37

student loan garnishment order, compliance (failure), 82

withholding failure, 74

Employer's Annual Federal Unemployment (FUTA) Tax Return, completion (requirement), 47

Employer tips

credit rules, 49–50

payment, negotiation/employer policy (nonusage), 46

report, 44, 45

responsibilities, 46–50

Employment-at-will condition, 13

Employment of Workers with Disabilities, 53

Employment (permission), Wage and Hour Division certificates (usage), 53

Enterprise coverage test, 135

Enterprise management, employee duty, 33

Equal Employment Opportunity Commission (EEOC), 244–245

Equal Pay Act (EPA), 156–158, 239

Equal pay, meaning, 157–158

Equal work, determination, 157

Equipment protection, 211

Escheat, 235–237

Exclusive remedy, 199

Executive employees, exemptions, 33

Executive Order 11246, 242

Ex-employee, complaint (DOL audit), 41–42

Exempt employee, deductions, 29, 37

F

Failure-to-file (FTF) penalty, 106

Failure-to-pay (FTP) penalty, 106

Fair and Accurate Credit Transactions Act (FACT), 240

Fair Labor Standards (FLSA), 21, 25, 38–51, 133–134, 191, 213, 239

Overtime Pay Requirements, 40